Second Edition

Cantabile

A Manual about Beautiful Singing
for Singers, Teachers of Singing and Choral Conductors

Katharin Rundus

ACKNOWLEDGMENTS

This book sets forth a systematic method of voice training that is based on a Spiral of Singing. As with the cultivation of all arts, these principles have been culled, borrowed, and appropriated from many different sources. The twelfth century French philosopher Bernard of Chartres has been quoted as saying that "we are like dwarfs on the shoulders of giants, so that we can see more than they, and things at greater distance, not by virtue of any sharpness of sight on our part, or any physical distinction, but because we are carried high and raised up by their giant size." I am thankful for the many "giants" in the field of vocal pedagogy, and I am honored to stand on their shoulders in cultivating the vocal art. I am deeply indebted to my teachers and mentors throughout the years who have patiently and generously shared their time and knowledge with this grateful student. I continue on the Spiral of Singing because of their tutelage. This group began with my father, Ivan Rundus, and prominently features Kathleen Darragh who overshadows all others. Much of the information presented here comes directly from many hours spent in her studio. Without her gentle teaching, generous spirit, and incredible knowledge, this book would not have been possible.

CREDITS
Special thanks to Steven Wirth who continues with me on the journey.
Illustrator: James Dowdalls
Photographer: Ryan Justin Chambers
Model: Natasha Valdes
Cover Art: Tommy Leon
Music Engravers: Lesley Sirianni and Lyndell Leatherman
Icons: Cris Hernandez
Editors: Elyce Berrigan-Dunlop
Layout and Design: Allan Robert Petker

Contents

The Cantabile Web Site

Please visit the Cantabile website at www.PavanePublishing.com. Click the Cantabile tab. You can send questions to Dr. Rundus and download 2-color versions of the anatomical figures. Updates and newsletters will also be posted periodically. In addition, more comprehensive explanations are included about several topics.

List of Figures

Introduction

Beauty • Freedom • Strength • Health

All singers, voice teachers, and choral conductors treasure and strive to attain these aspects of beautiful and skillful singing. As we deal with our voice students and choir members who are less-than-perfect singers, we admire and yearn for beauty in our own voices and in the voices we train. We prize a tonal quality that is freely produced, with well-controlled dynamics; we value an evenness throughout the range, and a resonance that is well projected, and we esteem voices that are strong and healthy.

But all too often these standards become wistful or wishful thinking as we struggle to exemplify or teach these principles of singing. Unfortunately, singing is not a "natural" activity for everyone, as any voice teacher will tell you after a first lesson, and these attributes of beauty, freedom, strength, and health are seldom inherent in singers. Unlike their instrumental colleagues, singing musicians cannot "trade-up" at the music store for a better instrument when their technique warrants it. The singer's technique and instrument are inextricably intertwined and developed over time; that is why singers seek out mentoring voice teachers who can build their instrument as well as coach repertoire and develop style.

Likewise, choral conductors rarely have singers walk into their rehearsals who do not need further voice training. Moreover, the choral conductor has many other demands and goals that must be addressed; in the midst of teaching sight singing, musicianship, concert deportment, or just trying to get the anthem ready for Sunday, it is easy to understand why more attention is not given to cultivating beautiful singing in the rehearsal. But choral conductors cannot purchase better instruments at the music store either; they must build them themselves, rehearsal by rehearsal, from their knowledge and experience, using the imagination of their singers.

This can seem like a difficult and overwhelming task. But like many formidable processes, singing can be broken down into much smaller and easier steps. With a systematic plan, time, and patience, singing will become a rewarding life-long journey. In this book, the longest journey begins with a map, and then a single step.

Singing is a skill-based motor activity that must be cultivated. It requires repetition and nurturing over a long period of time as the brain trains and develops both the minute and the large muscles that must be coordinated in order to sing beautifully. This kind of study flies in the face of our culture, which demands that our activities be fast and quick and not require our prolonged attention. It seems quaint to suggest to singers that they are beginning a pursuit that will require a lifetime of attention. But indeed, for the amateur as well as the professional, that is what is required: an intense focus on a spiral of learning that advances your knowledge and experience, and seemingly revisits the same subject over and over again. This cultivation of beautiful singing begins with what you already know, and leads you to areas of study that you don't know very much about, which then become familiar, allowing you to advance onward again to unknown material. All this occurs within the framework of revisiting principles of beautiful singing, and with each new visit, a greater depth of knowledge and understanding is gained; not a circle exactly, but a spiral. *Figure 1* on page viii is a graphic representation of a "spiral of learning for singing," which in this book will be referred to as the Spiral of Singing.

The purpose of this book then, is to provide a road map as well as a set of tools that are required on this journey of "spiral learning" about singing. It is written for and to the singer, but voice teachers or choral conductors may also find the information useful in their work and study. Nine major principles of singing will be discussed, and then numerous vocalises will be included that help cultivate each particular principle. You can use the book comprehensively by reading it cover-to-cover and practicing the exercises to cultivate the principles outlined, or you can use it like a handbook, consulting the index or chapter headings when you have a particular vocal problem that you would like to address. The format is also a road map that outlines how to teach beautiful singing from a scientific base of knowledge with additional use of imagination, metaphor, and simile. This information is intended to assist singers and teachers (and future teachers) in further developing their own pedagogy. In addition, choral conductors will be addressed in specifically noted sections, with information that is pertinent to voice training in a group setting that will cultivate beautiful choral singing. Chapter X is a brief outline of behaviors that foster vocal health in singers. Chapter XI addresses the need to teach singing as a motor learning skill, and encourages "deliberate, attentive" practice as the only pathway to improved vocal performance. There are also several appendices that contain referral information from the various chapters, including a guide to the International Phonetic Alphabet (IPA).

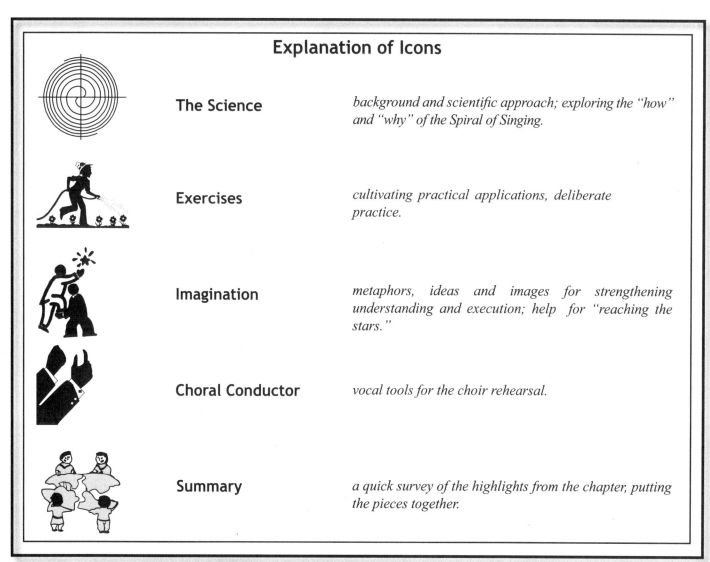

Explanation of Icons

The Science — *background and scientific approach; exploring the "how" and "why" of the Spiral of Singing.*

Exercises — *cultivating practical applications, deliberate practice.*

Imagination — *metaphors, ideas and images for strengthening understanding and execution; help for "reaching the stars."*

Choral Conductor — *vocal tools for the choir rehearsal.*

Summary — *a quick survey of the highlights from the chapter, putting the pieces together.*

Giovanni Battista Lamperti, the great nineteenth-century pedagogue said:

The singing voice is a "castle in the air,"
Imagination is its architect.
Nerves carry out the plans.
Muscles are the laborers.
The soul inhabits it. (Lamperti 88)

Turn the page and start on the spiral journey of "castle building."

The Spiral of Singing

Figure 1: A systematic vocal pedagogy illustrated in a spiral

This graphic, representing a spiral, contains principles of singing that will be discussed in this book. Singers will find in their voice study, as with any art, that the principles will be revisited over and over from varying perspectives, and with each revisit a new depth of understanding is likely to occur. This is why, although the graphic looks like a circle, it really represents more of a spiral. Learning can proceed in any direction on the spiral: clockwise, counter clockwise or skipping across. As a singer gains more technical mastery, more and more time is spent in the Musical Expressions area, but from time to time, even the best singers revisit all aspects of their singing.

RELEASE OF TENSION
& POSITIONING THE
INSTRUMENT

Release tension in legs, spine,
shoulders, arms and neck by
stretching and manipulation.
Align instrument by lining
up feet, hips, shoulders
and ears. Position rib
cage in a stable and
broad, but flexible,

the   sternum

Chapter I

Release of Tension and Positioning the Instrument

Chapter I

Release of Tension
and Positioning the Instrument

Background and Scientific Approach

Tension held in your body is the main enemy of beautiful singing. All singers, casual or professional, must work to release tension in their instruments. This does not mean that the body should be relaxed; singing is work and requires the coordination of many muscles. As you are singing, your muscles should be in a state of tonus: ready to act and respond.[1] Unfortunately, our busy lives too often leave us in a state of tension, with muscles taut, stretched to stiffness, and unable to respond quickly and smoothly. In the same way that good athletes prepare their bodies for physical activity by gently stretching and "warming up" the muscles, vocal athletes must prepare their bodies for the strenuous work of singing.

In singing we use both large muscle groups and small, minute groups. All of them need to be supple, and ready to respond quickly and smoothly to the demands made on them for singing. Shoulders need to be released, with a broad feeling across both the back and the chest. The breast bone or sternum should feel buoyant in a moderately high or tall position. The neck muscles must be released so the head sits balanced on the spine with the best possible mobility in every direction. The spine itself must be flexible as it supports the entire body, not stiff and unnaturally straightened. The chewing muscles that control the jaw must be released, so the jaw is free for articulation and vowel formation and modification. The other articulatory muscles, especially the tongue and the lip muscles, must be trained to release any untoward tension. Intrinsic and extrinsic muscles of the larynx must be released and ready to respond. The muscles of the torso must support the sternum and the ribcage without being stiff and inflexible. Released torso muscles will also help the arms to remain free. The diaphragm must flexibly expand as it descends or the singer will not get an optimal inhalation. In beautiful singing, the abdominal muscles work in resistance to the diaphragm, and they must be ready to act, not stiff and taut. The muscles of the pelvic girdle work in concert with the abdominals and the diaphragm to support beautiful tone, so they must start in a state of tonus.[2] Leg muscles, connecting the singer to the foundational ground, are also connected to the pelvic girdle. Singers notoriously hold tension in their thighs and calves, which may produce tension in the pelvic and abdominal muscles and can inhibit good support. Singers need to guard against locked knees, which is just another form of tension. Feet and toes need to be flexible and supporting, keeping the singer well balanced in the process of controlling the breath

---

1 Merriam Webster's dictionary defines "tonus" as "a state of partial contraction, characteristic of normal muscle."

2 This information will be covered in detail in Chapter 3, "Breathing for Singing."

for singing. The easy part is controlling each of these physical aspects individually. The hard part is coordinating and controlling ALL of these aspects at the same time, creating skillful and potentially beautiful singing. This is called vocal coordination.

When we say that the singers' bodies are their instruments, we are speaking more than figuratively. Quite literally, the entire body is involved in beautiful singing. All singers must learn to release tension throughout their instruments to get optimal performance; only then will the singing instrument be able to assume the important stance that enables "dynamic equilibrium," the foundation of beautiful singing. Depending on how tall the singer is, feet should be about 12 inches apart, weight balanced between toes and heels. The singer should feel firmly grounded to the floor, without any tension in the feet or calves. Thinking up from the feet and calves, the knees should be released and not locked. This not only enables the instrument's position, but also enables singers to move expressively as they are singing without looking "stuck" with stiff knees. Moving further up the body, the hips, shoulders, and ears should be in alignment, and the sternum will then be in the moderately high, but flexible position that pedagogues such as Richard Miller describe as the "noble posture" (30). The head sits centered on top of the spine, and when there is no tension in the neck muscles, the head and jaw can move freely to produce beautiful tone, and a natural looking expression.[3] This overall stance or posture of the body is called the singer's position. (See *Figure 2*.)

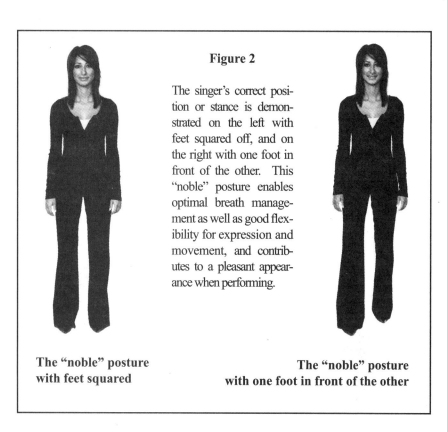

Figure 2

The singer's correct position or stance is demonstrated on the left with feet squared off, and on the right with one foot in front of the other. This "noble" posture enables optimal breath management as well as good flexibility for expression and movement, and contributes to a pleasant appearance when performing.

**The "noble" posture
with feet squared**

**The "noble" posture
with one foot in front of the other**

3 Those interested in a more in-depth discussion of body management or posture for singers are referred to the many fine books on the Alexander Technique, most notably those by Barbara Conable, published by Andover Press. These books are used by the Andover Educators Network and have special insights for singing musicians. Also by Conable, see *The Structures and Movements of Breathing* published by GIA Publications, Inc.

Exercises to Encourage the Release of Tension and Proper Positioning

♫ Stand with your feet apart, so they are lined up with your hips.

♫ Roll your shoulders forward, making BIG circles. Reverse directions.

♫ With hands overlapping in the front, bring elbows to shoulder level. Keeping elbows parallel to the ground, turn from left to right, releasing tension in the spine. (See *Figure 3*.)

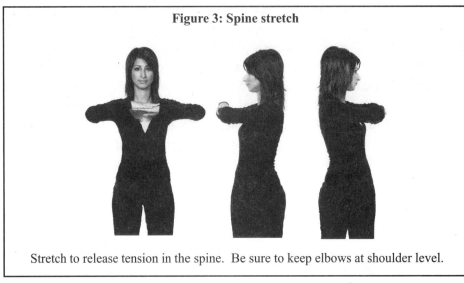

Figure 3: Spine stretch

Stretch to release tension in the spine. Be sure to keep elbows at shoulder level.

♫ Clasp hands over the head and then sway from side to side. Turn hands "inside out" and sway again. (See *Figure 4*.)

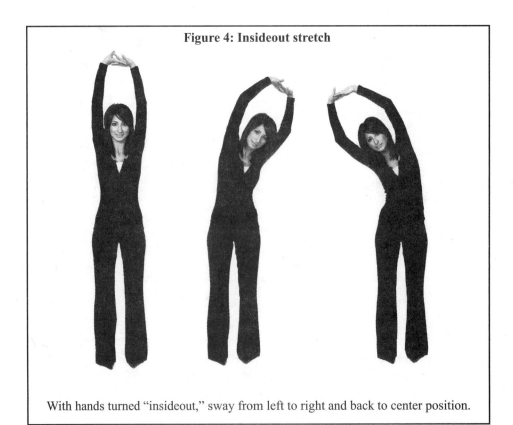

Figure 4: Insideout stretch

With hands turned "insideout," sway from left to right and back to center position.

♫ When you put your hands down, keep your sternum in this tall position; this is the position of singing.

♫ Now slump down allowing your sternum to move toward your abdomen, then lift it back up to the correct position. Note and feel the difference. Maintain this moderately high, flexible position when you sing.

♫ Inhale a yawn through your nose with your lips closed. Can you feel the open space in the back of your throat?

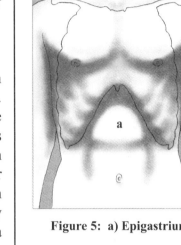

♫ Inhale deeply through your mouth in the position of the beginning of a yawn. Imagine that the air can go down your spine all the way to your tailbone. This helps release possible tension in your diaphragm and abdominal muscles. Placing your hand on your epigastrium (the area from the bottom of your sternum to your belly button, see *Figure 5*), gently pant like a small dog. This should feel free and easy, with your diaphragm moving smoothly to relieve any tension.

Figure 5: a) Epigastrium

♫ Shake your legs out one at a time. Release tension in your calves, thighs, and buttocks. After releasing any tension, get back into your singer's position with the moderately high, flexible sternum.

**Figure 6:
Side view of the "noble" posture**

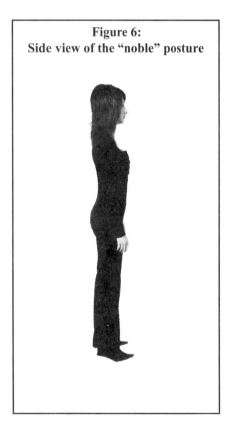

♫ Line up your hips with your shoulders and your ears, keeping your sternum moderately high and flexible. Check for knee locking and release it if it occurs.
(See *Figure 6.*)

♫ Clasp your hands over your head and stretch back slightly; then slowly move your hands forward toward the ground, leading with your head. Feel the release of tension in your spine. Then slowly, inch by inch, straighten up, back to your singer's "noble" posture.

♫ Gently move your head from the centered position toward either shoulder and then toward the other, mildly stretching your neck muscles. (See *Figure 7*.)

Figure 7: Neck stretch

♫ Then drop your chin toward your sternum and slowly (and carefully) rotate it 360 degrees in both directions. Resume your singer's position. (See *Figure 8*.)

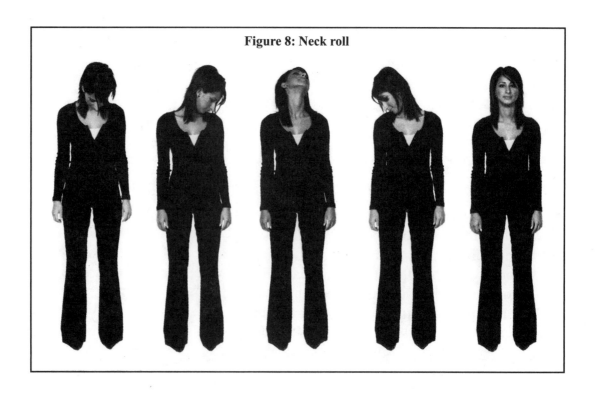

Figure 8: Neck roll

♫ Massage your temporalis muscles (the huge muscle on either side of your head, right above your ears) and then your two masseter muscles (below your cheek bones, connected to your jaw). (See *Figure 9*.) You can find these muscles by biting down on your molars and you will feel them bulge. Many singers carry enormous amounts of tension in these chewing muscles. Give them a gentle massage and tell them to release.

Figure 9: Temporalis and masseter muscles

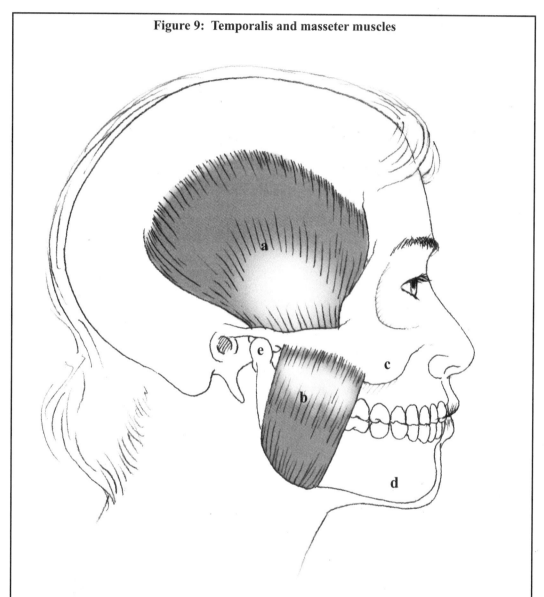

There are two powerful chewing muscles on both sides of the head. The temporalis muscles are attached at the temple and to the lower jawbone (the mandible). Masseter muscles are attached to the zygomatic arch (cheek bones) and also to the lower jawbone. Both muscles' function is to raise the jaw (or shut the mouth). Carrying tension in these muscles can lead to the inability to freely release the jaw properly for singing.

a) temporalis muscle
b) masseter muscle
c) zygomatic arch (cheek bones)
d) mandible (lower jaw)
e) condyle

♫ Release your jaw several times by separating your upper and lower molars. The action of your jaw should be back and down. Some people describe this as tilting your jaw, but the action is the same: back and down, not straight down and not jutted out. (See *Figure 10A, 10B, 10C, 10D* and *10E*.) The action should be tension-free and natural.

Figure 10A: Closed orientation of the jaw   **Figure 10B: Correct open orientation of the jaw**

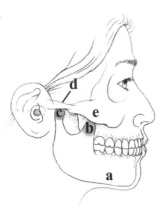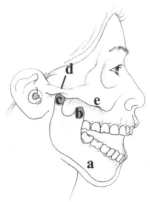

a) mandible (lower jaw), b) coronoid process, c) condyle, d) temporomandibular joint, e) zygomatic arch (cheek bones)

Closed orientation of jaw (10A) is shown in contrast to open or released jaw (10B) in singing. Note the angle of the jaw line as the jaw opens and tilts down and back. Also note the coronoid process (b) rotates slightly forward as the jaw rotates or tilts back.

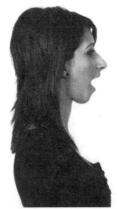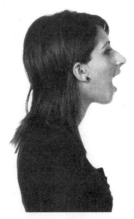

**Figure 10C:
Closed orientation of jaw in singer's "noble" posture**

Compare to anatomical drawing in 10A.

Figure 10D: Correct open orientation of singer's jaw

Note back and down position and compare to anatomical Figure 10B.

Figure 10E: Incorrect open orientation of singer's jaw

Head is tilted back: jaw is slightly jutted with muscle tension. This position will produce a shallow sound with less depth and warmth than the position in 10D, and it sets up tension in the throat and the neck.

♫ As you sing, be conscious of all these places that your body might be holding tension and address those places immediately. Tension will not resolve itself; you have to be aware of it and then consciously work to release it.

Some Common Images Used to Release Tension and Position the Singing Instrument

To release tension:

♫ Shake your whole body like a rag doll.

♫ Climb a tree with your arms.

♫ Raise the roof with your hands.

♫ Do the hula.

♫ Shake your legs like a dog is tugging at your pants.

To position your instrument:

♫ Stand like a royal king or queen in the noble posture.

♫ Present yourself as if you are "important."

♫ Stand as if you were a marionette with a string pulling up your head.

♫ Pretend that the string is attached to your sternum and is gently pulling it up.

♫ Pick up tall, heavy suitcases (Robison 183).

♫ Imagine that your body is really three triangles (with points down, on top of each other): head, shoulders, and hips. Your feet must be apart or your triangles will fall over (Feldenkrais 69). (See *Figure 11A* and *11B*, page 10.)

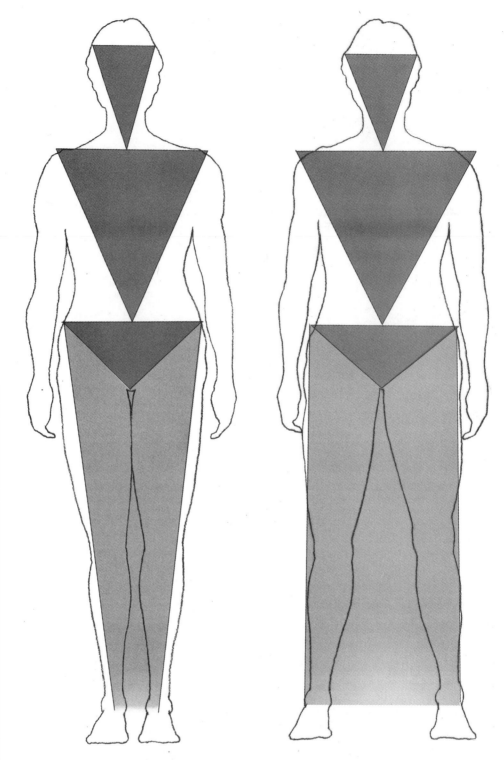

Figure11A: Incorrect   **Figure 11B: Correct**

Human body as three stacked triangles

Figure 11A shows an incorrect narrow stance. With feet together, the structure is unstable, in danger of tipping over. *Figure 11B* shows a correct broad-based stance. With feet apart, structure is stabilized, allowing a strong foundation from the ground and insuring stability for optimal breath management. This same broad-based stance can be achieved with one foot in front of the other, securing the same stabilization effect.

Especially for the Choral Conductor

All of the above activities and images work well in a group voice training setting. Every rehearsal, especially with groups that sing at the end of the day, should begin with an emphasis on releasing tension in the body/instrument and focusing the mind on coordinating all the muscles used in singing. Some groups like to start with back rubs, first turning right and then turning left before beginning stretches. The back rub treat might even get your singers to rehearsal on time! Be sure to allow at least three or four minutes for stretching and releasing the tensions of the day before you start to demand the hard work of singing from your choir members. The following is a suggested model to begin a rehearsal that incorporates the principles of releasing tension and aligning the instrument. The various components should be changed frequently from week to week to avoid boredom in the routine and to keep your choir engaged.

Begin by inviting the choir members to stand and spread out to find their own space, especially important if you rehearse in a crowded choir loft. Then invite them to do the following:

1. With your feet apart, roll shoulders forward and then back, making big circles.
2. Twist side to side with elbows out as shown in *Figure 3,* page 4.
3. Waggle jaw from side to side and up and down. Then give the massiter muscle (See *Figure 9,* page 7) a massage.
4. Shake out your entire body and end with your body in a slump.
5. Straighten your instrument into the "noble" posture, and check that your ears, shoulders, and hips are lined up. (See *Figure 6,* page 5.)
6. Inhale deeply into your body without changing the alignment, then exhale and notice if you are holding any tension anywhere. If you are, work to release it and then re-assume your singer's stance, tension-free.

You are acting as your choir's voice teacher, so you must take care to nurture and protect your singers' instruments. Be mindful of the following:

1. Overcrowding in choir lofts makes choir members uncomfortable and creates tension in their bodies, especially necks, shoulders and jaws. It is a nice problem to have, too many people and not enough room, but work out a way for your singers to have more space both during rehearsal and when they sing in worship or performance. They will sound and blend better as well.
2. If it is feasible, let them use music stands in long rehearsals to avoid arm and back strain.
3. Provide good lighting to avoid eyestrain, which also creates tension in the instrument.
4. Insist that they hold their music up and watch you over the top, avoiding the choir singer swayback slump.
5. Remind them frequently, sitting or standing, to align their hips, shoulders and ears every minute they are singing. Of course, they can relax when you are talking or rehearsing another section.

Release of Tension and Positioning the Instrument

Summary

♫ Every aspect of beautiful singing is dependent on the proper alignment of the instrument, your body.

♫ Proper alignment, or posture, is dependent on muscles, large and small, that are tension-free and ready to act (tonus).

♫ Here is a quick posture check: feet apart; knees, hips, shoulders, and ears aligned; sternum moderately high and flexible.

♫ Without a continuous "noble" posture, dynamic equilibrium cannot be maintained in the singing voice.

♫ Dynamic equilibrium is not only necessary for proper breath management, but also for proper phonation, resonance, and articulation.

♫ All these aspects, properly carried out, promote vocal coordination, crucial to freedom and beauty in the singing voice.

OPENING THE VOCAL TRACT

Release jaw, flexible and free of tension. Soft palate raised, but no tension in the pillars. Tongue flexible and independent. Throat open with the feeling of deep inhalation. Larynx low and stable, but not pressed down.

Chapter II

Opening the Vocal Tract

Chapter II
Opening the Vocal Tract

Background and Scientific Approach

Have you released the tension in your body? Is your instrument in your "singer's stance"? Then we are ready to examine the initial gesture of singing: opening the vocal tract. The vocal tract extends from the tip of the nose and the end of the lips down to the larynx, a little like the shape of a question mark. (See *Figure 12A*: Closed vocal tract, and *Figure 12B*: Open vocal tract for singing.)

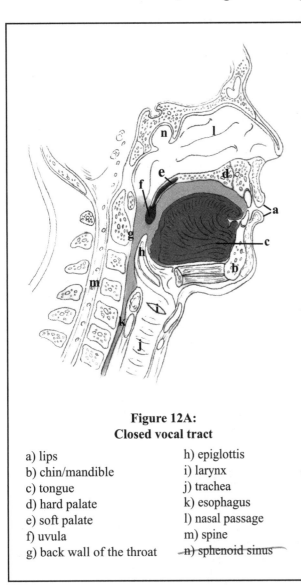

Figure 12A:
Closed vocal tract

a) lips   h) epiglottis
b) chin/mandible   i) larynx
c) tongue   j) trachea
d) hard palate   k) esophagus
e) soft palate   l) nasal passage
f) uvula   m) spine
g) back wall of the throat   n) sphenoid sinus

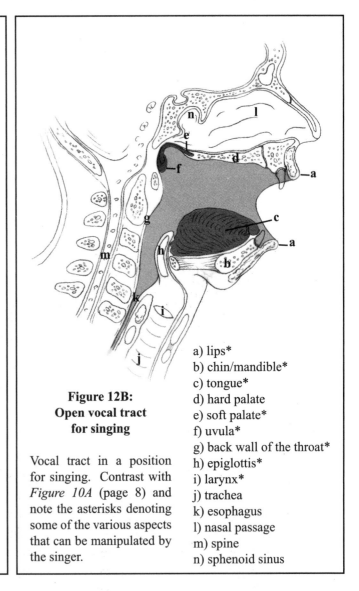

Figure 12B:
Open vocal tract
for singing

Vocal tract in a position for singing. Contrast with *Figure 10A* (page 8) and note the asterisks denoting some of the various aspects that can be manipulated by the singer.

a) lips*
b) chin/mandible*
c) tongue*
d) hard palate
e) soft palate*
f) uvula*
g) back wall of the throat*
h) epiglottis*
i) larynx*
j) trachea
k) esophagus
l) nasal passage
m) spine
n) sphenoid sinus

Acoustically, scientists compare it to a simple tube with one closed end (the larynx end) and one open end (the mouth). This will be very important later when we examine resonance, but for now it is enough to say that one of your jobs as a singer is to get your "singing tube" optimally open on inhalation so you can take in air quickly and efficiently without gasping. Equally important, this "open tube" or vocal tract will also encourage the right open shape to create beautiful resonance when you sing.

As you look at the two pictures, (see *Figures 12A* and *12B*) you can see several aspects of the vocal tract that you can control. Unlike most other wind instruments, the shape of the singing voice is in constant flux, with many moving parts, changing to accommodate vowels, pitch, color, and articulation. You can manipulate and control your lips (a), lower jaw (mandible) (b), and tongue (c); the pillars and the soft palate (e); the tissue in the back of your throat (g); and the position of your larynx (i). As a singer you also need to learn not to use your swallowing muscles, the constrictors (among others), (see *Figure 13*) when you sing. (Perhaps you have noticed when you are singing really well, that you get "spitty" with lots of saliva. That is because you have released your swallowing muscles, are swallowing less, and your saliva is accumulating in your mouth.)

Figure 13: Constrictor muscles

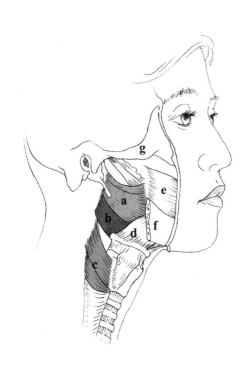

Upper, middle, and lower constrictor muscles are powerful swallowing muscles. Singers must learn to release these muscles habitually for singing, and especially to not use them for breath management and support. Other muscles labeled are the hyoglossus, a muscle that depresses the tongue, and the buccinator, the muscle that compresses the cheek against the teeth and contributes to lip puckering. Also note the mandible jawbone.

a) upper constrictor
b) middle constrictor
c) lower constrictor
d) hyoglossus
e) buccinator
f) mandible
g) zygomatic arch

Aspects of the Vocal Tract You Can Control

Unlike those other wind instruments that have a finite shape, your singing instrument must be in constant flux to accommodate different pitches, colors, and vowels. You have direct control over many of these movements, and it is important for every singer to understand that muscle movement, muscle tension, or the lack of tension, controls the various parts. The ability to isolate different actions (i.e. tongue independent from jaw) and to break certain affinities (like the tongue and soft palate frequently moving in concert) are important skills that have to be learned and practiced.

JAW

The action of the **jaw** is visually the most obvious. The jaw moves at the temporomandibular joint, which is located just in front of your ear opening. (See *Figure 14*.) The action that we are interested in for singing is the rotation of the condyles, the back part of the jawbone that sticks up from the lower jaw and almost touches the cheekbones on both sides. When you open your mouth correctly, the condyles rotate on a horizontal axis, causing the front of your jawbone (your chin) to tilt back and down. (See *Figure 15*.) The jaw's other action, translational movement, happens most notably

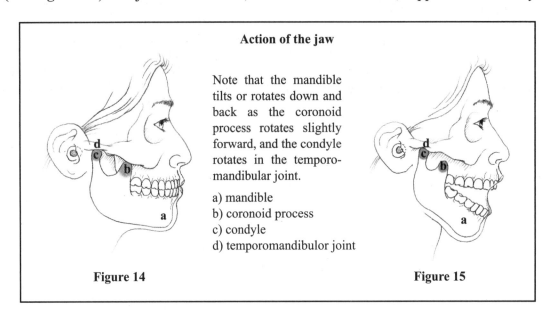

Action of the jaw

Note that the mandible tilts or rotates down and back as the coronoid process rotates slightly forward, and the condyle rotates in the temporo-mandibular joint.

a) mandible
b) coronoid process
c) condyle
d) temporomandibulor joint

Figure 14   **Figure 15**

when you jut your jaw. This gliding forward action of the mandible assists in chewing and grinding the teeth, but in singing we want to eliminate this action as much as possible to avoid a jutting jaw and the tension that accompanies it. Many times you will hear the expression "drop your jaw." As a matter of semantics, this statement is misleading; without dislocating from the joint, your mandible (jaw) cannot "drop down." It really tilts back and down. This tilting action brings the front coronoid process forward, (see *Figure 15*) which you can feel with your fingers. It doesn't "drop" either; it rotates forward. One of your jobs as a singer is to control and manipulate your jaw freely and effortlessly, so you can quickly change from one position to another to accommodate consonants, pitch, timbre, and vowel shape.

LIPS

Your **lips** have many actions that you can control. You can round them for vowels like [u], [o], and [ɔ] and release them for vowels like [i], [e], [ɛ] and [ɑ]. (For an explanation of the International Phonetic Alphabet (IPA) syllables, see page 182.) Both lips can compress to form certain consonants, and the lower lip and the upper teeth can form others. The lower lip, because of its attachment to the moveable lower jaw, is more mobile, and in turn the upper lip is more stable. Your job as a singer is to keep the lip muscles released and tension-free, ready to swiftly move as needed to form the correct shapes for vowels or consonants. You also need to guard against inappropriate pursing or grimaces with your lips that might detract visually from your performance.

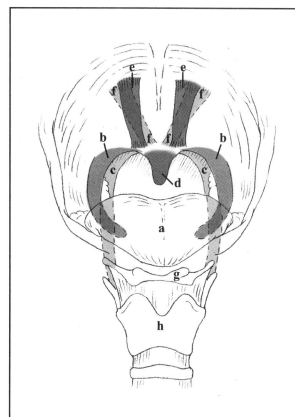

Figure 16:
Five muscles of the soft palate

Two sets of these muscles depress the soft palate: the palatoglossus (b) and the palatopharyngeus (c). The paired palatoglossus goes from the soft palate to the sides of the tongue and forms the front pillar seen in *Figure 17*. The paired palatopharyngeus goes from the soft palate down to the larynx and forms the back pillar seen in *Figure 17*. Three of the muscles elevate the soft palate: the azygos uvulos (d), going through the soft palate and ending in the uvula, the levator palatine (f), and the tensor palatine muscles (e).

a) tongue
b) palatoglossus
c) palatopharyngeus
d) azygos uvulos
e) tensor palatine muscles
f) levator palatine muscles
g) hyoid bone
h) thyroid cartilage

II

Opening the Vocal Tract

TONGUE AND SOFT PALATE

Your **tongue** is made up of many muscles that are intermingled. This means that if there is tension anywhere, it will manifest throughout the whole tongue. Your tongue is attached at its root to the hyoid bone, which in turn is attached to the larynx. Your tongue is also attached to the soft palate via the faucial pillars; so if you have tension in your tongue, you will probably have undesirable tension in your larynx and your soft palate as well. (See *Figure 16*.) For the majority of the time, (phonologists say about 70%) singers keep the tip of their tongue behind their bottom front teeth. Of course, it must move (quickly) to accommodate consonants, but it should always return to the position right behind the bottom front teeth. (It is like the position of shortstop in baseball. The shortstop positions himself between second and third base; however, when required, he shifts toward third base or second base, but always returns to his original position between second and third.) For an open vocal tract on inhalation, the tongue can also groove down the middle and lower slightly in the back, contributing to the open throat. (See *Figure 17*.) This is a good conceptual singing position from which the various other positions should spring. Remember, the back of the tongue is the front wall of the throat. One of your jobs as a singer is to keep your tongue tension-free, with the tip forward behind your bottom front teeth,[4] and your tongue slightly grooved; the groove should start in the back, not in the front by curling the tip. Like the shortstop, this position will enable you to quickly accommodate vowel shapes, consonants, and still maintain an open throat quality needed for beautiful singing.

---

4 In his 1922 book entitled *Caruso's Method of Voice Production: The Scientific Culture of the Voice* (New York: NY, Dover Publications, reprinted 1981), P. Mario Marafioti, Enrico Caruso's laryngologist and close friend, advocates covering the bottom front teeth with the tongue when singing vowels. This method obviously worked for the great tenor, although it is probably enough to keep the tip of the tongue forward and behind the bottom front teeth.

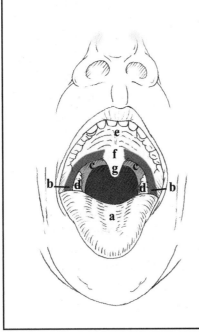

Figure 17: The grooved tongue

Shown here is a slightly grooved tongue which helps create more space in the back of the throat. Also illustrated are the faucial pillars with the tonsils nestled in between them, and the hard palate, soft palate, and the uvula.

a) grooved tongue
b) front pillars that insert into the tongue (palatoglossus)
c) back pillars that connect to the hyoid bone (palatopharyngeus)
d) tonsils
e) hard palate
f) soft palate
g) uvula

PILLARS AND SOFT PALATE

If you look in the mirror at your tonsils, you will note that they are nestled between two sets of **pillars**. (See *Figure 17*.) This area separates your mouth from your throat and is called the fauces. Also called the palatine arches, these pillars are two of the five sets of muscles that move the soft palate (see *Figure 16*), in this case depressing it. Their needed function is primarily swallowing, and as mentioned before, the swallowing muscles can create unwanted tension in singing. To maintain an open vocal tract, these pillars must be released and not resist the action of the other palatine muscles (the levator palatine, the tensor palatine, and the uvula: the muscles that lift the soft palate). (See *Figure 16*.) To say it in another way, the pillars and the soft palate muscles work in isometric antagonism to each other. Releasing any tension in the pillars will enable the palate to lift freely without the isometric tension. When the soft palate lifts freely, it creates more space in the back of the throat and blocks off the opening to the nasal passages. Both of these functions are important to beautiful singing, and one of your jobs as a singer is to learn to release tension in the pillars and control the action of the soft palate without adding tension.

BACK WALL OF THROAT

Looking further back in your **throat** (in the quest to release and open every aspect of the vocal tract) you see a lot of tissue and muscle that lies in front of your spine. If you do a vigorous yawn, you will see that this tissue will stretch, and if you could see it when you swallow, it would look constricted. Much of what you see is the result of the action of the three large muscles of the pharynx called the constrictors. (See *Figure 13*, page 15). The constrictors aid primarily in swallowing; they "squeeze" food down through your esophagus and into your stomach. (The esophagus is the tube behind your trachea that connects your mouth to your stomach. The trachea is your breathing tube. Both of these are shown in *Figure 12A* and *12B*, page 14.) When this swallowing action happens, your vocal tract closes. One of your jobs as a singer is to keep these constrictor muscles released and uninvolved in both inhalation and singing.

LARYNX

Finally, continuing down the vocal tract, at the far end of your trachea tube is your **larynx**. Your larynx is connected to and suspended from your hyoid bone as part of a complex system in your neck called the suspensory mechanism. For our purposes here, it is enough to know that you have external muscles, some of which primarily elevate your larynx and others that primarily depress it. For singing, we want to establish a stable equilibrium of the hyoid bone (the root of the tongue), which will ensure a stable but not rigid position of the larynx. Without this equilibrium, the vocal folds (contained in the larynx) cannot respond and vibrate freely with the controlled airflow from the lungs. The goal is for your larynx to be stable in a moderately low position, and to neither unduly rise nor depress with pitch. This position contributes to proper vocal fold function, helps maintain the open vocal tract that will enhance the lower partials of a tone, and helps create upper harmonic partials that contribute to the valued "singer's formant."[5] One of your jobs as a singer is to learn to recognize and feel the position of your larynx, in order to maintain the proper muscle coordination that will keep it relatively low and flexible (but not pressed down) and not rising with the pitch. (In all voice types, during extremely high singing, some laryngeal lifting may be necessary.) [6]

Exercises To Open and Release the Vocal Tract

IN GENERAL

Be sure you have released general tension in your body and that your instrument is aligned for singing.

Exhale completely through your mouth (releases your diaphragm) and then inhale deeply through your nose. Repeat the exhalation, and this time, inhale deeply through your mouth. Exhale through your mouth again, and feel as if you can inhale through your mouth and nose at the same time. Every time you inhale, feel the air enter your mouth, go across the hard palate, lift the soft palate, and go deeply into your body.

Inhale through your mouth as if you were yawning. You will feel a strong stretch that is too wide for singing. Now inhale warm air (not cold air) through just the beginning of a yawn. When you start to exhale, don't change the position of your vocal tract; keep it in that same position. Now, remembering that open feeling, practice inhaling through the shape of different vowels like [a] and [o] and then exhale through the same vowel space. This sets up the habit of singing on the gesture of inhalation.

Exhale with your hand in front of your mouth as if to warm up the palm of your hand. Think to yourself "inhale on the gesture of the beginning of a yawn, exhale (or sing) on the gesture of warming." When you exhale "warm air" it indicates an absence of constriction in your vocal tract. A constriction in your vocal tract will speed up airflow, which you will perceive as "cool air" similar to the "wind chill factor" in

---

5   These are issues of resonance, which will be examined in Chapter 5.

6   A full discussion of the suspensory mechanism can be found in Doscher, *The Functional Unity of the Singing Voice*, 44-55.

weather forecasting. Maintaining a sense of "warm air" flow on inhalation and exhalation and singing is one indication that you are not adding unwanted constrictions in your throat.

JAW

♫ Bite down on your back molars while you place your fingers about two inches under your ears along the jaw. You will feel a very big muscle bulging out. This is your masseter, a chewing muscle. Still biting down, place your fingers above your ears on your temple. The muscle bulging there is another chewing muscle, your temporalis. (See *Figure 9* on page 7). Give both of these muscles a gentle massage and tell them to release. If you are holding tension in these muscles, your jaw will not release properly, keeping the gateway to your vocal tract closed. After the massage, gently open and close your mouth several times and feel the release in your jaw.

♫ Think about opening the *back* of your jaw. Now do it, and feel the release of your masseter muscles.

♫ Think about what an 11-year-old says to her mom when she wants to point out stupidity. She says, "duhhhh, Mooooom." Say this word "duh" and think about separating your molars when you do. (This is sometimes called "the idiot jaw," but, of course, that is not politically correct.) Can you feel the release in your jaw?

♫ Put one finger on your chin and the other hand on the back of your head. Release your jaw back and down and notice that your head doesn't have to maneuver at all to move your jaw. Nodding your head is only for expression, not for jaw movement. (*Figure 10E* on page 8 shows this incorrect position.) Keep the back of your neck long, but not stiff.

♫ Put your index fingers in the hollow of your cheeks (under your cheekbone, the zygomatic arch) and your thumbs under the bottom of your jawbone (your mandible). Open your mouth slowly and feel how the mandible moves back and down toward your spine. At the same time, feel how the front notch at the top of your mandible (the coronoid process) moves forward into the hollow of your cheeks. (See *Figure 15* on page 16 and *Figure 10B* on page 8.) Notice that when the chin moves down and back, the coronoid process rotates forward. This is the proper movement of your jaw for singing. You should be able to do it quickly and freely.

♫ Waggle your jaw side to side and up and down. Does your jaw move quickly and freely?

♫ Put the knuckles of both hands right under the zygomatic arch and lower your jaw. Feel how that helps release your masseter muscles and frees your jaw for singing. (See *Figure 18*.)

**Figure 18:
Knuckles under zygomatic arch**

Knuckles placed under the zygomatic arch (cheekbones) to facilitate the release of tension in the jaw. Note also the relaxed tongue.

Do the exercise below (Exercise 1) with your hands in the position from *Figure 18*. Then do it without your hands. Practice this vocalise slowly, starting in your middle voice (sopranos and tenors: D major; mezzos and baritones: B flat or C major). As you are singing, notice the freedom you feel in your jaw when you release it on the [ɑ] sound.

Exercise 1

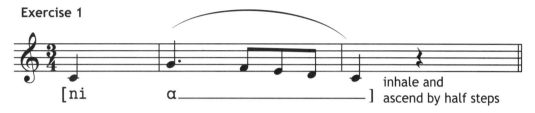

Now sing Exercise 2. As you toggle back and forth between [ɑ] and [i], the two vowel sounds work together to open the throat and bring the tongue forward.

Exercise 2

Exercise 3 adds flexibility and agility. Notice how your jaw must be released to do this exercise quickly.

Exercice 3

Exercises 4, 5, 6, 7. Here are several exercises that use a combination of [vi la] [va li], [va wa], and [vi wi]. The principles involved are: 1) the [v] sound (which feels as if the upper front teeth come forward) contributes to a feeling of a flat chin that encourages the proper jaw position; 2) the [l] sound (which brings the tip of the tongue forward and out of the back of the throat) contributes to our desired open throat; 3) the [w] sound (really a [u] sound, that involves the cheek muscles) brings the sound forward; and 4) the toggle between [i] and [ɑ] encourages a free and flexible jaw and tongue.

Exercise 4

Exercise 5

[vɑ wɑ vɑ wɑ vɑ wɑ vɑ wɑ   vɑ⌐] inhale and
                                                        ascend by
also: [vi wi vi wi vi wi vi wi   vi⌐] half steps

Exercise 6

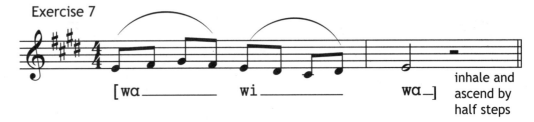

[vi la vi la vi li vi li   vi la vi la vi]

                                                        inhale and
                                                        ascend by
                                                        half steps

Exercise 7

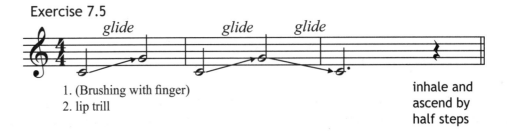

[wɑ_____ wi_____   wɑ⌐] inhale and
                                                        ascend by
                                                        half steps

LIPS

♫ While singing Exercise 7.5 use your pointer finger like a toothbrush and rapidly "brush" your front teeth. This will make your upper and lower lips move rapidly, releasing any lip tension (and will make you sound like a two-year old. Fun!).

♫ Alternate this action with a lip trill, a repeated b b b b b b sound, like "brbrbrbr, it's cold," as you ascend in the scale.

Exercise 7.5

glide   *glide*   *glide*

1. (Brushing with finger)   inhale and
2. lip trill   ascend by
                                                        half steps

TONGUE

♫ With your lips closed, say "mm-hmmm," as if you are agreeing with something someone said. Note where your tongue is; right behind your bottom front teeth, exactly where it should be most of the time when you are singing.

♫ Extend your tongue out of your mouth as far as you can (stick out your tongue) and then retract it rapidly (like an anteater). Then shake it rapidly from side to side. Gently jerk the root of your tongue down (make a sound like you are gulping a drink).

♫ With the tip of your tongue behind your bottom front teeth, pivot your tongue from side to side.

♪ Roll up the sides of your tongue like a sausage. (Some people genetically cannot do this).

♪ On one pitch in the middle of your voice sing [θɑ θe θi θo θu]. (Exercise 8)

Exercise 8

inhale and descend by half steps

On a five-note scale sing la da ra na da ta ra la da (Exercise 9). Use only the tip of your tongue.

Exercise 9

inhale and ascend by half steps

Sing Exercise 10 using only the tip of your tongue; keep your jaw released.

Exercise 10

inhale and ascend by half steps

Use a mirror to look at your tongue and throat. Watch what happens when you inhale through the beginning of a yawn. Now exhale warm air silently and gently on Ah, Ah, Ah. Can you see your tongue groove slightly down the middle? (The groove should start from the back of your tongue. See *Figure 17*, page 18.)

Check for undue tension in your tongue by gently resting your index finger along the groove. (Use clean hands or a latex glove). Do not press down or try to control your tongue, just let your finger be a reminder and guide. With your finger positioned on your tongue, sing a glide on "ah" from low in your voice to high. What does your finger tell you that your tongue is doing? If you feel your tongue stiffen, or pull back, or hump up, make note of this. Repeat the tongue release exercises above, and then try again to sing a glide without adding tension to your vocal tract via a constricted or tight tongue.

PILLARS AND SOFT PALATE

♫ Now look at your pillars in the mirror. There are two sets: the one in the front connects your tongue to your soft palate, (palatoglossus), the one in back (palatopharyngeus), connects your pharynx to your soft palate. (See *Figure 16*, page 17) Watch them as you do an elaborate yawn; they will stretch very wide and very tall. Watch them again as you say "Ah, Ah, Ah," like at the doctor's office. For singing, we want them to be comfortably arched, not stretched or pulled down. They also should feel supple to the touch.

♫ Put your index fingers in the sides of your mouth on top of your bottom molars. (You can do this with clean fingers or with latex gloves). Now gently move your fingers back further and feel the pillars as you sing one note in your middle voice. If they are resisting the soft palate, they will feel hard or stretched or contracted. If they do feel hard, pay attention to this, and see if you can consciously release them by inhalation until they feel soft and supple. Then begin singing again without adding tension in these palatal depressors. Remember, if you have tension in your pillars, you will have tension in your tongue and soft palate.

♫ Practice singing a single held note, and then sing scales with your fingers in your mouth monitoring the pillars. Notice and remember how it feels to release any tension in your fauces (the opening between your mouth and throat.) This may feel odd and awkward, but remember the words of the great voice teacher William Vennard: "One can condition reflexes to desired behavior, and the acquiring of most artistic skills begins with muscular independence" (Vennard 100).

In Exercise 11 go immediately to the [ŋ] on the first syllable. The [ŋ] brings your tongue and soft palate together, creating space in the pharynx; then the spring to the [ɑ] lifts your palate and opens your vocal tract.

Exercise 11

[ziŋ   ɑ_____]   inhale and descend by half steps

Variations on the same principle:

In Exercise 12 remember to go immediately to the [ŋ] sound and then spring to the vowel.

Exercise 12

[ziŋ ɑ ziŋ o ziŋ ɑ ziŋ o   zi_]   inhale and descend by half steps

In Exercise 13 be sure to *crescendo* into the eighth notes as you sustain the vowel.

Exercise 13

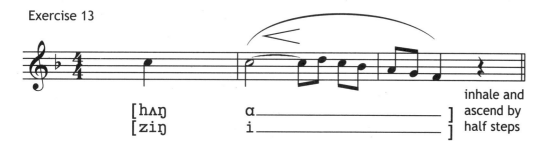

[hʌŋ   ɑ_____]   inhale and
[ziŋ   i_____]   ascend by
                                  half steps

In Exercise 14 the [k] and [g] also activate the soft palate/back of the tongue connection. Do the exercise slowly at first and gradually accelerate the tempo as your tongue can keep up. The glide will remind you to not add tension. Watch your soft palate in the mirror as you glide. Does it lift a little? Does the uvula (see *Figure 17,* page 18) seem to shorten a little?

Exercise 14

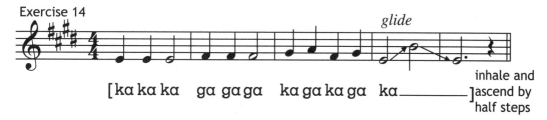

[kɑ kɑ kɑ   gɑ gɑ gɑ   kɑ gɑ kɑ gɑ   kɑ_____]   inhale and
                                                        ascend by
                                                        half steps

The following exercises open more pharyngeal space and strengthen the soft palate: (on each of the sing, sang, song words, go directly to the [ŋ] sound).

In Exercise 15 glide the octave on the [ŋ]. (Notice how the [i] vowel brings the tongue forward.)

Exercise 15

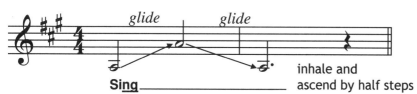

Sing_____   inhale and
                           ascend by half steps

In Exercise 16 glide on [ŋ] of "sang." The [æ] slightly broadens the tongue and the soft palate.

Exercise 16

Sing   **Sang**_____   inhale and
                                      ascend by half steps

In Exercise 17 glide on [ŋ] of "song." The [ɔ] slightly lifts the soft palate and grooves the tongue while they still maintain contact.

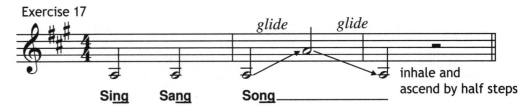

In Exercise 18 sing only the [ŋ] sounds of each of these words without the initial consonant and vowel on the octave glide. [ⁱŋ ᵃŋ ᵒŋ] Feel how your tongue and soft palate are working together to form these three postures and to open up pharyngeal space.

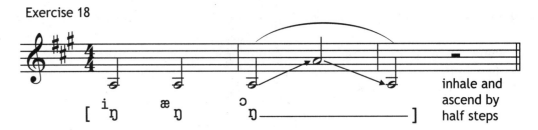

In Exercise 19 [ⁱŋ ᵃŋ ᵒŋ ɑ] after singing the three [ŋ] sounds, open up to vowel [ɑ] and descend on the scale notes. Can you sense how open your vocal tract feels? That is because you are training your soft palate to make more space.

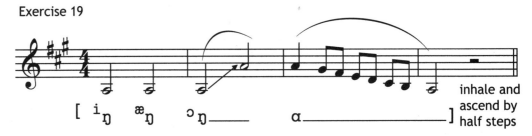

BACK OF THE THROAT TISSUE AND THE LARYNX

♫ To strengthen the neck muscles that support the larynx, stand in your singer's stance and gently move your head to one side as far as it will go and then gently stretch it slightly farther, holding the stretch for up to 30 seconds. (Build up to this.) Then repeat on the other side. Finish by rolling your head gently in a large circle first one direction, then the other. (See *Figure 7 and 8*, page 6.)

♫ Find your larynx by humming and feeling the vibrations with your fingers on your neck. Now swallow and feel how your larynx lifts to accommodate the swallowing action. Inhale the beginning of a yawn and feel how your larynx lowers. Finally, with your fingers on your larynx, swallow again, and at the end of the swallow, feel how your larynx reflexively releases into a low position that you might call a "not-swallow" position or an "un-swallow" position. Do this several times so you can remember what it feels like. This is an optimal position for your larynx. When you start to sing, remind yourself to let your larynx remain in this "un-swallow" position. In other words, work to keep your larynx in a comfortably low position without pressing it down.

♫ Additionally, the "un-swallowing" exercise helps to release your constrictor muscles in the back of your throat. These muscles will also release reflexively at the end of a swallow. Remember how this feels and incorporate that feeling into your singing.

♫ Use your hand to form a cradle or sling for your larynx. (See *Figure 19.*) Your larynx should rest gently in the area formed by your thumb and index finger as you form a letter "U" with them. Monitor the position of your larynx as you sing the following exercises, consciously working to let your larynx remain low and your constrictor muscles remain inactive. Do not hold or force the larynx down.

Figure 19: Cradled larynx

The singer cradles the larynx in her hand. The thumb and fingers can monitor for neck muscle tension while the "cradle" (area between thumb and index finger) monitors the position of the larynx. This exercise should be used only to monitor. Care should be taken that no pressure is applied to the larynx to manipulate it in any way.

In Exercise 20 glide on vowel [ɑ] and [o].

Exercise 20

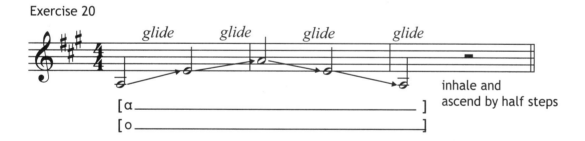

Exercise 21 adds range; does it seem like 1) your larynx is remaining relatively low, or 2) that there is some tension trying to pull it up? #1 is a better singing strategy; if you feel more like # 2, check for tongue and/or soft palate tension, give yourself a gentle neck massage and try again.

Exercise 21

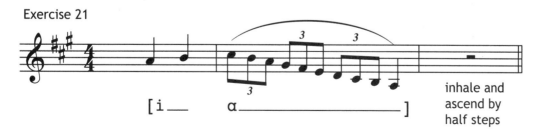

Some Common Images Used
To Encourage An Open Vocal Tract

General
- ♫ Inhale all the way down to the floor.
- ♫ Inhale all the way down to the lungs that you sit on, your bun lungs.

Open Pharynx
- ♫ As you inhale through your nose, "smell something wonderful" like coffee in the morning, or chocolate, or fresh flowers.
- ♫ Inhale a yawn through your nose (with your lips closed).
- ♫ You are listening to a friend and have to stifle a yawn. Do you feel how that opens your throat? (This gesture creates tension, however. When you sing you want this open feeling without the tension.)
- ♫ Warm your cold hands with a slow warming breath while exhaling. Contrast this with "blowing out the candles" that closes your pharynx.
- ♫ Use a warming breath to clean your glasses or to fog a mirror.
- ♫ Opening your throat is like the archer pulling back the string of his bow.
- ♫ Imagine that the back of your open throat is like a funnel. Tone is funneled forward to a focal point and then directed into the room. Keep your funnel open and three-dimensional but tension-free at all times (tall, broad and deep). (See *Figure 20*.)

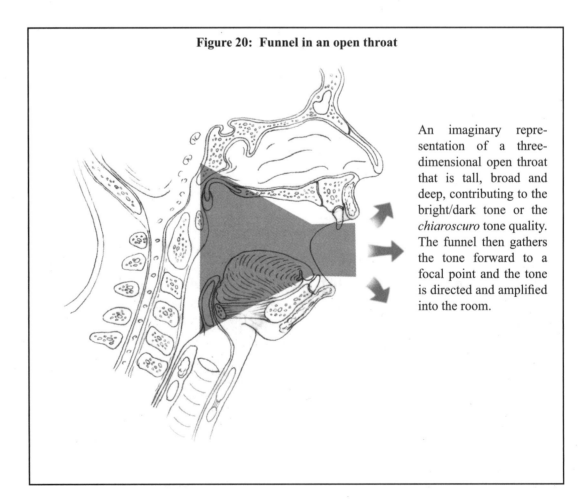

Figure 20: Funnel in an open throat

An imaginary representation of a three-dimensional open throat that is tall, broad and deep, contributing to the bright/dark tone or the *chiaroscuro* tone quality. The funnel then gathers the tone forward to a focal point and the tone is directed and amplified into the room.

Lift soft palate

♫ Smile at a secret friend across the room. Don't let anyone else see the smile. This is called the "inside smile."

♫ Think about a happy secret that you can't tell anyone.

♫ When you lift your soft palate, imagine a little cocktail umbrella opening in the back of your throat.

♫ When you lift your soft palate, imagine a heart shape in the back of your throat.

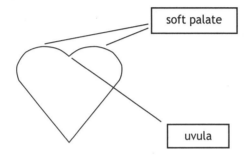

Release jaw

♫ Release your jaw as if you had very heavy lead fillings in your bottom molars.

♫ Imitate an idiot's jaw — say, "duhhh, mooom." (see page 20)

♫ Pretend you are asleep and your jaw becomes very loose, the position just before you start to snore.

♫ When you tilt your lower jaw back and down, imagine that tone flows out like from a teapot spout. "Just tip me over, pour me out."

♫ Tuck your lower jaw under your upper jaw (See *Figure 10B* and *10D* on page 8).

Especially for the Choral Conductor

The principle of singing with an open throat is one of the most important concepts you can teach your choir members; it should be a part of their regular "catechism" that you remind (nag) them about at every rehearsal. It is nearly impossible to get a beautiful choral blend in your group and good intonation if they do not understand and practice this principle. Further complicating the issue is that your singers undoubtedly come from different singing backgrounds and training and may have different concepts of "good" singing. Training the entire group to be aware of the different aspects of an open throat will solve many tonal problems and lead to a group cohesiveness and common purpose. As a choral conductor, you cannot possibly give everyone voice lessons. What you can do is provide information and training about basic principles of singing that everyone in your choir can practice and cultivate.

The following is a model that incorporates some of the principles set out in the chapter. As mentioned previously, the various components should be changed frequently to keep interest in the group.

Begin by leading the group through some tension-releasing activities and then help them to find the right alignment for singing (see Chapter 1 "Release of Tension and Positioning the Instrument" on page 4). Then invite them to do the following:

1. Inhale through your nose and smell something wonderful like chocolate, or fresh coffee, or the fragrance of a rose. Exhale. Now inhale through your mouth and feel the air lift your soft palate and open your throat. Exhale. It often helps to imagine that you can inhale through the nose and mouth simultaneously; this also contributes to an open throat feeling.
2. Inhale again and gently monitor your larynx with your fingers. Do not hold it down. Feel how it lowers as you inhale. As you exhale, maintain that low, unpressed position.
3. This time inhale with the beginning of a yawn and exhale as if you were warming up cold hands. Feel that the inhaled air is being warmed by the open throat as you inhale.
4. Still remembering that warming gesture, sing Exercise 1, page 21, (Ni-ah) to get the jaw released, the tongue active, and a feeling of openness.
5. Sing Exercise 12, page 24, (zing-ah / zing-oh) to activate the soft palate, the tongue, the jaw and the lips. Maintain the open feeling.
6. Sing Exercise 2, page 21, (wa-li wa-li) to add range, activate jaw, lips. Maintain open feeling.
7. Sing Exercise 3, page 21, (vi-va vi-va vi), which adds agility. Maintain the open feeling of the three-dimensional funnel as you sing this exercise.
8. At this point your choir is ready for the next step, breath-training exercises. Luckily, that is the next chapter!!!

Summary

♫ Opening the vocal tract is the initial gesture of beautiful singing.

♫ Many aspects of an open vocal tract are under your direct control.

♫ Your job as a singer is to:

Learn to control and manipulate your jaw freely and effortlessly so you can quickly change from one jaw position to another to accommodate consonants, pitch, timbre, and vowel shape.

Keep your tongue tension-free, with the tip behind your bottom front teeth, ready to move freely and quickly to accommodate vowel shapes and consonants, and still maintain an open throat quality that is needed for beautiful, resonant singing.

Learn to release tension in the faucial pillars, and to control the action of the soft palate without adding tension. When the soft palate lifts freely, it creates more space in the back of the throat (pharynx) and blocks off the opening to the nasal passages. Both actions are very important to beautiful singing.

Identify swallowing muscles and keep them released and uninvolved in both inhalation and exhalation/singing.

Recognize and feel the position of your larynx. This includes maintaining the proper muscle coordination that will keep it comfortably low and flexible (but not pressed down).

♫ Creating and cultivating an open vocal tract enables a singer to inhale efficiently and quickly, and sets up the right conditions to create proper resonance and beautiful singing on exhalation.

Opening the Vocal Tract

II

Notes

BREATHING FOR SINGING

Inhale with side ribs as well as diaphragm. Slow down the rate of exhalation by using intercostal and abdominal muscles. Use the concept of appoggio breathing - the voice "leans" on the breath.

Chapter III

Breathing for Singing

Chapter III

Breathing for Singing

Background and Scientific Approach

What could be more natural than breathing? One of my students joked with me at one point and said, "What's the big deal about breathing? I've been doing it all my life." Breathing is how the exchange of oxygen and carbon dioxide occurs in the lungs in humans (and many other living things). We call that exchange breathing for life. But breathing is also the engine of your singing voice, and that process is not exactly the same. That process, called breathing for singing, is not automatic; it requires attention, consistent training, muscle coordination, and your best effort.

As you are sitting around in everyday life, you breathe about 12 times a minute to maintain the oxygen levels that you need to function. Your inspiratory muscles (muscles for inhalation) expand your thorax (your chest cavity) in three dimensions: up and down, side-to-side, and front to back. This creates a negative air pressure in your lungs, and if your vocal track is open, air will naturally enter your lungs to even out the air pressure, and the exchange of oxygen and carbon dioxide takes place. In this breathing for life process, the inspiratory muscles then rebound to their original positions, the air is expelled, and the cycle starts all over again. When your body is at rest, your expiratory muscles (muscles for exhalation) are generally passive in this process.

In breathing for singing, singers need a much more active breathing cycle. The airflow and pressure described above are not strong enough to activate the vocal folds to create the vibrations needed for singing; never mind sustaining the long phrases of upward of 12 seconds or more. Although cyclical, breathing for singing is also irregular to accommodate long or short phrases and expression, so a different regulation process is needed. Singers' vocal folds need a slow, steady, well-coordinated stream of air that is well-regulated, responsive, and controlled. When this "dynamic equilibrium" is established in a singer's breath management, called by voice teachers the "*appoggio*,"[7] then the singer can go on to do the real work of singing, which is telling stories, expressing emotions, and creating beauty.

Friedrich Brodnitz describes the *appoggio*, or breathing for singing, as follows: "This much is certain: in true support the expiration is artificially slowed down by clinging as long as possible, after expiration has begun, to the position at the end of inspiration" (Brodnitz 62). There seems to be a lot of disagreement about the best way to do this among singers and voice teachers, but every singer, and certainly every teacher of singing, should have a clear understanding of the muscles and principles involved. It is true that you don't have to know how your microwave works to use it, but when

---

7 *Appoggio* or *appoggiare la voce,* Italian for "to lean" or to "support or sustain the voice." This breath management technique has come to us from the Italian school of singing and it involves a dynamic equilibrium between inhalation and exhalation muscles, and impacts other aspects of singing, such as resonance and registration.

it doesn't work, you call in a technician whom you expect to be knowledgeable about electronics. Singers need to know what is physically going on with their instruments, and breathing is one of the most fundamental physical aspects of the art. Responsible teachers will know how to answer questions and how to explain this basic aspect of singing.

So, how do we "cling to the position of inspiration for as long as possible"? It starts with alignment of your instrument. If you haven't read Chapter 1, "Release of Tension and Positioning the Instrument," go read it now, because this chapter is really a continuation of that information. If your instrument is not aligned optimally, with tension released throughout, then your breathing for singing will be compromised. Your inhalation and exhalation muscles cannot work optimally, providing the mechanism for the *appoggio*, if your body is improperly positioned. As we begin to examine the breathing mechanism for singing, the assumption is that your body is aligned for singing and you have cultivated an open throat so that air can freely enter your body.

Almost all singers and teachers agree that high chest or clavicular breathing is not an efficient way to create a beautiful tone, although you may see many singers doing it. This method entails lifting your chest on inhalation and letting it fall on exhalation, and is sometimes referred to as the breath of exhaustion or last resort. In extreme physical circumstances this method (combined with others) will get more oxygen to your body. But for singing, it allows very little control over the rate of exhalation, which of course is one of our goals in breathing for singing. It is enough to say that singers should avoid high breathing and should cultivate the diaphragmatic-abdominal method described here and used by so many successful singers and teachers. (I might add that if your instrument is properly aligned, you will be much less likely to use the inefficient high chest method.)

Much has been said (and imagined) about the diaphragm, and for good reason; it is the main muscle of inhalation. The name and the odd spelling come from the Greek *diaphragma*, meaning a wall or partition or barrier. And that is exactly one of the diaphragm's functions — it completely separates your thorax from your abdomen, your "vitals" (lung, heart) from your "vittles" (stomach, intestines, etc.). At rest, or at the end of exhalation, it nestles up inside your ribcage, attaching at the spine, sternum and the bottom ribs, creating a tight seal between your chest and abdomen. (See *Figure 21*.)

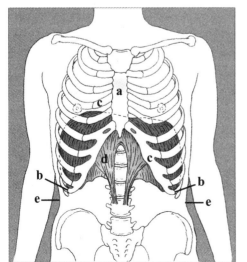

Figure 21: Diaphragm at rest at the end of exhalation

The dome shaped diaphragm is attached to the ribcage all the way around to the spine and creates a tight seal between the thorax and the abdomen. Note that the bottom complete rib is the tenth rib, and also notice the point on each rib approaching the sternum where bone becomes cartilage. The natural waistline is the place between the lowest end of the ribcage and the beginning of the hipbones.

a) sternum
b) tenth rib
c) rib cartilage
d) diaphragm
e) natural waistline

The diaphragm is shaped like a dome, or an upside-down bowl with an indentation in the top to accommodate your heart. Your lungs rest right on top of it and will move when your diaphragm moves. When your diaphragm contracts, it flattens out; it is actually a fairly subtle movement, descending about 1.5 centimeters (cm) when you are at rest and about 6 to 7 cm when you are singing (Zemlin 61). The flattening creates a vacuum in your chest and when you inhale, air comes in through your open vocal tract and fills your lungs. This downward movement accounts for the increased north/south dimension in your thorax mentioned earlier.

The flattening or lowering of your diaphragm also pushes against your viscera (all those abdominal organs) and you may feel them move out. This outward movement is sometimes mistaken as being your actual diaphragm, but it is not. As much as we would like to believe it, we cannot feel our diaphragms. What you can feel is your viscera being displaced by the movement of your diaphragm. You may also have a feeling of release and support in your pelvic girdle. This group of muscles (see *Figure 22*)

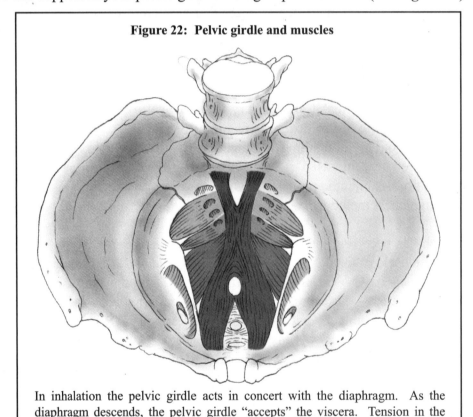

Figure 22: Pelvic girdle and muscles

In inhalation the pelvic girdle acts in concert with the diaphragm. As the diaphragm descends, the pelvic girdle "accepts" the viscera. Tension in the pelvic girdle will inhibit proper inhalation. This area also supports in breath management while singing.

acts as support for the viscera as it is pushed down by the action of the diaphragm. In inhalation the pelvic girdle acts in concert with the diaphragm. It is very important that your pelvic muscles be released and "accept" the viscera. If they are tense, they will resist the action of the diaphragm and inhibit a deep inhalation. At this point in quiet breathing, your diaphragm would discontinue contracting (flattening), and return to its at-rest position, the dome shape, as the air is exhaled. But for singing we use a strategy that works to keep the diaphragm in a flattened position for as long as possible after phonation has begun. Before we examine that, let's look at the other muscles that assist in inhalation.

As you look at *Figure 23*, notice that the ribs are not actually bone where they attach to the sternum, but cartilage. This gives them some flexibility in movement.

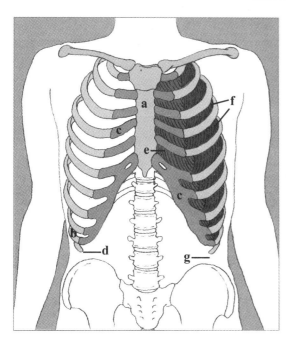

Figure 23: Thorax with intercostal muscles (diaphragm removed)

The left side of this diagram shows the rib bones without intercostal muscles. Ribs are numbered from the top down. The tenth rib is the lowest "complete" rib, and the eleventh and twelfth ribs are floating ribs. (The twelfth rib is not visible in this picture.) The right side of this picture shows the intercostal muscles, interior and exterior. Both sides show that the part of the rib that is closest to the sternum is made of cartilage.

a) sternum
b) tenth rib
c) rib cartilage
d) eleventh floating rib
e) interior intercostal muscles
f) exterior intercostal muscles
g) natural waist

The muscles that move the ribs are called the intercostals and they are tucked between each rib, one set external and one internal. (And yes, when you eat baby back ribs at Papa's Rib Joint, you get a great anatomical view of pig intercostal muscles. They work the same way.) When the external intercostals contract, they pull the ribcage out and up, similar to the movement of the handle on a bucket. (See *Figure 24*.)

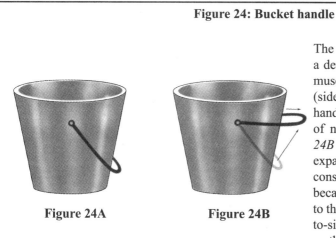

Figure 24: Bucket handle

Figure 24A   Figure 24B

The way a bucket handle moves can be a demonstration of how the intercostal muscles can move the lower ribs out (side-to-side) as well as up. In *24A* the handle represents the ribs at the end of normal exhalation. The handle in *24B* illustrates how the lower ribs can expand side-to-side because of their construction of bone and cartilage and because of their particular attachment to the sternum and the spine. This side-to-side expansion enables the *appoggio* method of breath management.

This side-to-side action increases the circumference of the thorax and provides the other two dimensions mentioned previously, side-to-side and front to back. With the inhalation action of the diaphragm and the external intercostal muscles, we have three-dimensionally increased the capacity of the thorax and set the stage for exhalation/singing. You have a lot of control over this movement, especially the side-to-side aspect. The dynamic equilibrium that you need for optimal breath management is only possible when your ribcage is expanded side-to-side. From this position comes the *appoggio* that will enable you to sing expressively and to cultivate healthy vocal habits.

Before we start to exhale, a mention should be made of the accessory muscles of inhalation, the scalenes and the sternocleidomastoids. (See *Figure 25*.) These muscles

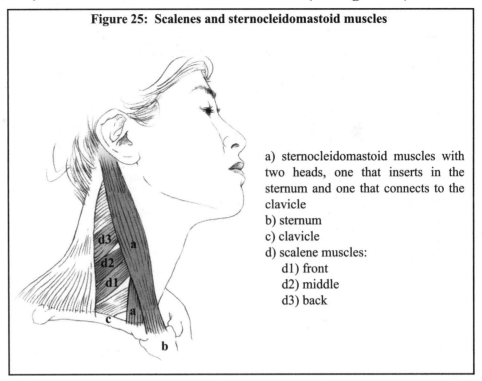

Figure 25: Scalenes and sternocleidomastoid muscles

a) sternocleidomastoid muscles with two heads, one that inserts in the sternum and one that connects to the clavicle
b) sternum
c) clavicle
d) scalene muscles:
    d1) front
    d2) middle
    d3) back

are classified as inspiratory, but if you have positioned your instrument correctly, you have already engaged them to elevate your sternum and slightly raise your ribcage to the "noble" position that is tall and flexible. (This does not mean to raise your shoulders.) If you find your chest lifting or heaving on inhalation, re-think your original singer's stance and cultivate this more useful position. It is too much work to lift your chest with every inhalation. Think how many times you would have to heave up and down to get through *Una voca poco fa*. (The Count and Rosina would never get married.)[8]

Finally, we reach the promised moment of exhalation, or in the case of singing, phonation![9] But Dr. Brodnitz has exhorted us to maintain the position of inhalation for as long as possible, or to artificially slow down the rate of exhalation as we are singing. This is where muscle antagonism comes in, between your muscles of inhalation and exhalation. You must activate your abdominal muscles to keep your inhalation muscles from immediately recoiling back to their at-rest positions. The abdominal muscles largely control this complicated balance between unregulated exhalation and the inhalation muscles, in order for us to deliver that slow, steady stream of air to the vocal folds. We tend to refer to these muscles as a group, sometimes just saying "our abs." In one manner or another, they are all attached to the ribcage, and they help maintain the circumference of the thorax during the controlled and slowed-down airflow required for singing. When activated, your abdominal muscles set in motion the dynamic equilibrium needed for us to follow Dr. Brodnitz' direction for support in singing.

---

8 "Una voca poco fa" is a *bravura* aria sung by Rosina in Rossini's opera *The Barber of Seville*. It takes splendid breath management to sing well.

9 Technically speaking, exhalation and singing are not equivalent. In ordinary exhalation, there is very little resistance to the airflow and the glottis or vocal folds are open. In singing, or phonation, the vocal folds are approximated and offer resistance to the airflow.

The largest and the strongest of these muscles are the external obliques. (See *Figure 26*.)

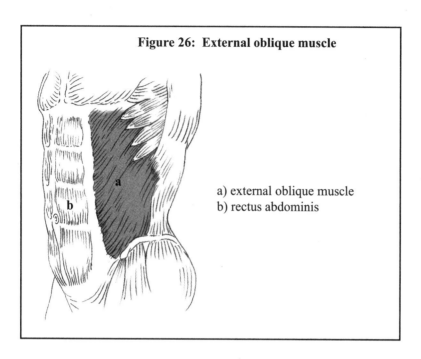

Figure 26: External oblique muscle

a) external oblique muscle
b) rectus abdominis

Like most of your muscles, they come in a pair, one on each side, and they are the closest to the surface of all your abs. They originate in the lower eight ribs and insert at your pelvis.

Underneath the external obliques lie the internal obliques. (See *Figure 27*.)

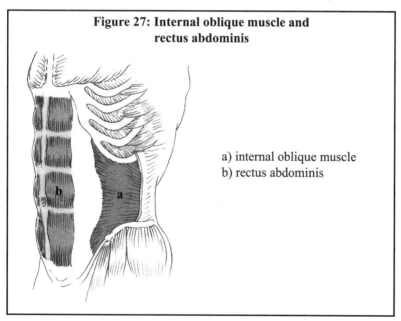

Figure 27: Internal oblique muscle and rectus abdominis

a) internal oblique muscle
b) rectus abdominis

Their directional course is opposite the externals, originating at the pelvis and continuing up to the last three or four ribs.

Going deeper into your body, under the obliques is the transverse abdominis. (See *Figure 28*.) Its muscle fibers course side-to-side, originating at the hipbone, the spine, and the last six ribs and inserting in the tissue in the middle of your body and at your pubic bone. Some of its fibers intertwine with the diaphragm.

Breathing for Singing   III

There is no clear agreement about the function of the rectus abdominis (see *Figure 27 and 28*) muscles in respiration; their primary function is to provide flexibility for the spine. They are classified as muscles of exhalation, but studies disagree about the actual function they serve in singing. Although they may aid in lowering the ribcage in exhalation, some voice teachers believe that they may contribute to

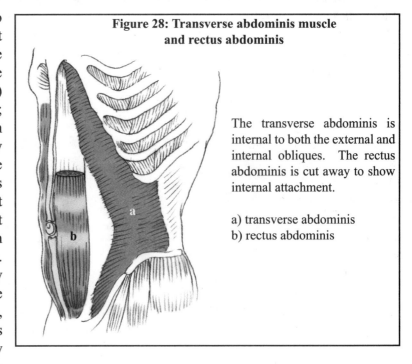

Figure 28: Transverse abdominis muscle and rectus abdominis

The transverse abdominis is internal to both the external and internal obliques. The rectus abdominis is cut away to show internal attachment.

a) transverse abdominis
b) rectus abdominis

stabilization of the thorax during exhalation as an extension of the sternum, kind of like a flying buttress resisting the outward pressure of the cathedral walls.

The quadratus lumborum (see *Figure 29*) begins at your hipbone, courses vertically

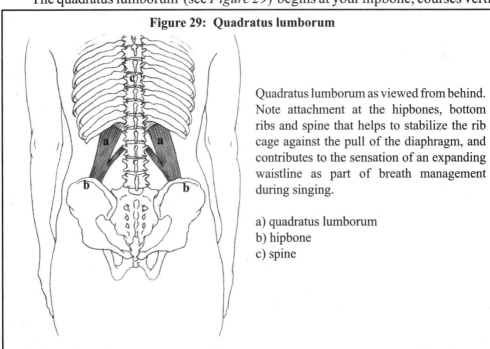

Figure 29: Quadratus lumborum

Quadratus lumborum as viewed from behind. Note attachment at the hipbones, bottom ribs and spine that helps to stabilize the rib cage against the pull of the diaphragm, and contributes to the sensation of an expanding waistline as part of breath management during singing.

a) quadratus lumborum
b) hipbone
c) spine

upward, and attaches to your bottom rib and to the lower spine. During phonation it can pull down on the bottom rib and help stabilize the ribcage against the pull of the diaphragm. It also is classified as a postural muscle and provides support for your lower back. You can feel the effects of this muscle when you use the Garcia position[10] to monitor your breathing.

10   The Garcia position is named for Manual Garcia, the nineteenth century pedagogue who advocated its use. The singer stands and crosses hands behind the back with palms facing outward. Used primarily to promote the "noble" posture, the singer can also feel the action of the 12th rib where the quadratus lumborum attaches.

The internal intercostals are not abdominal, but they are antagonistic to the external intercostals and contribute greatly to exhalation. They are located between the ribs, underneath the external intercostals, and their fibers form an X-shape with the externals. (See *Figure 23*, page 37.) This configuration enables and controls the unique movement of the ribcage. (Remember the bucket handle in Figure 24?)

On inhalation the pelvic girdle accepts and supports the viscera in order for the diaphragm to descend. Now on phonation, it works antagonistically, resisting the natural recoil action of the diaphragm, maintaining the up/down dimension of the thorax. Without this pelvic support, the abdominal muscles would not be as effective in resisting the inhalation muscles. You may experience this as extra support, low in your body, as you are singing, often described as "sitting into the breath." The important thing to remember is that all of these muscle actions are not static and tense, but dynamic and coordinated with all the other muscles in this breathing for singing mechanism. The great nineteenth century voice teacher Giovanni Battista Lamperti summed it up this way:

> *Singing is accomplished by opposing motions and the measured balance between them. This causes the delusive appearance of rest and fixity - even of relaxation. The singing voice in reality is born of the clash of opposing principals, the tension of conflicting forces, brought to an equilibrium.* (Lamperti 63)

Perhaps it appears that we are awash in minutiae identifying all these muscles; but too many times singers (and unfortunately their teachers/conductors as well) project the idea that breathing for singing is either magic or much too complicated to understand. Neither is true. The basic principles outlined here are fundamental to understanding the most efficient way to "support" in singing, as outlined so clearly by Dr. Brodnitz and others. The hard part is first understanding that all these muscles must work together in coordination to create the *appoggio*, and then training and cultivating the muscles to do what you want them to do. When a dynamic equilibrium is present throughout the entire singing instrument, the singing voice will be optimally vibrant, strong, and freely produced. The goal as you are singing is to have a perfect balance between inspiratory and expiratory gestures that allows only the perfect amount of airflow and pressure to reach the vocal folds for the desired pitch, timbre and expression. This coordination process is both physical and intuitive.

This chapter has outlined an overall view of a very complex coordinated breath management system. But don't forget that what we know for sure is that muscles are trainable even if they are a little stubborn. In the next section, you will find concrete, step-by-step exercises that will help you gradually cultivate your breath management. Give these exercises your full attention and train consistently. Remember that your ultimate goal is for your breathing for singing to be unconscious and intuitive, responding automatically to the demands of a beautiful, healthy and expressive singing performance.[11]

---

11 Those wishing a more in-depth discussion of breathing are referred to Zemlin, 33-99 and to Miller, 23-29.

Exercises To Encourage And Train *Appoggio* Breath Management

(These exercises assume that you have aligned your instrument and have cultivated an open vocal tract. They are not intended to be done all at the same practice session. The intent is to provide many different exercises for you to choose from as you establish your own practice routine.)

Finding and preparing the breath mechanism

♫ With your fingers, find your tenth rib on both sides. You don't need to count down; it is the last rib that is connected to your sternum (see *Figure 23* on page 37).

♫ Now find the top of your hipbone with your fingers.

♫ Place your fingers on the space between your tenth rib and your hipbone. This is your natural waistline but it is probably not where you wear your belt (see *Figure 23*). Your abdominal muscles are not exclusively located here, but it is a good point of reference. With your fingers on your natural waistline, do a light, delighted, lyrical laugh. "Ha ha ha ha ha." Do you feel these muscles engage? If you cough, you will feel them even more so. That engagement is the feeling that we want to be cultivating in these muscles. It is not pressed or tense, just engaged.

♫ Place your fingers on your epigastrium, (see *Figure 30*) the area just below your sternum. Pant like a small dog. Panting has almost nothing to do with actual singing, but it will help you locate and feel the effect of your diaphragm lowering and recoiling rapidly (more than in actual singing).

♫ With your fingers monitoring your tenth rib, completely exhale. At the end of exhalation, your diaphragm is in its "at rest" position, nestled up under your ribcage (illustrated in *Figure 21*, page 35).

♫ With your fingers still on your tenth rib on both sides, sniff in through your nose four times and expand your ribcage a little bit more with each sniff: "Sniff, sniff, sniff, sniff." Exhale and let your ribs recoil back to the "at rest" position. Repeat the sniffing and remember what it feels like to expand your ribs side to side.

♫ Now smoothly inhale through your nose (without sniffing) and expand your ribcage side-to-side and hold that position for a second. (You will never "hold" your breath while actually singing.) Your ribs are expanded and your diaphragm is in its contracted or flattened position. This is the position that Dr. Brodnitz wants you to maintain for as long as possible while singing (and I will add, without undue tension). Just make a mental note of what that feels like. Exhale freely, and feel how your ribs recoil back to their original position. Inhale and exhale several times, monitoring your ribcage action with your fingers.

Figure 30: Epigastrium

a) epigastrium

♫ Keep your left hand on your tenth rib and move your right hand to just below your belly button. Inhale, and note that when your ribcage expands, you can also feel the movement of your viscera as it is displaced by the flattening of your diaphragm. This is not a forceful movement. Your abdominals should not be engaged yet; on inhalation your abdominal and pelvic muscles allow your diaphragm to descend. Freely exhale and again feel the recoil. Repeat this a couple of times.

♫ Keep your left hand on your tenth rib and move your right hand to your natural waist. Inhale by expanding your ribcage. (Do you feel it with your left hand?) Exhale with short, sharp "sh" sounds. (See Exercise 22. In IPA [ʃ]. See Appendix Four, Guide to International Phonetic Alphabet, page 182.) Keep your ribcage in its expanded position and feel the engagement of your abdominal muscles at your waist. Do not let your ribs collapse! Repeat two or three times.

Exercise 22

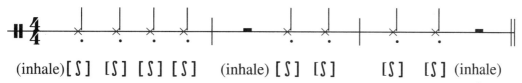

(inhale)[ʃ] [ʃ] [ʃ] [ʃ]   (inhale) [ʃ] [ʃ]   [ʃ] [ʃ] (inhale)

Now add a four count "sh" at the end. Do not let your ribcage collapse! (See Exercise 23.) You will feel your abdominals engaging as you "shhhh." Some people describe the feeling as a widening of your waistline. It is very important to keep your ribs expanded while you do this. Also, be sure to maintain your alignment. Check that ears, shoulders, and hips are all aligned. Repeat this "shhhh-ing" exercise several times.

Exercise 23

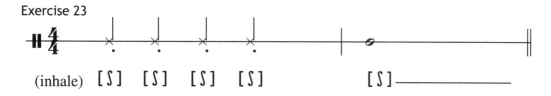

(inhale) [ʃ] [ʃ] [ʃ] [ʃ]   [ʃ]————————

Change "sh" to "s" and do the same exercise (Exercise 24). If you start to feel dizzy or light-headed, stop. Sit down.

Exercise 24

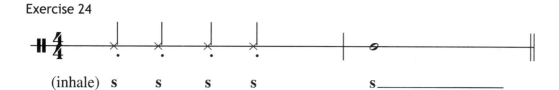

(inhale) s   s   s   s   s————————

Practice different regulations of your exhalation. Be sure to expand your ribs side to side on every inhalation. Be deliberate.

Breathing for Singing

a) Using an [s] sound, *crescendo* for four beats and *decrescendo* for four beats. (See Exercise 25.) Note how your abdominals respond to that new demand. Again, be sure your ribs stay expanded side-to-side.

Exercise 25

(inhale)   [s _____]

b) Use an [f] sound and maintain the same dynamic for eight beats: first *mf*, then *ff*, then *p*. (See Exercise 26.) Note how your abdominals respond to these new demands. Do your ribs stay expanded the whole time or at least to the very end?

Exercise 26

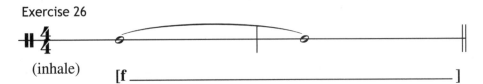

(inhale)

[f _____]

Now we start to add phonation, placing new demands on your exhalation.

a) This exercise begins with the [ʃ] sound that engages your muscles and then goes directly into tone. (See Exercise 27.) Start somewhere in the middle of your vocal range. Sopranos and tenors (high voices): D major is usually good. Mezzos and baritones (low voices): C or B major. Keep your abs engaged when you make the switch from unvoiced [ʃ] to the voiced vowel.

Exercise 27

(inhale) [ʃ] — [ʃi _____]

b) Sing the following exercise with an [m] hum. Be sure your lips are lightly together and your teeth are apart. (See Exercise 28.) You can take little sips of inhalation breaths between each *staccato*;[12] it will help you keep your ribcage out. Be sure your abdominals are engaged for the entire exercise, especially at the end on the *crescendo/ decrescendo*.

Exercise 28   *staccato*

(inhale) m   m   m   m   m   m   m   m   m____

12 *Staccato* means separated or detached.

c) Sing the same notes with an [m] hum, but this time use *martellato* instead of *staccato*. (See Exercise 29.) *Martellato* means "to hammer." In singing it means to put an emphasis on each individual note, using diaphragmatic pulses, but still connect one note to the other. This technique helps you keep your abdominals engaged. When you inhale, expand side to side and keep your ribs out for as long as possible while you are singing.

Exercise 29

d) Repeat the same exercise, but this time do it *legato*. Keep monitoring your ribcage and your waist muscles for the proper movements. (See Exercise 30.)

Exercise 30

Now sing Exercise 31. Feel the engagement of your abdominals as you *crescendo* into the vowel [u] and again as you glide up and down.

Exercise 31

Recognizing and building the *appoggio*

In Exercise 32 use a lip flutter or a lip buzz with ascending/descending glides. This is the motorboat sound you did as a child or the sound you make when you are cold, "Brrrrrr, it's cold!!!" Think about the connection between your lips and your abdominal muscles. If you cannot do this exercise, you probably have undue tension in your lips and cheeks, or your abdominals are really not engaged. Keep at it. This exercise trains a very important connection and will help you really feel the dynamic equilibrium in your instrument.

Exercise 32

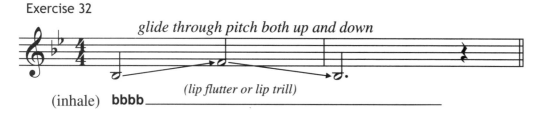

In Exercise 33 use a trilled or rolled "r" sound. Stretch the glide to an octave. This puts more demand on the breath. Keep thinking about the connection with your abdominals and always start with a strong inhalation expanding your ribs side to side.

Exercise 33

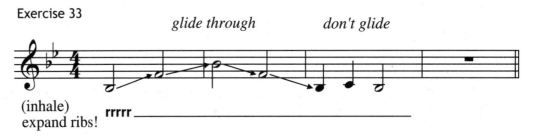

(inhale) expand ribs!   **rrrrr** _____

In Exercise 34 to add even more demand on your *appoggio*, combine both the motorboat sound with the tongue trill. (Yes, you can do this.) Glide through a full octave and back down again twice. This takes a lot more energy and effort. Remember in muscle training, "to do, first you over do." When runners are training, they frequently run with weights on their ankles or arms. This exercise is like that weight training; we tax our muscles in order to build them.

Exercise 34

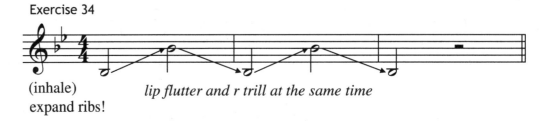

(inhale) expand ribs!   *lip flutter and r trill at the same time*

You can also use Exercise 34 to help identify your low pelvic support. Place a three-to four-inch inflated balloon between your thighs. (You can also use a three- to four-inch, small, very soft, ball.) As you are ascending in the glide with the lip flutter and rrrr trill, can you feel your thigh muscles gently pressing against the balloon? Now, can you feel a similar sensation in your low pelvic area? The idea is not to deliberately press on the balloon, but to use the balloon as a guide to discover those sensations that are already happening. These muscle actions are largely instinctive, but by being aware of them, you can condition them to assist you in singing (Vennard 25).

Use a regular drinking straw and inhale slowly through it to a count of eight, expanding your ribs side to side. Then exhale slowly through the straw for eight beats. Feel the connection with your abdominals and remember what this feels like.[13]

Still using the straw sing Exercise 35. Be sure to inhale through the straw and then sing into the straw; don't let the tone go into your nose. (Keep the soft palate lifted.)

13 There are many devices available commercially, called sports breathers or inhalation trainers, that are useful for adding resistance to both inhalation and exhalation. These devices enable singers' training and are in the category, as mentioned previously, of "to do, first you overdo." Many teachers equip their students with a 36-inch latex balloon attached to a tricycle handle. Students blow up the balloon both prior to a lesson and on a daily basis to strengthen respiratory muscles. The straw has the advantage of being cheap, more portable, and providing many of the same benefits. For more information and exercises using a balloon, go to www.PavanePublishing.com (Cantabile tab).

Exercise 35

(inhale)
expand ribs! (singing through the straw)   (inhale)

Sing Exercise 36 through the straw. Observe the *staccato* and *legato* indications and be careful not to use a hard glottal onset with the *staccato*.[14] Be sure to also inhale through the straw. Ascend by half steps.

Exercise 36

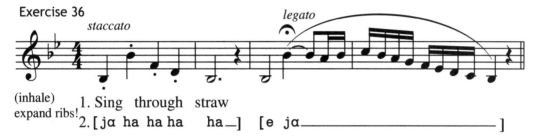

staccato   *legato*

(inhale)
expand ribs! 1. Sing through straw
2. [jɑ ha ha ha   ha—] [e jɑ————————————]

Sing Exercise 36 again with the IPA syllables printed. In order to keep the tone consistent you will have to engage your abdominal muscles. This is especially true as you go higher in your range and the further you get away from the point of inhalation.

Put a belt loosely around your ribcage. Inhale and notice if the belt expands.[15] Now see if you can sing Exercise 36 and keep the belt expanded. You can use the belt on any exercise. It is a good reminder to keep your ribs out for as long as possible when you sing. Exercise 36 is also a good exercise to use the Garcia position (page 40) mentioned earlier. Stand and cross your hands behind your back with your palms facing outward. This helps you maintain the "noble" posture and you can monitor your lower abdominal muscles as they support your singing.

More *appoggio* training exercises

As you sing Exercise 37, lean into the third note (the 3rd of the scale) and the third beat (tonic) to feel the abdominal engagement.

Exercise 37

(inhale)
expand ribs!   [i —   ɑ————————————]

---

14 More about this is coming in the next chapter. For now, just be sure to start each *staccato* note gently without a hard attack. (Not like when you've done something wrong, "uh-oh.")

15 The best kind of belt to use is either a stretchy one or the cloth ones like those that are part of the Boy Scout and Girl Scout uniforms.

Exercise 38 has both *staccato* and *legato* components. Learn them separately, but then sing the two parts as one exercise.

Exercise 38

(inhale)   ha ha ha   ha   ha   ha ha ha ha   ha ha ha   ha_____
expand ribs!

Exercise 39 also uses *staccato* and *legato* articulation. As in the other exercises, the *staccato* articulation helps your ribs to stay expanded. When you first start this exercise you can take little sips of breath between each onset, which will ever so gently remind your ribs to stay expanded. (Do not use a hard glottal onset.)

Exercise 39

(inhale)   [i   i   i   i   i_____ ɑ ɑ   ɑ ɑ ɑ_____] (inhale)
expand ribs!

Exercise 40 is an advanced exercise incorporating *staccato, legato, messa di voce*, and demands a flexible jaw as you ascend and descend. It is a "desert island" exercise. ("If you could only take one vocalise. . .")

Exercise 40

(inhale)   [jɑ hɑ hɑ hɑ   hɑ hɑ hɑ hɑ   hɑ hɑ hɑ hɑ   hɑ hɑ hɑ]
expand ribs!

[e   jɑ_____]

Exercise 41 is a cumulative exercise, requiring more and more control. It is also fun to measure your progress. How far in the counting can you go and still maintain good tone and engagement with your abdominals?

Exercise 41

Exercise 42 trains the *appoggio* as you descend. Starting in A major, tenors and sopranos should ascend by half-steps, with the high note no higher than E (C major) and then descend as low as is comfortable. Mezzos and baritones ascend to D or D sharp (B flat and B major) and then descend as low as is comfortable. Be sure to keep your abdominals engaged as you go low in your voice.

Exercise 42

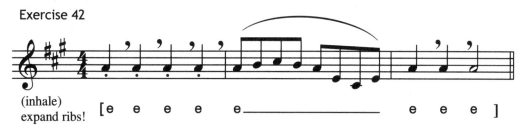

Exercise 43 will train your abdominals to anticipate when you need more support for high notes. Be sure to "lean" into the high note of each phrase (the sixth and the octave).

Exercise 43

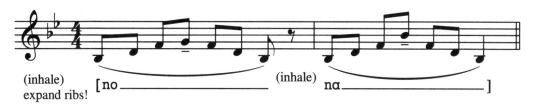

Exercise 44 teaches you to regulate your breath for long phrases that have an extra demand at the end. Use little sips of inhalation between the *staccato* notes to remind your ribs to stay out, and then notice how you must stay engaged with your breath all the way to the end of the phrase to accommodate the final octave glide.

Exercise 44

III

Breathing for Singing

Exercise 45 trains your breathing for a big power surge mid-phrase. Don't forget the little *crescendo/decrescendo* (*messa di voce*) on the octave and the hammerings on the triad down (*martellato*).

Exercises 46, 47, and 48 all cultivate the breath regulation needed to sing phrases of different lengths ascending and descending. If you take little sips of inhalation on the rests, you will also be reminding your ribs to stay out.

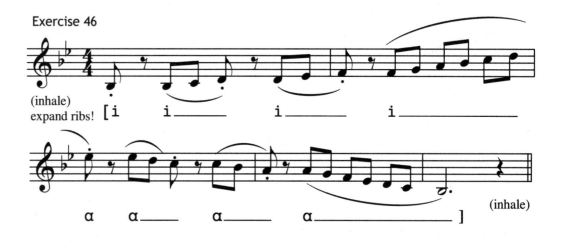

Exercice 48

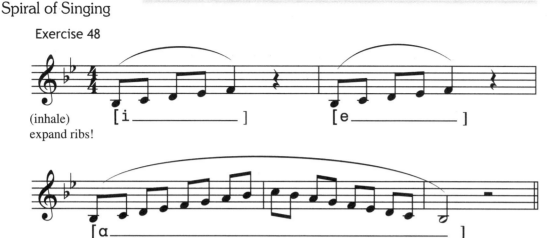

(inhale)
expand ribs!

[i_____]   [e_____]

[a_____]

Exercise 49 trains for melodic leaps and again to regulate for a breath demand at the end of a phrase. Really overemphasize the *martellato* on all the notes and don't forget to plan for the *crescendo* at the end.

Exercice 49

(inhale)   No_____
expand ribs!

Exercise 50 trains the *messa di voce* technique that is so important to expressive singing. Keep the tempo slow so you have time to do a really beautiful *crescendo/decrescendo* on the dotted quarter notes. Notice if you are trying to control this *messa di voce* gesture with your neck or throat muscles instead of your abdominal muscles. (See *Figure 31* and *32*, page 53.) If you feel any tension in your neck or throat, stop; give yourself a little neck massage, inhale a couple of yawns and try again.

Exercice 50

(inhale)   [lu_____
expand ribs!

_____]

Some Common Images Used to Encourage
Appoggio Breath Management

♫ Your ribs and diaphragm are like a fireplace bellows pointed toward the ceiling. When you pull the two handles apart, it is like the ribs expanding.

♫ "Don't blow out the candle; don't even let it flicker." This is the admonishment given by the Old Italian masters of singing to their students to encourage healthy tone with no wasted breath or breathiness.

♫ "Optimal breath management is like optimal gas mileage." With your car, you want to get the best mileage you can from each tank and still get where you want to go in a timely manner. Breathing for singing is like that; too much or too little airflow does not get your desired result. You have to train to get the optimal amount of tone for each inhalation.

♫ On inhalation, feel the expansion in your back where angel wings would sprout.

♫ Notre Dame Cathedral's flying buttresses are an excellent example of resistance. Think of your abdominal muscles as being flying buttresses for your support.

♫ Inhale all the way to the floor.

♫ Inhale into the lungs you sit on (your "bun lungs").

♫ Like the learning experience Goldilocks had, your lungs should feel neither "hungry" for air nor "overstuffed" with air, but "just right" or satisfied.

♫ Think back to Feldenkrais' three triangles mentioned in the alignment section on page 10. There it was noted that if your feet were not apart, stabilizing the bottom triangle, you might fall over. Now look at *Figure 31*. When you inhale for singing with your ribs expanded, you stabilize the middle triangle side to side. When you engage your abdominal muscles, you further stabilize the middle triangle out and down. It is not a stretch to imagine that if you don't stabilize the middle triangle in that manner, then your top triangle (your head and neck) will try to stabilize your body with tension in your neck and throat, putting undue pressure on your larynx (see *Figure 32*). It is obviously better to stabilize at the middle instead of at the larynx.

Figure 31: *Appoggio* **posture and breath management stabilizes the body**

Figure 32: Incorrect stance inducing undesirable neck tension

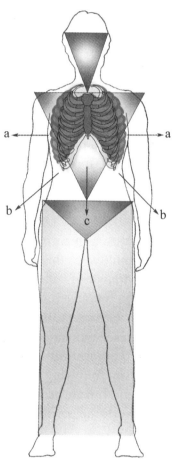

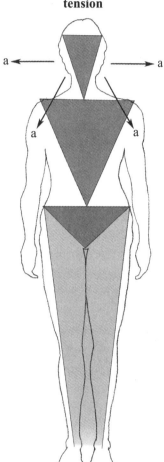

Starting from a broad-based stance, the middle triangle of the body is stabilized with correct inhalation as demonstrated with arrows "a." When abdominal muscles are engaged in breath management, the body is further stabilized as indicated with arrows "b" and "c."

a) top arrows at ribcage
b) middle arrows
c) arrow pointing down

With feet tightly together, this narrow stance tends to destabilize the core of the body. Neck and shoulder muscles are likely to attempt to compensate with unwanted tension as indicted with arrows "a." This can adversely affect the larynx's ability to vibrate freely and can compromise resonance in the vocal tract.

a) arrows at neck and shoulders

Especially for the Choral Conductor

Your choir's corporate ability to sing with adequate breath management will be the determining factor in their intonation, phrasing, beauty of tone, diction, and musicality. Like any physical, muscular skill, breathing for singing must be cultivated and maintained. This important training and maintenance job is your responsibility because you are your choir's voice teacher. Even if most of your singers have had some training in breath management, you must help them maintain the muscle tone needed to progress musically as a group. Our singing coordination is really a case of "use it or lose it." Your singers need (and want) correct information about how breathing for singing really works, and they need a training regimen that is practical, understandable, and not complicated. The basic principles outlined in this chapter should be regularly inculcated into your choir's culture and attitudes, as they take pride in their ability to sound beautiful and musical as a result of their trained breathing. The vocalises at the start of your rehearsals should give information and provide training, and then you will need to remind your choir about those principles (that they already know and have practiced) in the course of singing their repertoire. Singers will progress in their skill in a spiral manner: learning something new, practicing it, mastering it, revisiting it, and then learning something new as the spiral continues. This is the definition of art: a skill that is acquired by experience, study, and observation.

All of the exercises outlined in this chapter can be used in a group setting. It is important that all of the singers participate and are committed to the process. This attitude will come from your leadership, modeling the importance of consistent training for the good of the whole. Time is always a precious commodity in a rehearsal, but the time spent here will be regained in efficiency in other parts of the rehearsal; you won't have to stop to correct as many breathing/support problems. You can quickly remind your singers of the principles and of the results they got in the warm-up, and then apply that memory to the repertoire they are currently singing. The following is an example of a weekly (or daily) regimen that will maintain and build breath management in a group, and is designed to work in a ten-to fifteen-minute warm-up period.

Warm-up Regimen

1. Release tension and align the instrument
Begin by inviting the group to release tension in their bodies with shoulder rolls and various stretches as outlined in the previous chapter. Then remind them to get into their singer's stance by checking alignment of ears, shoulders, and hips, or by some other method. Vary this from week to week. Remind them that their breathing for singing depends on proper alignment of their instrument. Then invite them to follow you through the following instructions and exercises.

2. Establish an open throat
Release your jaw back and down, and let it stay in that position for a moment, as if your bottom jaw were very heavy. Waggle it back and forth. Thrust your tongue out of your mouth and then pull it back a couple of times and mentally remind it to stay loose. Inhale through the beginning of a yawn and exhale on your hands as if warming them.

3. Identify aspects of the *appoggio*

With your fingers on your tenth rib, do Exercise 23, page 43, together as a group two or three times. Remind them to always expand their ribs on inhalation. Then change the consonant to [s] (Exercise 24, page 43) and have them move their fingers to their abdominal muscles between their tenth rib and their hipbone. Repeat that two or three times. Remind them to feel and remember the engagement of their abdominals. (It is okay to call them waist muscles.)

4. Training inhalation for *appoggio*

Now add phonation with Exercise 27 (page 44). Start in the general lower middle of your singers' vocal range, usually B flat major, B major, or C major. On each repetition remind them to expand their ribs on inhalation and maintain that position for as long as possible. Do five or six repetitions, each time ascending by a half step.

5. Training abdominal engagement for *appoggio*

Proceed to Exercise 30 (page 45), starting in the key where you ended and descend. Ask them to notice that their abs engage on the *crescendo* and the *messa di voce*. Do five or six repetitions descending each time by a half step.

6. Training coordination of inhalation and singing with abs engaged

Model Exercise 39 (page 48) for them so they can see your ribcage expand on each of the little inhalations between the *staccato* notes. Invite them to join you and to make sure their ribs are staying expanded for as long as possible.

7. Putting all aspects of breathing for singing together in one exercise

Begin Exercise 41 (page 49) on "five by five." Ask how many made it to the end in one breath. Go on to "six by six." How many made that? No cheating in the middle of the phrase! Keep the ribs out and the abdominals engaged ("widen your waist") for the entire exercise. Remind them to release their jaw on "a-way."

8. Summation

Use the "W's" as a quick reminder of *appoggio* breathing.

   a) <u>Widen</u> (expand) your ribs on inhalation and keep "wide" as long as possible.
   b) Sing with a <u>warming</u> breath.
   c) Feel a <u>widening waist</u> for abdominal engagement while singing.

9. Apply to something new

Remind them that now when they sing the Mozart (or Craig Courteney, or Eric Whitacre, or Handel or Brahms, or whatever it is) that they need to notice their ribs expanding on inhalation and their abdominal muscles' engagement while they are singing.

Summary

♫ Breathing for singing, unlike breathing for life, needs to be trained and maintained.

♫ Singers' vocal folds need a slow, steady, well-coordinated supply of air that is well-regulated and controlled, in order to phonate properly.

♫ Many voice scientists and teachers believe the Italian *appoggio* method of breath management is the optimal strategy for breathing for singing.

♫ The *appoggio* technique is dependent on proper body alignment, sometimes referred to as "the noble posture."

♫ In inhalation, the external intercostal muscles work to expand the ribs so the diaphragm can fully descend to the position of inhalation.

♫ In singing, the abdominal and internal intercostal muscles resist the recoil action of the inhalation muscles to maintain the position of inhalation for as long as possible. This is the basis for the "dynamic equilibrium" needed for a singing tone that is beautiful, free, healthy, and expressive.

♫ Although complex, the various components of this breathing for singing process are well documented in the scientific community and can be cultivated and trained. Consistency of practice, an unambiguous understanding of the respiratory mechanism, and clear goals will lead to the vocal coordination that will free the singer from mechanically induced anxiety, and will allow for creativity and expressivity in performance.

ONSETS
AND RELEASES

Onset of tone is coordinated between breath and glottal closure. Sound is neither breathy nor pressed. Glottal stops are not used to initiate sound. Upper harmonics are initially apparent and tone has immediate presence. Releases are also coordinated, with harmonics apparent to the end of the tone. Tone is not stopped by a closure of the glottis, but by cessation of breath.

Chapter IV

Onsets and Releases

Chapter IV

Onsets and Releases

Background and Scientific Approach

We are ready for another step on our spiral road map. So far we have positioned the instrument to sing, we have prepared the instrument to receive air efficiently, and we have prepared the breath mechanism to provide the air needed to start the vibrations at the glottis (the opening between your vocal folds). Have you noticed that so far, in theory you haven't made a sound? After all that, we are finally ready to phonate: to deliver that slow, steady stream of well-coordinated air to your vocal folds. They in turn will start to vibrate, and those vibrations will be delivered to your resonators (the vocal tract), and ultimately, to someone's ears, to be perceived as singing.

You need just a little information about the structure of this amazing vocal organ, your larynx. As mentioned earlier, it is suspended in your neck from your hyoid bone. Its biological function is to protect your lower respiratory tract. Your larynx is really just a valve on top of your trachea, connected at the front, with the ability to open and close at the back. (See *Figure 33*.)

Figure 33: Cross-sections of the vocal folds

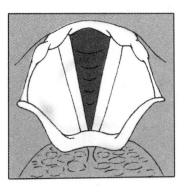 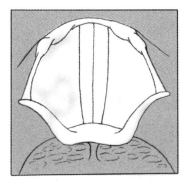 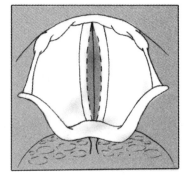

33A is a view from above which shows the vocal folds abducted or apart for inhalation and exhalation.

33B shows the vocal folds adducted or approximated for phonation, the closed phase.

33C indicates the opening and closing action of the vibrating vocal folds during phonation.

This valve function serves to prevent air from escaping from the lungs, to prevent foreign substances from entering the lungs, and to expel those substances if they start to invade. Its structure is made out of nine distinct cartilages, three of them paired (the arytenoids, the corniculates, and the cuneiforms) and the remaining three unpaired (the thyroid, the cricoid and the epiglottis). (See *Figure 34*.)

Figure 34: Nine cartilages of the larynx

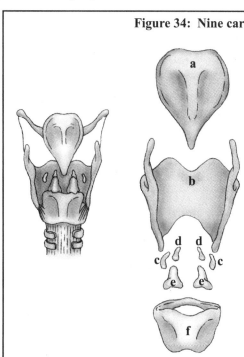

The illustration on the left depicts the cartilages as viewed from the back. On the right, the structure is "exploded" so the nine distinct components can be seen in isolation.

a) epiglottis
b) thyroid cartilage
c) corniculates cartilage (paired)
d) cuneiform cartilage (paired)
e) arytenoids cartilage (paired)
f) cricoid cartilage

They are all connected and interact by way of intrinsic (internal) ligaments and muscles. You have very little direct control over their actions. You can't say to yourself, "Now, thyroarytenoid muscle, lengthen a little." What you can do is learn to control their actions by trial and error, remembering what your successes feel like, and then reproducing them again and again (like our Spiral of Singing, on page viii). A good mantra to remember this principle is "the memory of how it feels is your main method."

The other function of your larynx is to communicate thoughts and feelings through singing or speaking. For our purposes we are mostly interested in the action of your vocal folds when singing. Each of them contains a thyroarytenoid muscle and a vocal ligament. (See *Figure 35*.)

Figure 35: Cross-section (coronal) of the vocal fold

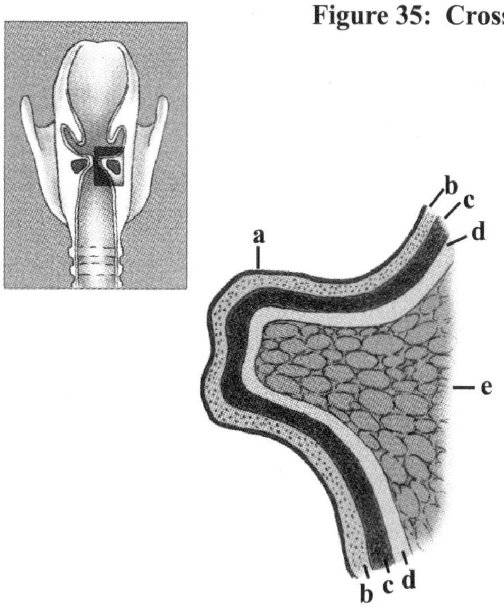

From the surface moving internally, the vocal fold has five different layers:
a) the epithelium
b) the superficial layer
c) the intermediate layer
d) the deep layer
e) the muscle

Voice scientists use two other schemes to describe the entire vocal fold. The three-layer scheme as follows:
1. the **mucosa**, which includes the epithelium (a) and the superficial layer (b),
2. the **ligament**, which is the intermediate (c) and deep layers (d), and
3. the **thyroarytenoid muscle** (e).
The two-layer scheme consists of the **cover** (epithelium and superficial and intermediate layer) and the **body** (deep layer and the muscle).

IV

Onsets and Releases

More about "floppy" vibration at www.PavanePublishing.com

The vocal folds are both loosely covered with a mucous membrane, which is an important factor in how they vibrate. The vibration begins when you deliver that slow, steady stream of well-coordinated air to your vocal folds. Voice scientists call this action myoelastic-aerodynamic. (Stay with me now!) Myoelastic means muscle (myo) that moves (elastic); aerodynamic means the motion of air and the forces that act on it. When air goes through your larynx on its way to your vocal tract, certain aerodynamic properties suck the vocal folds together and then re-open them in a physics principle called the Bernoulli Effect (Vennard 38-39). As applied to singing, scientists call this action "flow phonation."[16] At the same time, the "myoelastic" element works as a self-sustained oscillator, also contributing to a very complex vibration mechanism.[17] Voice scientists refer to this complex vibration as "floppy," meaning that the muscle, ligament, and mucosa have the ability to vibrate in more than one mode, not just back and forth like sharply clapping your hands together, but like a ribbon undulating with many rippling motions. And remember that your vocal folds are very tiny; when they are closed (adducted), for men they are about 15-22 mm long; for women, 9-13 mm. What is really important for us to know is that this myoelastic-aerodynamic "floppy" vocal fold action, coupled with sharp, clean onsets, creates the most desirable complex vibration or sound wave. This is the raw material that is acted on in the resonators to create the most beautiful singing tone. (Did you get this far? Read it again if you need to. It is complicated but important.)

This brings us back to the Spiral of Singing. This "floppy" vibration production works best under certain optimal circumstances. An incorrect head position, a tight jaw, tense neck muscles, a tense soft palate, a tense tongue, or tense laryngeal muscles are all counterproductive to this complex vibration. It is also dependent on that muscle equilibrium aspect that you set up on inhalation and are maintaining as you sing. Your vibratory mechanism has now become a part of the dynamic equilibrium in your entire instrument, and this vocal coordination of breath and phonation can be trained and controlled. And as with any skill, it must be maintained and cultivated or your ability will diminish. This is why singers continue to revisit and cultivate all the principles of singing over and over. It is not like learning math where two plus two will always be four. Singing is intuitive, not linear. There is always more to learn and add to your artistry.

So in summary, the "floppy" mode of vibration is the optimal way to phonate for singing, and the goal is to produce and send these pulses of air to be acted upon by your resonators. Voice scientists tell us that how you start and stop these pulses (the onset and release) will determine the quality of that floppiness and thereby the quality of your tone.

For the onset of tone, you have three choices, and you can practice and control all of them. The two extreme choices are 1) the pressed onset (sometimes called a glottal attack) and 2) the breathy onset. The optimal choice, flow phonation, is called 3) a coordinated onset. Sometimes this onset is also called a "silent h" onset. Beginning the tone this way, with a balance between the two extremes, will produce the most sound for the least amount of work.

---

16 Flow Phonation is further defined and discussed in Sundberg, 79-81.

17 Ingo Titze's comprehensive book, *Principles of Voice Production*, 80-109 provides an in-depth discussion of all these properties.

It is probably easiest to understand the coordinated onset in contrast to the other two less desirable ones. Imagine that your vocal folds are pressed together so hard that no air can get through. That would be the most amount of work for no sound or vibration. If some air gets through these pressed vocal folds, it is called a pressed phonation onset and it requires a high air pressure to move air through those very stiff vocal folds. There is also a lot of muscle pressure at work to keep the folds pressed together. The initial sound is like a grunt and is loud and unpleasant. Other names for this sound are the glottal attack, the hard attack, or a glottal stroke.

Now think about the other extreme of that vocal fold posture. Imagine that your folds don't come together at all, producing no vibration, no sound, and requiring no work, no muscle pressure. Then, if the folds partially come together (but not entirely) and vibrate a bit, that is called a breathy onset. Characterized by low air pressure, the sound is weak and breathy, with air escaping along with tone.

With the coordinated onset the goal is for the vocal folds to adduct (come together) precisely when the breath flow begins, with the right amount of air pressure, to make the desired tone and pitch. This perfect combination is controlled by the brain and ear and although an intuitive process, you can practice and cultivate it. (Several exercises will be given at the end of this chapter to guide you in this important skill.) This is what many choral conductors and voice teachers call "singing on the breath" and as mentioned previously, it is the most efficient combination of airflow and muscle pressure, and it provides the best "floppy" action of the vocal folds.

The tone produced at the glottis is called the glottal source. Oddly enough, to the human ear, this tone will only sound like a buzz, but it contains all the frequencies in your tone that will be acted on by the resonators. The resonators will either enhance or attenuate (weaken) frequencies, but the resonators do not create frequencies (more about this in the next chapter). That is why the "floppy" action of the vocal folds is so crucial; it creates the richest variety of frequencies to be sent along to the vocal tract to be converted into beautiful singing tones. Optimally, these harmonics will be created immediately, so that adjustments don't have to be made after the tone begins. That is one reason why the onset is so crucial.

How tone is stopped, the release, is equally important. Abruptly closing the vocal folds (a "hard" release), to choke off the sound at the end of a phrase, has an unpleasant sound, even though it is used on occasion to express emotion. Used habitually, this action can cause some damage to the vocal folds and become annoying to the listener. Perhaps more importantly, how you release the tone sets up the next onset. If you are pressing to stop the tone, you are likely to begin the tone that way, to the detriment of your "floppy" vibration.

The soft release is the other extreme. Allowing the vocal folds to gradually separate at the ends of phrases while the breath is still flowing has a trailing off effect on the tone. It also disturbs the dynamic equilibrium of your breath and can cause your instrument to collapse. And like the "hard" release, this "soft" release will also affect your next onset, increasing the likelihood that you will begin with a breathy sound.

The best release, like the onset, is a coordinated one, where the vocal folds abduct (open) precisely as the airflow is turned around and inhalation begins. This ensures a consistency of tone quality throughout each phrase and within each musical paragraph as tone begins and ends. This constant balance between "hard" and "soft" onsets and releases is a major contributing factor to *legato* singing and freedom in the voice, a product of dynamic equilibrium in both breathing and phonation. It seems we are back to that Goldilocks lesson that was apparent in breathing; a well-coordinated onset is "just right."

Exercises to Encourage Coordinated Onsets and Releases

Continuing on our Spiral of Singing, it is assumed that prior to beginning these exercises, you have released tension in your instrument, prepared an open vocal tract, and you are cultivating a proper dynamic equilibrium for your breathing in order to support a healthy phonation. All these exercises are not intended to be done in one practice session; the intent is to provide many different exercises for you to choose from as you establish a regular practice routine.

Begin Exercise 51 by singing just one sustained pitch in the middle of your range, holding for three beats and then inhaling on the fourth.

Exercise 51

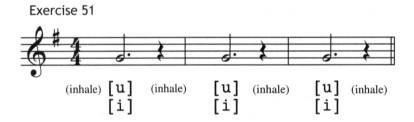

Listen carefully for the quality of the tone throughout the entire three beats. Does it start well with a "silent h"? Does the tone continue consistently? Does it end with the cessation of breath, but not a breathy trailing off? Repeat on several different pitches on both vowels [u] and [i]. Do the onsets and releases change as you ascend? Descend?

Exercise 52 adds short repeated notes with some *legato* to maintain breath equilibrium. Begin in the middle of your vocal range and listen carefully for how you start and stop the repeated pitches at the beginning and end.

Exercise 52

Exercise 53 now adds higher repeated pitches as well. Start in the low part of the middle of your voice and carefully differentiate between the *legato* pitches and the repeated ones.

Exercise 53

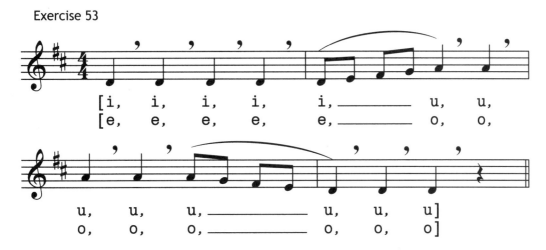

Exercise 54 adds eighth notes on the onsets, requiring more quick muscle action. Begin with a tempo that is comfortable and gradually push yourself to go faster.

Exercise 54

Exercise 55 is made up entirely of eighth notes. Again, begin with a comfortable tempo and gradually go faster as you are able.

Exercise 55

Exercise 56 increases the speed with triplet rhythms. As you get going on the challenge of getting the right rhythms and right notes, don't forget to listen for the onsets and releases. If they are breathy or hard, slow down the exercise until you can do it well with coordinated onsets and releases.

Exercise 56

Exercise 57 is similar to Exercise 56, only longer. You are training your muscles for endurance and consistency. When this is going well, begin Exercise 58, which is the same exercise only with *legato*. Be sure to take care with the new onset when you change vowels.

Exercise 57

[i, i, i, i, i, i, o, o, o, o, o, o, o—]
[e, e, e, e, e, e, ɑ, ɑ, ɑ, ɑ, ɑ ɑ, ɑ—]

Exercise 58

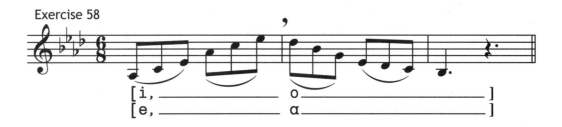

[i, —————————— o ———————————————————]
[e, —————————— ɑ ———————————————————]

Exercise 59 now has vowel changes more frequently, requiring quick articulation of the tongue and jaw; it presents a double coordination problem: larynx muscles AND articulators! Listen to be sure they don't get in each other's way. Exercise 60 adds some *legato* singing, and Exercise 61 even more. Don't lose sight of the goal: clean beginnings and endings for each onset, whether there is *legato* singing in between or not.

Exercise 59

[i, i, ɑ, ɑ, i, i, ɑ, ɑ, i, i, ɑ, ɑ, i]

Exercise 60

[i, i, ɑ, ɑ, i, i, ɑ, ɑ, i— ɑ— i]

Exercise 61

[i, __ ɑ, __ i, ɑ, __ i, __ ɑ, __ i]

Exercise 62 adds a descending pattern to the onset/release practice.

Exercise 62

[u wɑ]   [u wɑ]   [u wɑ, ɑ, ɑ]

Exercise 63 and Exercise 64 add more articulation practice with the onset/release pattern.

Exercise 63

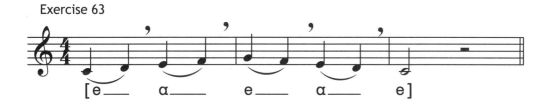

[e___ ɑ___ e___ ɑ___ e]

Exercise 64

[i_____ e   i_____ e

i_____ e, __ e, __ i_____ e]

Exercise 65 and Exercise 66 use actual words instead of just vowel sounds. As you add the other consonants, go slowly so you can hear and feel your onsets and releases. It is true that sometimes in singing English we deliberately add glottal or hard attacks for expression or clarity, but we want those glottals to be a matter of choice and not habit. Practice these two exercises without any glottal. Then add a few (gently please) to experiment with how glottal onsets can change the meaning.

Exercise 65

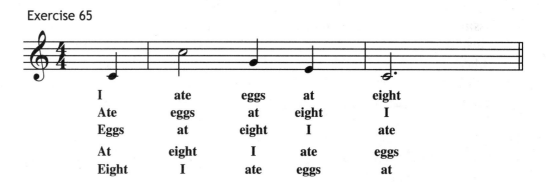

I	ate	eggs	at	eight
Ate	eggs	at	eight	I
Eggs	at	eight	I	ate
At	eight	I	ate	eggs
Eight	I	ate	eggs	at

Exercise 66

I ar - rived ear - ly while Ed - na ate.

Some Common Images Used to Describe Coordinated Onsets and Releases

♫ The voice rides on a constant pillow of air. Suspend the first tone on that pillow and keep the others floating.

♫ Begin tone by the permission of the breath. Tone also ends by permission of the breath.

♫ Think the tone and then sing the breath.

♫ Send out a continuous column of "silent h."

♫ Initiate tone on the gesture of inhalation.

♫ Onsets should be gentle but firm, like a ballerina putting her foot down after a lift. She doesn't stomp it down or place it tentatively, but with practiced gentleness and firmness.

Especially for the Choral Conductor

Training your choir to become aware of the three different ways of initiating and stopping tone is an important factor in the beauty of your choir's sound and in their ability to be expressive. Unlike individual voice training, where the extremes of onset and release are highly discouraged (breathy and hard), there are many times in choral singing when, for emotional reasons or for clarity of text, you may request your singers to corporately use a breathy or glottal attack. This is an interpretive choice and should be made by you and not by your singers because they have individually habituated a particular onset and release pattern.

So the issues for the choral conductors to address are:
- ♪ Teaching your choir the difference between the three onsets and releases
- ♪ Making sure as a rule, that they understand the vocal health and vocal efficiency implications of not using the coordinated onset/release
- ♪ Cultivating with your choir the control to exercise any of the three onsets and releases as a choice
- ♪ Training them to listen to themselves within the group to be sure they are singing onsets and releases in the manner you have prescribed, almost always the coordinated onset/release

How vocal folds work

If you place your hands together like you are praying, you get a pretty good model of how the vocal folds function i.e. fingertips only together: abduction; fingers and palms completely touching: adduction; fingertips and base of palm together with middle of hands undulating: phonation. (See *Figure 36A, 36B, 36C*). This is a three second rehearsal demonstration, and you will be surprised at how many singers don't

Figure 36: Hand demonstration of how vocal folds work

 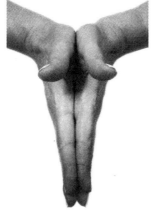 

36A: Abduction-vocal folds open for inhalation and exhalation

36B: Adduction-vocal folds touching for closed phase of phonation

36C: Open phase of phonation.

Example of a rehearsal demonstration of how vocal folds work, viewed as a cross section looking "down a throat" from the pharynx toward the lungs. Thumbs could represent the arytenoids cartilages. Compare this figure with *Figure 33*, p.58.

During phonation the vocal folds alternate between 36B and 36C, but with an undulating open and closing motion, beginning with the bottom of the vocal fold nearest the lungs. Voice scientists call this a "floppy" phonation.

know how their vocal folds move. Then demonstrate with your own voice a "hard" onset, a "breathy" onset, and then a coordinated onset (called the "silent h" onset). In the course of this demonstration, mention that a habitual "hard" onset can cause muscle fatigue and perhaps damage, and that the breathy attack causes laxness throughout the entire instrument. Continue with vocal exercises that help them recognize and cultivate a healthy coordinated onset and release pattern. A suggested sequence for one rehearsal is outlined below. (Any of the vocal exercises listed in this chapter can be used with a group.) It is assumed that your choir has released tension, prepared an open vocal tract, and established breath management.

A Rehearsal Sequence

♫ Begin with Exercise 67: one note initiated and stopped four times and then held. Have them repeat with a "hard" glottal onset for negative practice. Then have then do it with a "breathy" onset, again for negative practice. Then have them begin each note with a silent, coordinated "h." Tell them that most of the time they will corporately use the silent "h" onset. Reinforce that the noise partials created by individual "breathy" and "glottal" onsets, because of their high frequencies, will carry over the coordinated onset of the whole group (one rotten apple. . .).

Exercise 67

[i,   i,   i,   i,   i]

♫ Go immediately to Exercise 52, page 62, which is similar to Exercise 67 with added *legato*. Remind them to listen and feel individually, and to listen corporately for the proper onset.

♫ Now go to one of the exercises that uses eighth notes, (Exercise 54, page 63; Exercise 55, page 63; or Exercise 59, page 64). Gradually speed up the tempo to train flexibility.

♫ Now use Exercise 65, page 66, to demonstrate how different onsets can affect meaning. "I / ate eggs at eight" has a different feel than "Ate eggs at eight / I." Reinforce that everyone in the group is responsible to reproduce the requested onset pattern. Individually they do this by listening and by feel.

Summary

♫ Vibrations for your singing instrument are created in your larynx.

♫ The larynx is made up of small cartilages and muscles that interrelate in a complex manner, and are also affected by external muscles.

♫ The larynx has a biological function: keeping foreign matter out of your lungs.

♫ The other laryngeal function is one of communication and expression. It is the vibrator of your singing instrument.

♫ The larynx's scientific function is described as myoelastic (muscles that move) aerodynamic (motion and forces of air).

♫ A "floppy" mode of vibration creates the richest variety of frequencies to be acted on later in the resonators.

♫ There are three ways to initiate and stop the vibration (the onset and release). The "hard" onset (too much muscle and air pressure), the "breathy" onset, (too little muscle and air pressure), and the coordinated onset, (optimal muscle and air pressure initiated simultaneously). Singers should train to consistently produce the coordinated onset.

♫ A coordinated onset with a "floppy" mode of vibration produces the most amount of sound for the least amount of work.

♫ There are times in singing that either the glottal or breathy onsets might be used for expression. This should be a matter of taste and choice, not a matter of habit or inability.

IV

Onsets and Releases

IV

Notes

RESONANCE

Vibrations are optimzed and refined to produce a solid "core" sound. Each vowel has a distinct shape that has an optimal sound throughout the range.

Resonance

Chapter V

Resonance

Background and Scientific Approach

Fully realized, beautiful resonance should be the goal of every singer, and like the other aspects of singing, it needs to be continually cultivated and trained as part of the Spiral of Singing we have been exploring. Although it is necessary to have a linear approach to each topic in each chapter (including this one), it needs to be restated that all functions of singing are interactive. If you think of a Slinky toy, which is a good spiral, you know that if you move one part of it, the whole toy moves. So as we are examining different aspects of the Spiral of Singing, don't forget that it is all interconnected and interdependent. This is especially true of resonance.

A simple definition of resonance is when sound waves from one source are intensified or enriched in some other way. In singing, vibrations made at the glottis are enhanced, enlarged, reinforced, and some are attenuated in the resonators to get a beautiful singing tone. Before they get to the resonators, the vibrations that are created at the glottis are called the glottal source. The sound created there, directly from the vocal folds, is not a beautiful, fully realized tone; it is more like a buzz. But if the optimal conditions with the breath and phonation have been met, this sound source will be very rich in harmonic frequencies, carrying all the frequencies that are needed, to be turned into beautiful tone in the vocal tract. It is also conversely true that if the frequencies are NOT created at the glottis, then they cannot be enhanced, or enriched, or enlarged in your resonators. You can only amplify what is already provided. The resonators do not create frequencies, they just interact with the frequencies created at the glottis, enhancing some and attenuating others.

The Source/Filter Theory of Vowels

Voice scientists agree that your primary resonators are your pharynx (throat) and your mouth.[18] (Your nasal cavities also contribute but only on nasal sounds when your soft palate is down.) They compare these two spaces to two tubes that are coupled together with one end closed, at your larynx; and one end open, at your lips. (See *Figure 37.*)

---

18   A comprehensive discussion can be found in Titze, 136-168.

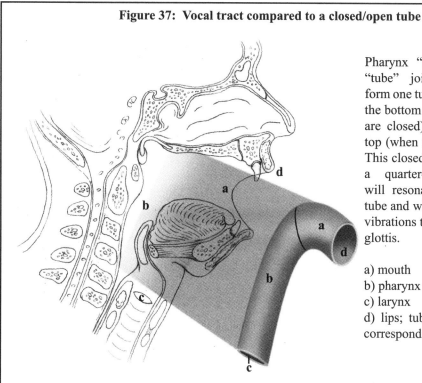

Figure 37: Vocal tract compared to a closed/open tube

Pharynx "tube" and mouth "tube" joined together to form one tube that is closed at the bottom (when vocal folds are closed) and open at the top (when the lips are open). This closed/open tube, called a quarter-wave resonator, will resonate like a simple tube and will filter the source vibrations that come from the glottis.

a) mouth
b) pharynx
c) larynx
d) lips; tube is labeled with corresponding parts

More about spectral analysis and quarter-wave resonators at www.PavanePublishing.com [Cantabile tab]

Even though your resonators can constantly change shape, this closed/open tube (called a quarter-wave resonator) will resonate like what physicists call a "simple tube," and in singing will act as a "filter" of the "source" vibrations that come from your glottis. How this tube filters these vibrations will determine which vowel is perceived, and you will determine that filtering process by how you shape your resonators, primarily your throat and mouth. Stated in another way, by your direct control of your vocal tract, you can determine not only what vowel you sing, but the degree of resonance (or lack thereof). This process, when your vocal tract acts upon the glottal source, is called the source-filter theory of vowels.[19]

With the use of several graphs, we can illustrate this manner of creating resonance. Imagine that the sound emitted from your glottis contains around 40 frequencies from 145 Hz to 5000 Hz. (145 Hz would be baritone D3, the D below middle C. 5000 Hz would be really high, beyond the highest note of the piano.)

At the glottis, the first frequency would be the loudest and each subsequent frequency would be perceived as softer and softer. (The actual fall-off is about 12 dB per octave.) This is the buzz sound (mentioned on page 72) with no help from the resonators, called the glottal source. *Figure 38* shows a graph, called a power spectrum, of all the harmonics in a glottal source (see *Figure 38*).

---

19 Much of the original research in this area has been carried out by Johann Sundberg. See *The Science of the Singing Voice*, 49-133 for a complete discussion of the voice source and the source-filter theory of vowels.

Figure 38: Glottal source shown as a Power Spectrum

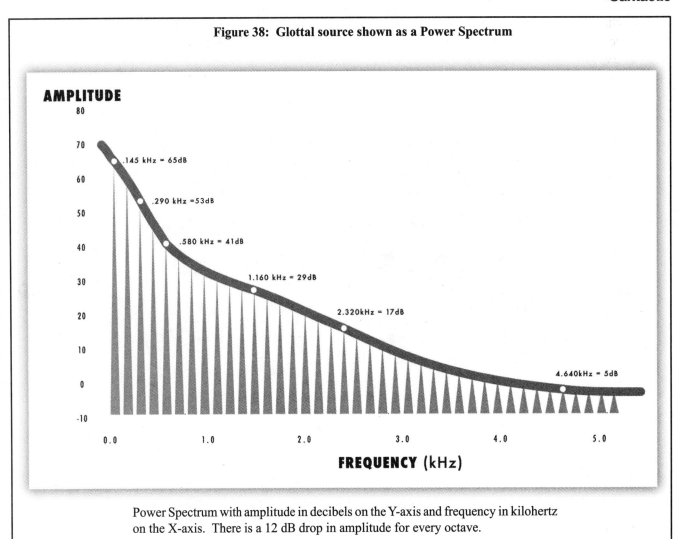

Power Spectrum with amplitude in decibels on the Y-axis and frequency in kilohertz on the X-axis. There is a 12 dB drop in amplitude for every octave.

The frequencies read across the bottom from 0.0 to 5.5 kHz, the X-axis; this is the "spectrum" aspect of the graph. The amplitude in decibels (dB) is from bottom to top on the left-hand side, the Y-axis; this is the "power" aspect of the graph. You can see how the loudest frequency is the fundamental pitch, in this case 145 Hz, and all the subsequent harmonics get softer at the rate of 12 dB per octave.

Now we begin the filtering process. Imagine that you make the front of your vocal tract tube smaller in diameter than the back of your tube. How do you do that? You bring your tongue forward and shape the vowel [i]. The vowel we are creating here is [i] as in "see." Because of the scientific laws of the quarter-wave resonator, some of those frequencies from the glottal source will be enhanced, made stronger, and perceived as louder. Some of those frequencies will be attenuated, made softer, or will disappear all together.[20] Appelman's research (226) tells us that a well-resonated [i] vowel will have peaks of amplitude strength at 300 Hz, 1950 Hz, and 2750 Hz. So imagine on the chart that the frequencies right around 300 Hz are "pulled up," (intensified or perceived as louder) and also the frequencies right around 1950 Hz and 2750 Hz are "pulled up" (enhanced or enlarged or reinforced). And also imagine that

20 Formant frequency values are taken from D. Ralph Appelman, The Science of Vocal Pedagogy, 226.

all the other frequencies are attenuated or diminished. Those areas of frequencies that are "pulled up" or strengthened are called formants, and the first two will determine what vowel sound the human ear will perceive. *Figure 39* and *40* are spectral analysis examples of a professional baritone singing an [i] vowel. (See *Figure 39* and *40*.)

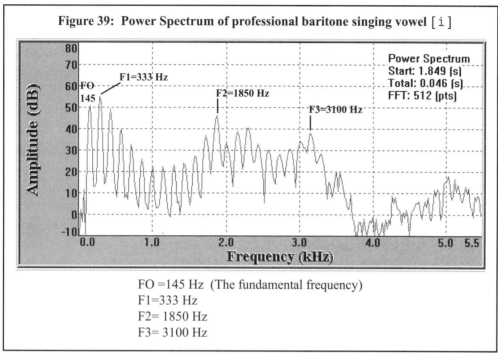

Figure 39: Power Spectrum of professional baritone singing vowel [i]

FO =145 Hz (The fundamental frequency)
F1=333 Hz
F2= 1850 Hz
F3= 3100 Hz

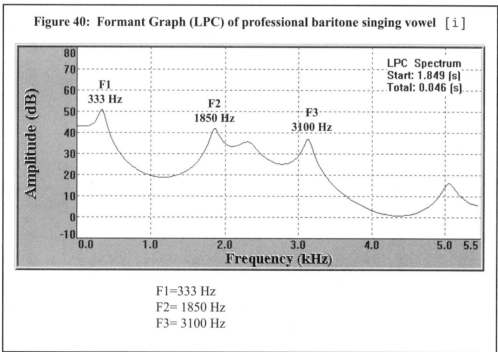

Figure 40: Formant Graph (LPC) of professional baritone singing vowel [i]

F1=333 Hz
F2= 1850 Hz
F3= 3100 Hz

Figure 39 is a Power Spectrum that shows all the individual harmonics and their amplitudes. Note that the first harmonic is around 145 Hz and this represents the fundamental pitch that we perceive as around D3. Immediately to the right of 145 Hz is the next prominent harmonic, around 333 Hz, very close to the norm in Appelman's research. The second area of strength is at 1850 Hz, very close to the 1950 Hz ideal. The third area of strength is around 3100 Hz, a little high but close to the norm, and well within the 2800-3200 range that we expect in singers for the third formant. *Figure*

40 is an LPC spectrum of the same sound showing the formant peaks at 333 Hz, 1850 Hz, and 3100 Hz (note that an LPC graph does not show the Fundamental Frequency of 145Hz). This baritone is singing a vowel that our ears will recognize as an [i] and it will sound "in resonance," because he has shaped his resonators skillfully into that particular shape. Keep in mind that pitch is not necessarily a factor, especially in your mid-range. If your tube is in the [i] shape, the most intense frequencies will be somewhere around 300 Hz and 1950 Hz (a little higher for women). You have "filtered out" all the frequencies that don't contribute to the [i] sound, leaving only those that do. Remember that your resonating tube is a coupling of your throat and mouth space.

Now imagine that we change the shape of the tube, making the front part relatively larger than the back part. How do you do that? From the [i] position you release the middle of your tongue down, and the back part of your tongue releases or grooves. The tip of your tongue rests gently behind your front teeth. You release your jaw, which makes the front of your tube larger than the back portion of your tube. We are forming the vowel [ɑ] like "father" in English. Now different frequencies will be "pulled up," or favored, or strengthened. According to Appelman (226), the first area of enhancement for [ɑ] will be around 700 Hz; that is the first formant. The second area of enhancement or formant will be around 1200Hz and the third for this [ɑ] vowel will be around 2600 Hz. Again these formant values are not determined or much affected by pitch. And to state it again, if the spectral analysis shows these values, then it means that the singer has "filtered out" the frequencies that don't contribute to a resonant [ɑ]. So let's see how our baritone does with the [ɑ] vowel. *Figure 41* and *42* show the same professional baritone singing [ɑ] at G3, the G below middle C. The Power Spectrum (*Figure 41*) shows the first harmonic at 193 Hz; that is the fundamental pitch that we will hear at G3, the G below middle C. The next peak area is at 597 Hz, labeled F1 or Formant 1. Formant 2 (F2) occurs at 1087 Hz, F3 at 2604. These values match pretty well with Appelman's ideal values, so our ear will hear this as a resonant vowel [ɑ]. The formant graph (LPC), *Figure 42*, gives a clearer picture of the peaks in this particular sound at that particular moment.

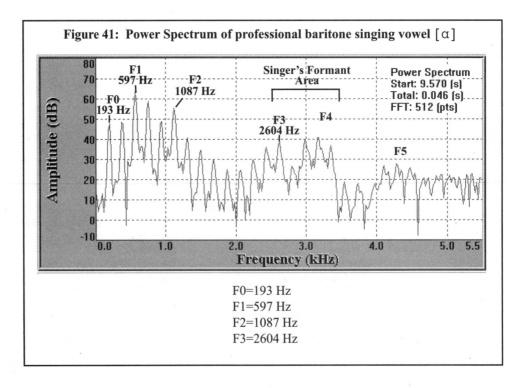

Figure 41: Power Spectrum of professional baritone singing vowel [ɑ]

F0=193 Hz
F1=597 Hz
F2=1087 Hz
F3=2604 Hz

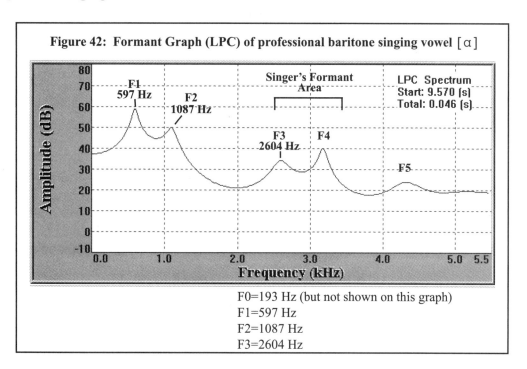

Figure 42: Formant Graph (LPC) of professional baritone singing vowel [α]

F0=193 Hz (but not shown on this graph)
F1=597 Hz
F2=1087 Hz
F3=2604 Hz

V

Resonance

Of course it follows that all vowel sounds will come from a unique optimal shape formed by your coupled resonator tube (vocal tract), and the sound produced by each unique shape will be perceived and recognized by the human ear as that particular vowel sound.

You may also notice in *Figure 41* and *42* that there are several other "mountains" or formants. The third formant (third from the left) has been named the "singer's formant." In trained voices, it appears at about 2800 Hz to 3400 Hz. This formant or area of intensity is perceived as the singer's "ring" and it is what enables us to hear a trained singer's voice (not amplified electronically) over the sound of the entire symphony orchestra. The third, fourth, and fifth formants contribute to the timbre or color of your voice. Unlike the first two formants that are about the same from voice to voice and determine the vowel, the "color" formants (F3, F4, F5) will vary more from singer to singer.

So to sum up, the sound source, created at the glottis, contains many frequencies or partials, also called harmonics. Your vocal tract, which is your resonator and is under your control, changes into different positions that will intensify some frequencies and attenuate or decrease others. The intensified frequencies are called formants. The first two formants determine the vowel sound that will be perceived, and the others determine the singer's "ring" and vocal colors.

Titze (Principles, 165-167) summarized the relationship of the vocal tract and the formants and they are paraphrased as follows:

> If you lengthen the vocal tract, you will lower all frequencies. This will "darken" the tone (see further explanation in box on page 78). You can lengthen the vocal tract by lowering your larynx or protruding your lips. Conversely, if you shorten your vocal tract, by raising your larynx or spreading your lips, all the frequencies will raise. This will be perceived as "brightening" the tone. Any combination of larynx movement and lip protrusion will effect the perceived darkness or brightness of the tone.

Opening your mouth or releasing your jaw will raise the first formant. This is what singers do when they modify the vowels as they ascend in pitch.

If you constrict the front of your vocal tract (your mouth), you will lower formant one and raise formant two. This constriction is made primarily with your tongue. The poster child for this position is vowel [i] where the tip of the tongue is behind the bottom front teeth and the rest of the tongue moves forward, making more space in the throat and less space in your mouth.

If the back of your vocal tract (your throat) is relatively smaller than the front (your mouth), you will raise the first formant and lower the second. The poster child for this position is vowel [ɑ]. This is a bit counter-intuitive, because we think of the "ah" sound as having an open throat. In fact, the throat is open, but relative to your mouth with an open jaw, the throat space is less than the mouth space. Of course the tongue position is also a contributing factor; it should be flattened and grooved.

All manipulations (deliberate or not) in any part of the vocal tract tube, including the soft palate, the pillars, and any soft tissue, will affect the sound. That is why we spent that time in Chapter 2 opening the vocal tract and working to release tension there. We want to choose the shape of the vocal tract according to what vowel and color we desire, and not have that determined unconsciously or by bad vocal habits. Making those choices is what singers and teachers and choral conductors do constantly in order to produce the most beautiful resonant tone that will then serve the emotional expression of the repertoire being sung.

A clarification (almost) about "dark," "warm," "light," and "bright" vowels

Many times singers and voice teachers refer to "dark" vowels or "bright" vowels. These terms can be confusing and mean different things to different people.

Phoneticians classify vowels according to the position of the tongue in forming the vowel sounds. The vowels [i] [ɪ] [e] [ɛ] and [æ] are formed with the body of the tongue shifted forward and are called front vowels. The order listed here is from most forward going back. Traditionally, these vowels have been perceived as "bright" because the second formant is higher, giving more high frequencies in the tone.

Vowels [u] [ʊ] [o] [ɔ] and [ɑ] are formed with the body of the tongue shifting back and are called back vowels. The order listed here is from the most back to more forward. Traditionally, these vowels have been perceived as dark, because in contrast to the front vowels, the second formant is lower, giving fewer high frequencies.

Front vowels and back vowels have also taken on the qualities of "light" and "warm" respectively. Further confusion has come about because of some voice teacher's and singer's reluctance to refer to "back" vowels, because "back" is associated with a "throaty" or swallowed tone, a negative tonal choice.

The gold standard in resonance has traditionally been a balanced resonance between "dark" and "light" qualities: the *chiaroscuro*, borrowed from visual art. This quality demands a dynamic equilibrium between front and back vowels on every pitch and with every vowel. When a tone is overbalanced, it is common to encourage "a warmer vowel" to counteract an overly forward resonance, and to encourage "more brightness" to counteract too much back resonance.

There is plenty of imprecision in this labeling of resonance balancing, and we would all do well to begin to use the proper scientific terminology. However, singing is an art, and in some cases, metaphors and similes are better suited to appeal to our imaginations. Scientists define and explain, poets feel and communicate. Singing artists combine and use both of these disciplines for an outcome that affects our spirits in a manner that is deeper than mere words.

The "tone factory" and the "vowel factory"

So let's start making those resonance choices. Most voice teachers agree that your pharynx (throat) should be as open and unconstricted as possible for all of the vowels. [21] This means that your larynx is not elevated, the back wall of the throat is not constricted, the soft palate is lifted and the tongue is in a state of tonus (ready to act), not jammed back into your throat, and is slightly grooved. Just for a semantic choice, let's call this area, from your larynx to your pillars, your "tone factory" and think of it as the place where your resonance is manufactured. (See *Figure 43.*)

Now think about the area from your faucial pillars forward, your mouth. For our purposes here, let's call this area the "vowel factory." The "vowel factory" will be manipulated by releasing your jaw, by moving your tongue, or protruding your lips. This area largely controls how you form your vowels. (See *Figure 43.*)

Figure 43: "Tone" and "Vowel" factory

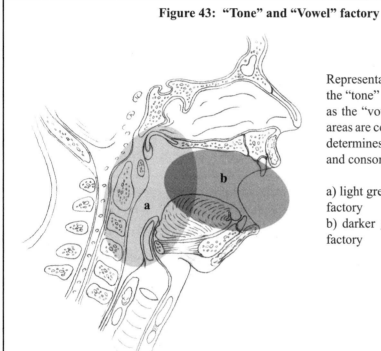

Representation of the pharynx as the "tone" factory, and of the mouth as the "vowel" factory. How these areas are controlled and manipulated determines resonance, vowel sounds, and consonant articulation.

a) light grey oval: pharynx/tone factory
b) darker grey oval: mouth/vowel factory

So as an exercise, let us analyze the vowels [i][ɛ][e][ɑ][o][ɔ][u] according to how they are formed in your "vowel factory." Starting with [ɑ], let's characterize this vowel as tall. Your soft palate is lifted, your tongue is low and slightly grooved, your jaw is released, and your lip muscles are not involved. Your "tone factory" of course remains open and free. Now, if you move your tongue to form the vowel [i], you will bring it to its most forward position in singing. As your tongue comes forward, it narrows the front of your vocal tract and opens up more space in the back of your vocal tract by moving the front wall of the pharynx forward. Your "tone factory" does not collapse and remains open and free. You will also probably close your jaw a little. We will now release the tongue back by increments toward the [ɑ] position, always keeping the tip of the tongue behind the bottom front teeth. Starting from the [i] position, form the vowel sound [e]. Did you notice how your tongue

21 The open pharynx is also an important element to produce the singer's formant. Titze, 238-241, and Sundberg, 121, both explain that the pharynx cross-section opening needs to be at least six times the opening cross-section right above the glottis (the epilarynx) to produce the "singer's formant."

released back somewhat? Now form the vowel [ɛ]. Your tongue releases back again. The goal is to keep your "tone factory" open and tension-free while your tongue is making the adjustments for these tongue vowels [i][e][ɛ]. Each of these vowels has a distinct posture (shape of your tube) and that posture will vary according to pitch, becoming a little more open as you ascend. One of your jobs as a singer is to find the optimal place for each of these tongue vowels on each pitch, and to habituate and cultivate it so it becomes intuitive.

Similarly, lets examine the vowels formed with the lips. Again, if you begin with [ɑ] and then move your lips to form [u], you will find your lips in their most forward position. Try to maintain the feeling of a low tongue that is grooved when you move your lips forward. Of course you should not add any tension to your tongue or pull it back. Now shape the vowel [o]. Notice how your lips release a bit; they are still rounded but incrementally less so. Again, try to maintain the feeling of the low, grooved tongue. Now shape [ɔ]. Although still somewhat rounded, you have incrementally released your lip position, heading closer toward the original [ɑ] position. Finally, release your lips and form the tall [ɑ] vowel, which brings you back where you started. There should be no residual tension in your lips and you should still be retaining the feeling of a tension-free (not relaxed) tongue. And as with the tongue vowels, your "tone factory" should remain open the entire time, feeding beautiful tone to be shaped in the "vowel factory" by the tongue, or the lips and the jaw.[22] Each of these lip vowels also has a distinct posture that will change according to pitch. As a singer you must learn to choose intuitively and precisely which posture to use for each vowel and then modify it accordingly as you ascend. The goal is always to maintain freedom, and to maintain a "core" tone (the open "tone factory") that remains optimally resonant through the range. Don't forget that all this is dependant on the dynamic equilibrium of your breath management, and a well-coordinated onset to create all the frequencies needed to produce these various vowel sounds. It all happens interactively and instantaneously.

The above exploration may not be entirely scientifically accurate, but it serves the purpose of making you aware of the different shapes that are required for resonant singing and how they are formed. All of the vowels are formed by the interaction of your coupled closed/open tube, adjusting at one end or the other. Any tension in the system will distort the tone and will likely cause problems elsewhere in order to compensate.

As in all things in singing, the key is balance (coordination or a dynamic equilibrium) between opposing forces or ideas. In the case of resonance, we value a three-dimensionality of tone, a tone that has both "brightness" and "darkness," and a forward focus. Voice teachers refer to this as the *chiaroscuro* quality of resonance, literally from the Italian, meaning the light/dark tone. Certainly there are different ways to sing a particular vowel; you want to be able to choose the sound that is resonantly fully realized (three dimensional), freely produced, and serves the thoughts and feelings you are projecting in your singing.

22 In English, Italian, and Spanish, tongue and lip vowels are never "mixed"; if your lips are forward, your tongue is not. French and German both use "mixed" vowels, an example being: lips in [u] postion, and tongue in [i] position together produce the [y] sound, commonly called the German umlaut "ü" or the French "u."

Exercises to Encourage Optimal Resonance

As in previous chapters, the assumption when you start these exercises is that you have released tension in your instrument, aligned it properly, you are cultivating *appoggio* breath management, and understand and practice coordinated onsets. Now on the Spiral of Singing, we add cultivating resonance. True to the spirit of the spiral, you may have to go back and review some of the other elements. Don't hesitate to do this; singing is an art requiring practice and experience over time. And as in the other chapters, these exercises are not meant to be done in one setting, but gradually added to your routine, choosing what is appropriate for your level of accomplishment and goals.

Shaping an open "Tone Factory"

♪ Begin by inhaling the beginning of a yawn. Exhale a warm breath into the palm of your hand. This helps you to remember the feeling of an open throat at all times during inhalation, exhalation, and singing.

♪ Inhale through the beginning of a yawn and silently exhale vowel [ɑ]. Remember what it feels like to maintain that openness. Do this with other vowels like [o] and [u].

♪ Now remembering that openness, with your lips closed say "um-hum" like you are agreeing with someone on the telephone. It should feel "hummy" or "buzzy" at your lips, but "easy" at your larynx (no pressure or tension).

♪ Maintaining the same "hummy" quality, separate and then close your lips, saying "mum-mum-mum-mum." Keep the pitch in your high mid-range. This is one of the first sounds you made as a baby (and it eventually turned into "ma-ma").

♪ Now take the [m] sound out, and say a *legato* "uh-uh-uh-uh" (no glottal onset, please). Your jaw should be moderately open, your tongue tip behind your bottom front teeth. This is the neutral vowel [ʌ] when it is stressed, and [ə] when it is unstressed.

Now sing this neutral vowel [ʌ] on one note in Exercise 68. Notice how it feels open and released.

Exercise 68

[ʌ— ʌ— ʌ— ʌ—]

Now in Exercise 69, toggle back and forth between [ʌ] and [ɑ] without taking any breaths.

Exercise 69

What feels different between the two vowels? If you have a mirror, look inside your mouth while you toggle back and forth. Ideally, when you shift to [ɑ] you should see your jaw release down a little bit and your tongue drop down a bit in the back. You may be able to see your tongue groove a little (starting in the back) and your soft palate may lift a bit. If you put your finger on your neck where your larynx is, you may feel it lower slightly. All of these changes, from [ʌ] to [ɑ] will help you feel and recognize a pretty good [ɑ] sound, with its own posture and sensation. The [ɑ] helps you to form the tall dimension, or north/south dimension, of your "tone factory."

Now toggle back and forth between [ɑ] and [i] in Exercise 70.

Exercise 70

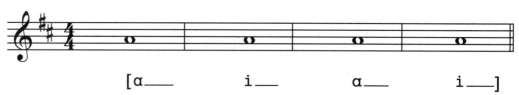

What changes do you notice? Does your tongue "front" or come forward? This motion establishes the front-to-back dimension of your "tone factory." The back of your tongue is the front wall of your pharynx. When you move your tongue forward to create [i], you clear out space in your throat or deepen the space in the back of your pharynx. (Think like a stage is deep or like depth perception in a painting.) Remember what that feels like, to have added that space to your tall space [ɑ]. We have established the feeling of two of the dimensions, top-to-bottom and front-to-back.

One dimension to go! In Exercise 71 toggle back and forth from vowel [ɑ] to [æ].

Exercise 71

Does it feel like your tongue broadens a bit, especially in the back? (Don't let the sound become nasal. Keep your soft palate high and don't let your tongue touch your soft palate.) This is the east-west or side-to-side dimension of your "tone factory."

With these three tongue postures, you have established the outer limits of the three dimensions of your pharynx (throat). Sing Exercise 72 and feel how it encourages you to keep all three dimensions open and free.

Exercise 72

[ɑ i   æ i   ɑ i   æ i   ɑ__]

Repeat six times, ascending by half-steps each time. This exercise is like putting a brand new tube sock on your foot; the sock will adjust to match your foot's shape. Pretty soon your muscles (stubborn but trainable) will assume this more open shape intuitively and you will "naturally" sing with an optimal open throat ("tone factory"). Remember how this feels and always try to have this open feeling behind all of your vowel sounds. When things start to feel "tight," stop, inhale the beginning of a yawn, and exhale on the warming gesture. Then remind yourself to sing through that warming gesture, shaping an open "tone factory."

In Exercises 73, 74, and 75, practice the various tongue positions from most forward (close) to back. Do each one two or three times, ascending by half steps, noticing how your tongue moves. Be sure to keep your throat open; just because you move your tongue, it does not mean you have to collapse your "tone factory." Be sure to expand your ribcage on EVERY inhalation.

Exercise 73

[ɑ i   ɑ__ i__ ɑ__ i__ ɑ_]

Exercise 74

[ɑ i   e   i__ e__ i__ e__ i_]

Exercise 75

[ɑ i   e ɛ   e__ ɛ__ e__ ɛ__ e_]

Now sing Exercise 76 ascending by half steps (a) through (h). Always begin the next repetition with the vowel you just sang. Make sure the initial [m] is forward and "easy" (no pressure at the lips or larynx) and the "tone factory" is open as you sing the tongue vowels. The [m] sound helps to keep the tone forward and focused.

Exercise 76

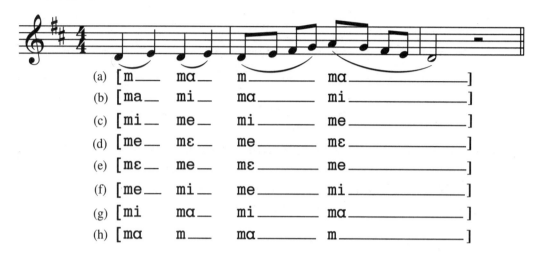

Exercise 77 now incorporates the [ŋ] sound. The combination of this sound with the tongue's postures of [i][e][ε] also exercises and trains your soft palate.

Exercise 77

Exercise 78 emphasizes some agility while still exercising the tongue systematically.

Exercise 78

Exercise 79 combines agility, tongue movement, onsets and releases, and *appoggio* breath management practice, especially if the *messa di voce* is observed at the end.

Exercise 79

Exercise 80 combines the systematic tongue practice with duple articulation and onset practice. If sung by a group, it can be done as a canon (parts entering at the asterisk) and will help tune thirds. Be sure to release the jaw gradually as you ascend to allow for vowel modification. The four permutations are not intended to be done at one time, but to be introduced as variations of each other.

Exercice 80

Exercise 81 can be used with any combination of tongue vowels. Three examples are suggested.

Exercise 81

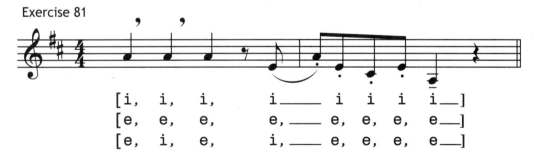

Exercise 82 emphasizes *legato*.

Exercise 82

Exercises 83, 84, and 85 shift to lip vowels. The same principles apply. Keep your "tone factory" open as you are manipulating your lips. Breath management, of course, remains important. Add Exercise 84 and 85 as soon as you can easily differentiate the four different positions.

Exercise 83

Exercise 86 works especially on the shift from [α] to [ɔ], which is especially troublesome for American English speakers. Remember that [α] has no lip tension or rounding at all; [ɔ] does have slight rounding of the lips. It is the difference between "collar" ([α]) and "caller" ([ɔ]), " body" and "bawdy."

Exercise 86

Exercise 87 requires facility in no particular order of the lip vowels. It is especially important to notice if your "tone factory" is open during this exercise. Sing it very elegantly.

Exercise 87

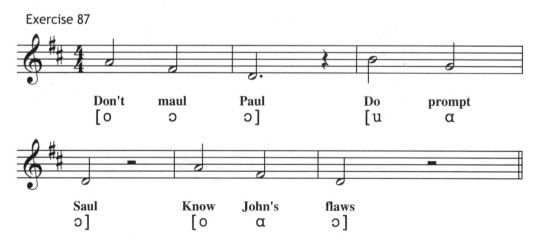

Exercise 88 goes from rounded lips (forward) to neutral. With a group it can be sung as a round, parts entering at the asterisk.

Exercise 88

[lu_____ lo_____ la_____]

Exercise 89 adds range. It also teaches vowel modification (release your jaw as you ascend) and will help tenors and baritones to access the *passaggio* (more about this in the Registration chapter on page 99).

Exercise 89

[e   o   e   o   e   o o o o o]
[e   u   e   u   e   u u u u u]

Exercise 90 adds the expressive element of *messa di voce*. Be sure to use only the tip of your tongue for the [l] sound. With a group it can be sung as a round, parts entering at the asterisk.

Exercise 90

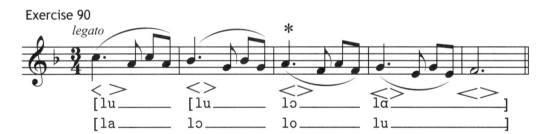

[lu_____ [lu_____ lɔ_____ lɑ_____]
[la_____ lɔ_____ lo_____ lu_____]

Exercise 91 teaches tongue independence while differentiating lip vowels.

Exercise 91

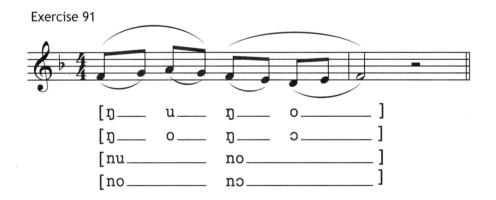

[ŋ___ u___ ŋ___ o_____]
[ŋ___ o___ ŋ___ ɔ_____]
[nu_____ no_____]
[no_____ nɔ_____]

Some Common Images
Used to Encourage Resonant Singing

♫ Imagine that a funnel's wide end is in your throat ("tone factory") with the narrow end extending through your hard palate and beyond your lips. The back of the funnel represents the three dimensionality of your pharynx. Tall is [ɑ], deep is [i], broad is [æ]. Don't let your funnel collapse as you sing. The front of the funnel represents the focus of the tone (see *Figure 20*, page 28).

♫ Imagine that your mouth and throat are the shape of a pear with the blossom end toward the back. This enables "pear shaped tones" when you sing.

♫ Sing the breath but think the tone.

♫ Feel as though you can sift the breath from underneath your eyes.

♫ Think of tone as going out, over, and down, like a half-circle starting at the glottis, forming an arc to the head, and then out and down.

♫ Suspend the first tone and keep the others floating.

♫ Tone is disembodied spirit. In Greek, "breath" and "spirit" mean the same thing, which in regard to singing, speaks for itself.

♫ Imagine that when you inhale, you create a large fish bowl. When you start to sing, you place a beautiful fish (tone) in the bowl that can swim freely.

♫ As you sing higher, imagine that your head is lighter.

Especially for the Choral Conductor

Unified, blended vowels are imperative in any choir. Every singer in your choir must understand the importance of this and work to be a part of that blend. Without uniform vowels, your choirs will be limited in their tuning, choral blend, choral diction and musical expressiveness. The principle of unified choral vowels is a macro example of the dynamic equilibrium theme expressed over and over in earlier chapters. The disparate singers in the choir must balance their individual resonance with each other. Without this choral discipline, there will be no choral blend, just singers competing to out-shout each other.

Among all the other tasks that you have to do as a choral conductor, imposing this discipline may be the most important. It is your responsibility to imagine a tonal preference or ideal. Then you must inspire and train your singers to share and realize that ideal. This is similar to what individual singers do with their personal tone. They imagine it (usually with help from a teacher) and then train to sing with that particular tonal choice consistently. Without a choral tone ideal, you will be at the mercy of 20 (or 50 or 90) individual voices trying to impose their tonal ideal on each other.

Part of acquiring this tonal ideal is learning about how your instrument works. Your instrument is a collective group of people with this myoelastic-aerodynamic, constantly changing, singing voice. They can make a lot of sounds (beautiful and not) and are looking to you to mediate the vocal choices they can make. You need to understand what your "instrument" is capable of doing and then train them and give them the tools that they need to realize your tonal ideal. If you have an auditioned choir, you do some of this in the audition process, weeding out the singers who you are sure cannot realize your ideal tone, and encouraging those who are already in line with your goal or who you believe can develop the skills needed. If your choir is not auditioned, then you have the wonderful opportunity of cultivating every singer in the group to appreciate and participate in the beautiful goal of choral singing you have imagined. People love to learn how to improve their voices. They want to be given reasonable and attainable goals and to be treated with respect as they work to be consistent with your ideal sound.

If your choir is having trouble realizing your choral goals, then "slice the loaf thinner." Break down your musical concepts and ideas into smaller concrete objectives that everyone in the room can do, and then proceed to more difficult concepts as the group is ready. An example: You have asked your altos to sing with more resonance with almost no results, so you ask them to sing with an open throat. Perhaps there is still no appreciable difference because they all have a different concept, or no concept of an open throat. However, if you ask them to create a warmer sound by releasing their jaws (lowering all the formants, but of course, you don't tell them that) and then sing the phrase, they will hear a difference. Then ask them to sing through the beginning of a yawn or any of the other techniques discussed here. Keep refining. Now they have some tools, something concrete. Now they have a closer idea of the tone ideal you are asking them to produce.

The following is a suggested plan for preparing your choir to sing resonantly and uniformly together. You will notice that it doesn't try to fix individual problems, but it trains and cultivates the group to sing corporately with an ear toward your choral ideal. Don't dwell on the negative. Strive for the positive and the negative will correct itself. As with earlier chapters, the assumption is that your singers have released tension in their instruments, they are cultivating *appoggio* breath management, and they have released and opened their vocal tracts in preparation for resonant singing. (You have perhaps started with one or two of the exercises from previous chapters.)

Have your choir sing the Choral Variation of Exercise 69 (page 82) shown below. Do not change to a new chord until the vowel is unified and the chord is in tune.

Exercise 92

Now have them sing Exercise 72, page 83, in unison, first slowly and then faster. Listen carefully and correct if the vowels are not unified. Tell them that these three vowels represent the extreme postures in their "tone factory": tall, broad, and deep. If you have a funnel, use it as a visual image of an open throat.

To activate their soft palate, have them sing Exercise 77, page 84. Depending on your choir, it might be a good idea to have them toggle back and forth between only two of the "tongue" vowels instead of all four, i.e. [ŋ, ɑ, ŋ, i, ŋ, ɑ, ŋ, i, ŋ, ɑ]. And then [ŋ, i, ŋ, e, ŋ, i, ŋ, e, ŋ, i]. Use any combination.

Now have them sing Exercise 80, page 85, as a round (usually have basses, then tenors, then altos, then sopranos, but you can mix this up). Continue to carefully listen for open throat ("tone factory") and vowel unification. Remind them about releasing their jaw as they ascend for vowel modification. Sometimes it helps to write the vowel changes on a whiteboard or easel. The object is not to stump them, but to unify vowels according to your tonal ideal. Remember, longer tube (vocal tract) = warmer vowels; shorter tube = brighter vowels. (See page 77, the Titze principles.)

Depending on the expertise of your group, have them sing either Exercises 83, 84, or 85, on page 86. If they differentiate the three lip vowels to your satisfaction, you can go directly to Exercise 85. If not, then "slice the loaf thinner" and begin with Exercise 83.

Have them sing Exercise 87, page 86, to help differentiate the lip vowels out of order. If they have difficulty, back up to Exercise 85 or 86.

Now have your group sing either Exercise 88 or 90, page 87, as a round (next group starts at the asterisk). By now they should have an excellent idea of your choral tone ideal with each of these vowels. (If not, then "slice the loaf thinner" at the next rehearsal; go slower, be more concrete.) Ask (demand) that everyone in the group listen three ways: to themselves, to their direct neighbors, and to the whole group.

This is choral listening, much different than the listening they do when they sing by themselves.

Any of the "Resonance" exercises can be adapted for choral use. The important things for you, the choral conductor, are to:

1. LISTEN for the choral tone that you want to cultivate and work to eliminate tone that is not consistent with your tonal ideal
2. WATCH that everyone is correctly shaping the individual vowels with no tension while keeping their "tone factory" open
3. TRAIN your choir to listen chorally as outlined above

Summary

♫ Resonance is defined as when sound waves from one source are enhanced or enriched or intensified in some other way.

♫ Your primary singing resonators are your pharynx (throat) and your mouth.

♫ Your vocal tract resonators (primarily your throat and mouth) will obey the scientific laws of an open/closed-end tube, a quarter-wave resonator.

♫ Vibrations created at the glottis, called the glottal source, will be acted upon in the vocal tract resonator, depending upon the resonators' shape. This is called the source-filter theory of vowels.

♫ How you shape your quarter-wave tube (resonators) determines which vowel will be perceived and the timbre of your voice.

♫ One strategy for improving resonance is to cultivate and maintain an open and three-dimensional pharynx ("tone factory") while shaping tongue and lip vowels in the mouth ("vowel factory").

♫ The optimal resonance in "classical" singing is described as *chiaroscuro*, which is a balance between light and dark tone color.

Resonance

V

Notes

REGISTERS

Registers are balanced
and the transitions blended.
Range is seamless
with no register
events.

Chapter VI

Registers
of the
Voice

Chapter VI
Registers of the Voice

Background and Scientific Approach

Voice teachers have been describing different registers of the voice and expounding contrary theories about them for hundreds of years. Even into the twentieth century there was much disagreement about registers; some teachers advocated for just one register, others for as many as seven. Although early pedagogues could not agree on how many registers there were, they could agree on a definition. Manuel Garcia (the voice teacher who invented the laryngoscope) defined registers in a singing treatise published in 1841. Paraphrased here, he said that a register is a series of sounds, from high to low, that are of equal quality, and that those sounds are produced by the same mechanical principle. Other pedagogues have added that those mechanical functions include the way the vocal folds vibrate, the shape of the glottis, and the amount of air pressure.

Historically, it was hard to argue with successful teachers about how many registers there were because there was not a good way to observe the internal movements of the larynx. The issue was further clouded by the fact that singers felt sensations in different parts of their bodies. High notes seemed to vibrate in their heads, low notes seemed to vibrate in their chests, which gave rise to the terms "head register" and "chest register." Because of the work of mid-twentieth century speech and voice scientists like Janwillem van den Berg and William Vennard, we now know that registers are defined by certain events that happen in the larynx, not in the resonators. And as with all things in singing, the registers are highly dependent on coordination between aerodynamic (breath) functions and myoelastic (muscle) functions.

Most voice scientists and teachers now agree that there are two different singing registers (as defined by Garcia), one for the upper range and one for the lower range. They also agree that successful singers use a strategy of mixing and blending them in the middle of their voice to produce an evenness of the range throughout the singing instrument. (This mixing or blending creates the so-called middle register, often referred to in current pedagogy as the third register.) The mechanical changes occur in the larynx, but these changes are very sensitive to other aspects of singing, especially breath management, and to a certain extent, resonance cavities. Singers may feel sensations in other parts of their bodies, but the actions are laryngeal. For our purposes here we will refer to the upper register (head) as the light mechanism, the lower register (chest) as the heavy mechanism, and the mixture between them as the middle voice. When speaking of women's voices, the middle voice may be further differentiated by referring to an upper middle and a lower middle. There are also transitional areas in a singer's range where the registers overlap. These connection areas or "bridges" are sometimes referred to as the *passaggio* (Italian for "a passage" or a "thoroughfare between").[23] In men's voices, the transitional area that bridges into the light mechanism usually requires the most attention in voice training. In women, depending on the voice type, both transitional areas (from heavy mechanism to lower middle, and from upper middle to light mechanism) can be troublesome.

Untrained singers tend to favor one register over the other and may have difficulty making the transition from one to the other. Before the 1960's, when the popular music ideal was a derivative of the big band sound (think Frank Sinatra), most untrained men's voices sang predominantly in heavy mechanism and women in light upper mixed mechanism to harmonize. When the Beatles became famous worldwide in the early 1960's, they largely sang in light mechanism (some would say falsetto). Untrained singers, mimicking this popular sound, began to use the other register: for men, the lighter mechanism, for women, the heavier mechanism, again to harmonize. So in our voice studios today, it is not unusual to find a beginning young male singer unable to use the rich, warm sounds associated with heavy mechanism, and likewise, young, untrained women's voices unable to successfully bridge into their lighter mechanism. This is the opposite of what was found in earlier generations.

However, our goal for traditional singing, both solo and choral, is to create a seamless range in all voices, seemingly without any register breaks or interruptions. So let's explore this mysterious phenomenon that has engendered so much discussion and controversy among singers and teachers.

When you are singing in your heavy mechanism, the whole mass of your vocal folds vibrates. This means that more air pressure is needed because there is more mass to move. Your vocal folds open and close first at the lower edges, near to your lungs and away from your mouth. Compared to the lighter mechanism, they are relatively thick because of the contracting action of the thyroarytenoid muscles, the muscles that run longitudinally through your vocal folds, hereafter referred to as the TA. The vocal folds also vibrate with a large amplitude in this register, which means that they move relatively far away from the center before coming back to a firm closure (see *Figures 44* and *46*, page 96.)

The sound source from this heavy mechanism, which is dominated by the action of the TA, is loud and rich with harmonic partials that are very important to full tone.

VI

Registers of the Voice

23 For comprehensive, scientific discussions of the issues agreed upon or disputed by voice teachers and voice scientists, see Titze, 252-275 and Doscher, 171-195. Miller (115-149) agrees about laryngeal function, but uses different terminology and identifies "register events." Vennard (66-79) presents a balance between science and practical application.

Figure 44: Action of the thyroarytenoid (TA) muscle in transverse cross-section

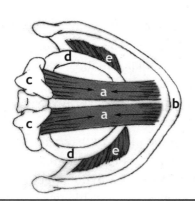

Contracting action of the muscle fibers causes the TA muscle to shorten and thicken. This action and muscle posture is the dominant characteristic of the heavy mechanism, but generally neither the heavy nor light mechanism acts exclusively or independently of the other.

a) thyroarytenoid (TA) muscle
b) thyroid cartilage
c) arytenoid cartilages
d) cricoid cartilage
e) cricothyroid (CT) muscle

Figure 45A and 45B: Action of the cricothyroid muscle in sagittal cross-section

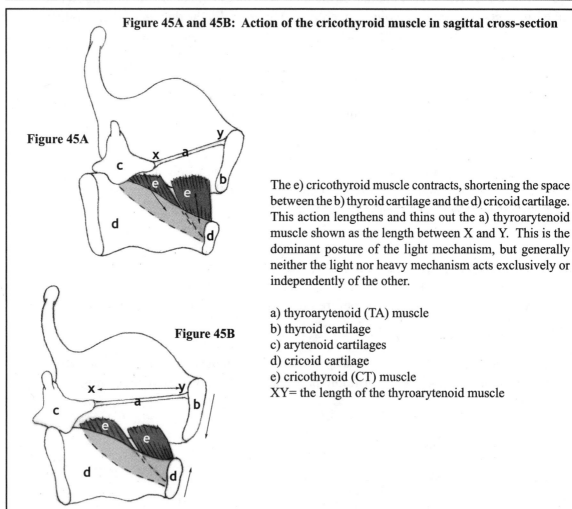

Figure 45A

Figure 45B

The e) cricothyroid muscle contracts, shortening the space between the b) thyroid cartilage and the d) cricoid cartilage. This action lengthens and thins out the a) thyroarytenoid muscle shown as the length between X and Y. This is the dominant posture of the light mechanism, but generally neither the light nor heavy mechanism acts exclusively or independently of the other.

a) thyroarytenoid (TA) muscle
b) thyroid cartilage
c) arytenoid cartilages
d) cricoid cartilage
e) cricothyroid (CT) muscle
XY= the length of the thyroarytenoid muscle

Figure 46: Graphic representation of the heavy mechanism

Top picture represents a transverse cross-section

1 2 3 4 5 6

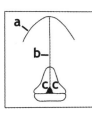  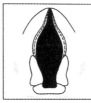  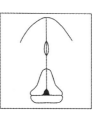

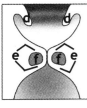 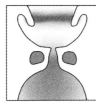 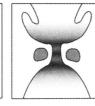 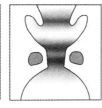  

1 2 3 4 5 6

Bottom picture represents a frontal cross-section

1) **Bottom**: Air pressure builds beneath the closed glottis with the vocal folds adducted (closed).
   Top: Closed glottis looking from above.
2) **Bottom**: The vocal folds begin to open from the bottom up as air molecules push through. Note that the TA muscle is part of the vibration.
   Top: Glottis begins to open.
3) and 4) **Bottom**: The vocal fold continues to open from the bottom up.
   Top: Glottis continues to open and widen.
5) **Bottom**: Vocal folds begin to close starting at the bottom.
   Top: Glottis begins to close and narrow.
6) **Bottom**: Vocal folds almost completely closed at the end of the cycle.
   Top: Only the very edge of the glottis remains open prior to complete closure as the cycle ends and air pressure begins to build again.

a) thyroid cartilage
b) closed glottis
c) arytenoid cartilages
d) false vocal folds
e) vocal folds
f) thyroarytenoid muscle

inset rectangle identifies e) vocal folds

(Drawings are based on Vennard, 64-65)

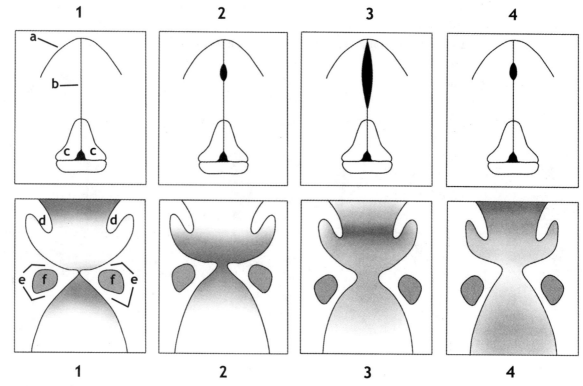

Figure 47: Graphic representation of the light mechanism

Top picture represents a transverse cross-section.

Bottom picture represents a frontal cross-section

1) **Bottom**: Air pressure builds beneath the closed glottis with the vocal folds adducted (closed). Notice that for the light mechanism only the edges of the vocal folds are involved and the TA muscle has moved to the side.
   Top: Closed glottis looking from above.
2) **Bottom**: Edges of the vocal folds separate, creating a puff of air or vibration.
   Top: Glottis begins to open.
3) **Bottom**: Vocal folds continue to separate.
   Top: Glottis continues to open. Notice that the amplitude, the distance the vocal folds move from the center line, is less in light mechanism than in heavy.
4) **Bottom**: Vocal folds begin to close, building up air pressure again beneath the glottis.
   Top: Glottis almost completely closed as air pressure builds and the cycle begins again.

a) thyroid cartilage
b) closed glottis
c) arytenoid cartilages
d) false vocal folds
e) vocal folds
f) thyroarytenoid muscle

(Drawings are based on Vennard, 72)

inset rectangle identifies e) vocal folds

When you sing with your light mechanism, only the inner margins of your vocal folds vibrate. Because of the action of the cricothyroid muscles (from now on referred to as the CT) the folds are stretched from back to front and are under high tension. (See *Figure 45A, 45B* and *47*.)

This posture provides much less resistance to the airflow, and often the glottis does not even completely close. Now the folds vibrate with a small amplitude, meaning that they don't move too far away from the center, and as mentioned previously, often don't completely touch when they do come to the center. Most importantly, in the muscle antagonism between the TA and the CT, the CT becomes dominant, and the TA becomes more and more passive (or at least relatively passive) and falls off to the side, allowing vibration in only the outer layers of the vocal folds in the upper range.

But, of course, neither of these actions is exclusive of the other. Remember that dynamic equilibrium thing? The truth is that most voice teachers want a balance of these two registers or mechanisms (except in the extremes of the ranges), which will provide an evenness of color and dynamics through the entire singing range. They train their students to intuitively balance the antagonism between the TA and the CT, and to give that balance special care as they sing through the transition areas (the *passaggio* areas) from one register to the other, creating what is often described as blended, mixed, or middle register. This requires a singing strategy in which some pitches can be produced in more than one way, as singers bridge through the area in their voices where normally a change would abruptly occur between registers. Of course, there are individual differences between voices, and different singers with their teachers, will make a judgment as to how far ascending or descending the mixtures will extend. Each voice type has its own particular challenges, which will be addressed later, but in general, singers with register issues such as belting or carrying the heavy register too high, need to "lighten" their mechanism sooner (or lower in the range) by using less TA and more CT as they ascend while keeping the two mechanisms in balance. These muscles are not under direct control, so these behaviors must be learned intuitively, by trial and error, and habituated. Singers can then express and project thoughts and feelings in performance, as their voices sound perfectly seamless. It is very much like observing the ballet. From the back of the orchestra section the dancers appear to be flying and weightless; only from the front rows can you see the muscle control and strength that is required to make it seem effortless.

Exercises to Encourage
Unified Registers for Singing

Have you released tension in your instrument? Are you in your singer's stance? Is your vocal tract open and ready to shape vowels flexibly? Have you been cultivating your *appoggio* breath management and coordinated onsets? Then you are ready to think about how you manage and unify your registers.

For Women

♫ Pretend you are hungry and you just sat down to a great meal prepared by someone you like. Say "mmm mmm mmm mmm" and slide all around your range low and high. Now start high in your voice and glide down: m↘ m↘ m↘. It should feel buzzy on your lips and easy in your throat.

♫ Do the same exercise with [n] and with [ŋ]. Start comfortably high in your voice and glide down to a comfortable low pitch. It should feel buzzy in your "mask" (front part of your face) and easy in your throat.

Sing Exercise 93 into a regular drinking straw, as if it were an instrument or a kazoo. (Be sure to hold it with your hand so you don't create tension in your lips. Also be sure that no sound is coming out of your nose.) Sopranos start in G major and descend to B flat major. Mezzo-sopranos begin in G flat major and descend to A major. Altos begin in F major and end in G major. Keep the sound forward, into the straw. This vocalise is designed to start in the upper middle of your voice and take you down to lower middle. The straw helps keep the registers balanced.

Exercise 93

(Singing through a straw)

Still with the straw, begin in the key where you stopped, (Sopranos: B flat; Mezzos: A; and Altos: G) and practice Exercise 94. As you are singing, notice any "rough" spots. If you do, sing that glide again and lighten your voice as you approach that spot. It is important to keep the tone forward and focused into the straw. Sopranos ascend to G major, Mezzos to F major, and Altos to E major. This vocalise starts in lower middle register and takes you to the top of upper middle.

Exercise 94

Without the straw, sing Exercise 95 gliding on the [ɛ] vowel of "Ben" (Soprano – G major, Mezzo-soprano – F major, Alto – E major). As you go lower in your voice, add a little heaviness to the bottom note, but always be sure to return to the lighter quality on the high note. Go as low as you would like, always being sure to return to the lighter quality to begin the next repetition. This helps the transition from upper middle register to lower middle.

Exercise 95

Sing Exercise 96 without getting heavy at the bottom. Sopranos start in E Flat major, Mezzos in E major, and Altos in F major. In the descending repetitions, start adding weight **but only** on the last note of each repetition. This trains varying degrees of TA involvement as you descend. Be sure when you begin the next repetition that you start "light."

Exercise 96

Exercise 97 now varies the point where you add noticeable heavy mechanism. Sopranos start in E flat major, Mezzos in E major, and Altos in F or F sharp major. The object of the exercise is to shift the point of register change around; in those transition areas, you can sing different degrees of registration on the same note.

Exercise 97

Exercise 98 helps to bridge and unify from the top down and then return to the top without adding too much weight. Sopranos start in C major and ascend by half steps to E major. Mezzo-Sopranos begin in B flat and ascend by half steps to D major. Altos begin in A major and ascend to D flat major.

Exercise 98

Exercise 99 and Exercise 100 help to strengthen the upper transition (from middle to light mechanism) and unify through the rest of the range. Exercise 99 uses *staccato* and Exercise 100 is all *legato*. Begin as noted and ascend by half steps to the top of your range.

Exercise 99

Exercise 100

Exercise 101 is an advanced exercise that encourages breath regulation, range extension, and will help unify registers. Do it first on [u], then [e], and then finally with Ferdinand Sieber's[24] syllables: *ni po tu la be da me.* You can start anywhere in the sequence, but if you start with "ni," the highest note will be "la" and will facilitate creating space as you ascend. Sopranos should start in C major, Mezzos in B or B flat major, and Altos in A or A flat major. On all three exercises, be sure to make more space as you ascend, by releasing your jaw.

24 Ferdinand Sieber, 1822-1895, Viennese voice pedagogue.

Exercise 101

[u_____

[e_____

ni po tu la be da me ni   po tu la be da me ni po

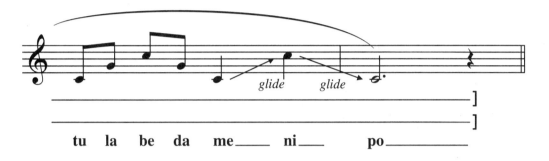

glide   *glide*

tu   la   be   da   me___ ni___   po___

For Tenors

Begin the same way as suggested for the women, starting on page 99 and going through Exercise 94, but with the following changes:

Use the "mm mm mm" sound to glide all around in your range. Then change to [n] and [ŋ].

For Exercise 102, use the straw, begin in G major, and descend. Stay on the light side of your voice, not getting too heavy as you descend to B flat major. The straw keeps the sound forward and the registers balanced.

Exercise 102

(Singing through a straw)

Exercise 103 begins near the bottom of your voice around B flat major. Use the straw and glide through the octave. As you approach the top, lighten your voice, but not to falsetto. When you reach E flat or E Major, use vowel [u] instead of the straw. Keep gliding through the octave, staying on the lighter quality of your voice, but again, don't use falsetto. Keep your breath engaged and be sure that you keep your body aligned as you ascend. Do not lift your chin (or your larynx) as you approach the top notes. Be sure to release your jaw and sing the [u] very tall on the top.

Exercise 103

glide

Starting in F major and ascending by half steps, sing Exercise 104 and keep the notes short and light, and in this exercise, don't sing falsetto. Remember the forward feeling you had when you sang through the straw and keep that feeling in your voice. Be sure your onsets are coordinated and you aren't using hard glottal attacks.

Exercise 104

Exercise 105 now brings *legato* into this transition area and then brings the voice down into the middle. Ascend by half steps and only go as high as you can keep it tension-free without going into falsetto. Be sure that the [e] vowel is very open, with a released jaw. Increase airflow as you ascend and do not raise your larynx. Do one more repetition than you think you can.

Exercise 105

Exercise 106 works gradually through the transition area half step by half step, as you ascend for each repetition. It is important to go gradually; we are trying to train a very delicate balance between the TA and the CT muscles. Only ascend as far as you can without going into falsetto. Keep the tone forward. If you have trouble with this, you can sing it into the straw to remember that forward feeling. As you work at this daily, you will keep adding range and beauty and confidence to your top notes. Increase airflow as you ascend and do not raise your larynx.

Exercise 106

To release any tension caused by Exercise 106, sing Exercise 107 at a fast tempo and descend by half steps.

Exercise 107

Exercise 108 works carefully through the transition area from heavy to light register. Do not add tension as you ascend by half steps or lose your head alignment. Keep the back of your neck taller than the front.

Exercise 108

[no ___   ne ___   no _____]

Exercise 109 practices ascending through the transition and then descends. It should be practiced on all vowels. On each repetition ascend by half steps.

Exercise 109

[jɑ,   ɑ _____]

For Baritones and Basses

Begin in the same manner as the women using "mm mm mm" as a glide all through your comfortable singing range, then change to [n] and [ŋ]. Keep the front of your face buzzy and an easy feeling in your throat.

Keep that same buzzy feeling and sing Exercise 110, first on [m] hum (lips together, teeth apart) and then on the suggested [mo] and [mu]. As you descend, keep the feeling "easy" (tension-free) in your throat and the tone warm and full. Repeat a half step lower until you descend to your lowest note.

Exercise 110

[m _____]
[mo _____]
[mi _____]

Starting where you ended (somewhere around G major or lower) begin Exercise 111 and ascend by half notes, just until you begin a transition into your light mechanism, somewhere around E major, F major, F sharp major, or G major. The *crescendo* on the fifth of the exercise helps to maintain the *appoggio,* and the shift from [o] on ascent to [e] on descent will help to unify the range (a warm vowel to ascend, a brighter vowel to descend).

Exercise 111

[no_____ e_____]

Now glide as suggested in Exercise 112. Do it first through a straw, and then with [i] on the bottom, gradually changing to [u] as you ascend, closing to [i] as you descend.

Exercise 112

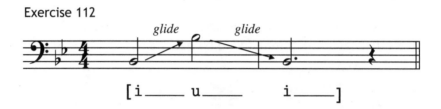

[i____ u_____ i____]

Exercise 113 will help the low male voice to bridge into the light mechanism without adding tension. Begin in lower middle of the voice (B flat major is probably good) and ascend up to A or B flat major, as far as you can go without adding tension. Toggling back and forth between [i], a bright vowel, and [u], a warm vowel, will keep the voice in balance and help keep the throat open as you maneuver through the upper transition. Keep your larynx in a comfortably low position, but don't press down.

Exercise 113

[u, i, u, i, u_____]

To build strength through the transition areas, practice Exercise 114 in E flat or E major and ascend by half steps. Work carefully and gradually, without adding tension in your neck or throat. Only ascend as high as you can sing tension-free, while still making a beautiful sound. Be sure you release your jaw as you ascend to make plenty of space for the vowel. You will gradually train the balance between your TA and CT that will allow you to bridge from the heavy mechanism upward into the lighter mechanism.

Exercise 114

[no_____ nu_____]

Exercise 115 is an advanced exercise that encourages register unification, *appoggio* breath management, and range extension. Be sure to release the jaw as you go higher, keep your head and neck in alignment, and think about your soft palate as you ascend. Does it lift a little? (That would be a good thing.)

Exercise 115

[i————— o— o— o—————]

Some Common Images
Used to Encourage Unified Registers

♫ Imagine that your head expands like a balloon as you ascend.

♫ Show more "rabbit teeth" as you descend and more "fish mouth" when you ascend.

♫ Think high on low tones and low on high tones.

♫ One way to think of unified registers is to think of hanging clothes on a line with clothespins. Heavy mechanism tones are like bed sheets, mixed tones like dishtowels, and light mechanism tones like handkerchiefs. They are all different sizes, but they are all attached at the same place. The clothesline is like a unified vocal line.

♫ Learning to sing with unified registers is similar to learning to drive a car with manual transmission. When you first start learning to shift, it is awkward and jerky. As you gradually gain skill, passengers can't even tell when you make the shifts. That is the goal of unified register singing.

♫ Every heavy mechanism tone must have some light mechanism in it. Every light mechanism tone must have some heavy mechanism in it.

♫ Blending or mixing the registers is like a bowl of vanilla ice cream with chocolate syrup. You can mix varying amounts of the syrup into the ice cream to make either milk chocolate ice cream or dark chocolate ice cream or various degrees between the two. You can do the same thing with your registers.

Especially for the Choral Conductor

Your singers, especially if they are "untrained," will come to your group with all different concepts and terminologies for their registers. Even the trained singers will probably have disparate vocabularies and training. One of your jobs is to define words so they all know what you are asking for in terms of how they negotiate registration. With that knowledge they can then be trained to listen and then discern when they are not producing the sound quality that you desire as their director. Using the terms "heavy" and "light mechanism" are desirable because they are a more accurate description of how the registers are produced, unlike "head" and "chest" registers. Once the new terminology is introduced, it puts everyone on an even playing field without the perhaps confusing leftover language from voice teachers and previous conductors. Singers are perfectly capable of using different vocabularies in different settings. You need to clarify **your** terminology and be consistent with it.

You as the conductor are now faced with cultivating your tonal ideal in respect to registration. This is compounded by the fact that different voice parts have different register issues and problems. There are advantages to having your entire choir cultivate a predominantly light mechanism sound; it is easier to blend and to tune. But the sound can lack expression and excitement and eventually wears on the ear and sounds monochromatic, colorless. Encouraging a heavier mechanism mix in your group will give you more timbre options. But taken to the extreme, it may cause your group to develop blend and tuning problems within the sections as well as in the entire group sound. It would appear that, as in all things we have discussed here, the answer is to find a balance that encourages beautiful, healthy singing, and that conforms to your ideal choral tone concept, which, of course, includes a pleasing choral blend, excellent intonation, and exciting color options. A free vocal production throughout the range of every singer (that will also encourage beautiful individual singing) will only enhance the beauty of your choral sound. The example of the string section of the professional orchestra is applicable here. The individual players do not play like soloists, but modify their sounds to blend with the section. It doesn't mean that they play poorly or softly, just differently. They must play well to be able to blend in the first place! It is a difference in degree, not in kind. With that in mind, below you will find some common choral registration issues for individual voice types and some suggestions for how to improve them.

Sopranos

Sopranos will tend to tighten and sing sharp in the upper transition area (anywhere from C^5 to F sharp^5), creating tension for the upper middle and head voice, which makes them sound shrill. They are also likely to start their heavy mechanism too high and press as they descend (especially if they have done belting or a lot of popular singing), which can make an unblendable sound that will not tune. Sometimes they have difficulty singing in the middle of their voices around B^4 and C^5 (the C above middle C) because they have not cultivated their upper middle voices in deference to musical theater or popular music training.

Some choral solutions: Watch carefully that they don't anticipate tension as they approach the upper middle of their voice. Encourage freedom and openness through E⁵, F⁵, and G⁵. Be mindful that constant singing in this tessitura creates tension, fatigues the voice, and may cause intonation problems. Allow them to "mark" (to sing lightly or even an octave lower as appropriate) after several repetitions if you have to drill this spot for other considerations. Be sure to vocalize the whole group from the top down and remind the sopranos to stay predominantly in their light mechanism; in choral singing, sopranos hardly ever use full-on heavy mechanism except for effect. Use glides from the top down and then bottom up with the whole group to develop an evenness of range.

Altos

Altos tend to use too much heavy mechanism all through the range. They sound pushed as they ascend and pressed as they sing low. In their lower range the sound tends to be foggy, unfocused. Sometimes that fogginess is also in the middle voice and they may have trouble transitioning to upper middle voice and above.

Some choral solutions: Remind them not to push "out" their voice, but to let it bloom, especially as they ascend. Remind them not to press as they descend but to brighten or close the vowels for clarity. When you are vocalizing the entire group from the top down, use glides and bright vowels to descend [i][e][ɛ] and warm vowels to ascend [o][u]. When the section sings in their upper middle voices, be sure they are using proper breath management so the tone is clear and energized. Be mindful when you choose repertoire; make sure they get to sing more notes than middle C⁴, D⁴, and E⁴.

Tenors

Tenors tend to carry too much weight into the transition to the light mechanism and then the voice breaks or shouts above that. They may press their voices the higher they go with high larynx positions. They tend to become breathy and unfocused on the bottom of their voices.

Some choral solutions: As tenors enter the transition area to light mechanism, remind them to stay light, but to sing with more energy. Be sure they understand that "light" does not mean less energy or support. Watch carefully that they do not lift their chins as they ascend and that they keep their heads and necks in alignment. Singing through this transition requires an open throat, an unlifted larynx, an arched soft palate, and sometimes a slight pout or fish mouth with the lips to lower the formants — so watch that they are not adding tension that would inhibit those actions. Vocalize the whole group from the top down with bright vowels, and as you ascend, use warm vowels and train them to release their jaws. *Staccato* singing through the transition helps them not to "set" or habitually tense as they approach. Build this area half step by half step. When some of your singers cannot manage this *passaggio* area without "shouting," it is better for them to sing lighter, even toward falsetto. Falsetto is NOT a substitute for developing evenness through the range, but it is less damaging to the instrument and will blend better in the choir than carrying a shout to the top.

Baritones and Basses

Basses and Baritones sometimes do not know how to access their light mechanism, so they just quit singing at the transition point and say it is "too high." Adolescent boys can be acculturated to avoid a high-pitched voice, speaking or singing, and may affect a low timbre quality that is usually full of tension; this may influence how they produce singing tone then, and later in life.   Low male voices tend to lose focus on the bottom similar to altos. Usually, flexibility needs to be developed.

Some choral solutions: Especially during warm-ups, give these low male voices permission to sing lighter all through the range. Have them access their upper voice by using falsetto and then help them add weight to this sound in a tension-free manner. Watch carefully that they are not pressing their voices to sound darker or "more mature." Remind them that their larynxes should feel "easy" as they sing, comfortably low, although not depressed, and without tension. When they approach low notes from above, use bright vowels to encourage clarity. As they ascend into the light mechanism remind them to stay light and not push and be sure they are allowing enough space by releasing their jaws. Practice eighth note runs and *arpeggios*, reminding them to stay light in order to develop flexibility.

Adolescent Voices

Adolescent voices need careful nurturing. Their voices are **developing**; they really don't have a complete instrument until they are in their early twenties (this will vary by voice and gender). They must not be pushed into singing with a vocal quality that they are not developmentally ready or able to produce. Avoid literature that is too vocally demanding, even if they can "sing the notes." This takes a lot of discipline on your part as their choral conductor; of course you would like the thrill of more demanding literature, but remember that teenagers sometimes don't have the same voice two days in a row because of all the changes. Be patient and value vocal freedom above a "mature" sound or dynamic extremes.

Suggested vocalises to work on register issues with a group

Begin the voice-building session in the usual way, emphasizing release of tension, alignment, cultivating *appoggio,* and developing resonance. Then have the entire group glide through their range of notes on [m]. Demonstrate for them, starting in the middle, going up to the top, down to the bottom, and ending in the middle again.

Demonstrate Exercise 116 using the "brrrrr" sound (this is sometimes called a lip flutter or a lip buzz or a liptrill). Start in D major and ascend, ending in F or F sharp major.

Exercise 116

br-r-r-r_____

Now demonstrate Exercise 117. Remind them to stay on the light side of their voices and then have them do four repetitions descending by half steps. Then start again and have them ascend for four repetitions. Watch and listen carefully for tension and make sure they release their jaws as they ascend.

Exercise 117

[no ___   ne ___   no _____]

Next, demonstrate Exercise 118. Ascend by halfsteps and tell the low voices, altos, and baritone/basses to drop out when it gets too high, but that they should always do one more repetition than they think they can. Remind the tenors and sopranos to stay open by releasing the jaw as they access the top of their voices, and to do one more repetition than they think they can do. Watch carefully for signs of tension in all sections.

Exercise 118

[o _____   o   o o o o   o _]
[y _____   y   y y y y   y _]
[e   e   e e e e   e _]

End with Exercise 119. Do it first in unison and then in a round. Begin in C major and descend for two repetitions to B flat major, and then begin in C sharp major and ascend to E flat or higher if your basses can do it without adding tension. With a group it can be sung as a round, parts entering at the asterisk.

Exercise 119

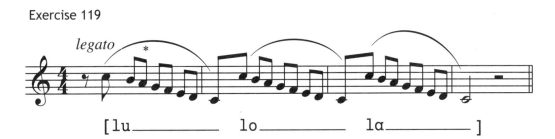

[lu _____   lo _____   la _____]

Summary

♫ Although there may be disagreement and discussion about how many singing registers there are, most voice teachers and scientists agree that a register is a series of sounds from high to low that are of equal quality and are produced by the same mechanical principle.

♫ Singing register events (or "shifts") are primarily laryngeal, although they are sensitive to breath and resonance factors.

♫ Voice teachers train their students to balance the muscle antagonism between the thyroarytenoid and cricothyroid muscles in the larynx to bridge through the passage from one register to another.

♫ One method of describing the register postures is: heavy mechanism for low tones, light mechanism for high tones, and a mixture or balance of the two referred to as the middle voice. Transitional notes that connect the registers are referred to as bridges or as the *passaggio* (Italian for "a passage").

♫ The goal of traditional voice training for both solo and choral singing is a seamless range from low to high, with no apparent register events. This enables the singer to freely express musical thoughts, ideas, and stories without being concerned about mechanical adjustments that are needed to express the full range of the voice.

Registers of the Voice

VI

FOCUS OF THE TONE

Tone has both point and space, or a chioroscuro (bright/dark) quality. Tone projects forward in the room and resounds throughout the room. Singer's Formant is present. Tone is clear but has dimensionality.

Chapter VII

Focus
of the
Tone

Chapter VII

Focus of the Tone

Background and Scientific Approach

The focus of the tone in singing may well be in the category of "I don't know what it is, but I sure know it when I sing it or hear it." This is not a great beginning for a scientific examination of something that every voice teacher and singer values and works to attain. The problem is that the ability to "focus" tone or "place the tone" or "project" is dependent on kinesthetic sensation or feeling as well as sound. Paraphrasing Lamperti again, after all is said and done, scientific or not, the memory of how a tone feels, and the ability to reproduce that memory over and over again, is really our only method. The skill needed to "focus the tone" is acquired through trial and error (remembering how it feels) and the development of a personal tone concept that is consistent (ability to reproduce it over and over again).

However, the concept of "focus" or "ping" or "singing in the mask" can be somewhat deconstructed, and it certainly can be trained. Although this sensation is referred to in many ways, for our purposes here and for consistency, we will call it "focus." Not surprisingly, it turns out that focus is another example of balance or coordination in singing. In our Spiral of Singing, so far we have been concerned with alignment, openness, breathing, phonation, resonance, and registers. All these concepts and skills now contribute to how the tone is projected or focused into the room.

When something is focused, it is gathered together, concentrated, or comes to a point. The Italian term is *raccolto* or *raccogliere* meaning "to gather." In these terms, focus is an action, and in singing, focusing the tone means to find an optimal balance between space and point, warmth and brilliance. It is really a function of dynamic equilibrium in resonance. There are several components to it. Vennard says that the first issue of focus is to correct breathiness (Vennard 150). When a breathy onset is corrected with proper breath management and glottal closure (the well-coordinated onset), then the tone will sound more focused. As noted in the earlier chapter on onsets and releases, without the "floppy" and coordinated onset creating a rich harmonic palate to begin with, the resonators cannot do their job of enhancing the sound. Teachers sometimes ask for more "energy" (breath) to correct this fault, and with that increased breath energy, many times the tone seems to focus (gather) forward, even coming to a point.

The second issue also has to do with harmonic scientific principles. In the earlier chapter on resonance we learned that our singing tone is partially determined by the relationship of the size and shape between your throat and your mouth, and that this balance creates both the vowel that our ear perceives, and the color or timbre of the tone. The chapter then went on to describe particular vowel shapes and how they were formed, and the way scientists use the measurement of formants (strengthened frequencies) to define vowels. On an LPC graph, such as those that are provided in Chapter 5 (*Figure 40*, page 75 and *Figure 42*, page 77), the vowels are defined by formants one and two, usually labeled F1 and F2. When we speak about the focus of the tone, we are referring to further refinements of those vowel shapes that define the timbre or color. And without getting too technical ("too late," some of you are saying), those changes in timbre, or focus, are measured by the other formants in the spectrum, usually three, four, and five (F3, F4, and F5). On any given vowel, while F1 and F2 remain the same (defining that vowel) these upper harmonics can shift, creating different colors and intensities that some voice scientists believe account for the focus or placement sensations that singers experience. (See *Figure 48, 49, 50* and *51*.)

Figure 48, 49, 50 and 51:
Spectral Analysis of vowel sound [i] with different points of focus

VII
Focus of the Tone

The four graphs on pages 116-119 show a professional soprano singing an [i] vowel with four different focus points or sensations. The graphs show that the same vowel, on the same pitch, can have several different colors or a different focus, and the ear will still hear and distinguish the vowels as [i].

The top chart in each diagram is a power spectrum with frequency (pitch) shown on the horizontal axis from left to right, and amplitude shown on the vertical axis up and down. Frequency in this case is measured in kilohertz and amplitude in decibels. The various spikes show all the harmonics in that single pitch at that particular moment labeled H1, H2, etc. The pitch being sung is G4, which is represented by the first spike from the left and is labeled .398.24 kHz. Each of the subsequent spikes is about .398 kHz higher. (.785 kHz, 1.175 kHz, 1.572 etc.)

The bottom chart in each diagram is a vowel space diagram that graphs the first formant (F1) on the vertical axis and the second formant (F2) on the horizontal axis. These are the two formants that determine which vowel will be perceived by the ear. The seven crosses represent Appelman's (Appelman 226) vowel formant standards for the seven Italian vowels. The one of interest here is vowel [i] with F1 = .400 kHz and F2 = 2.250 kHz. Any vowel sound with F1 near .400 kHz and F2 near 2.250 kHz will be perceived as [i].

Figure 48 - 51 continued

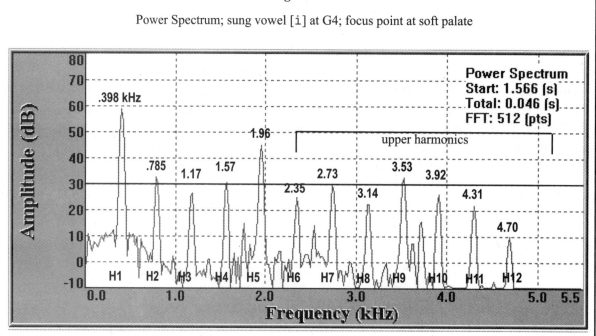

Figure 48A

Power Spectrum; sung vowel [i] at G4; focus point at soft palate

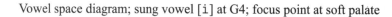

Figure 48B

Vowel space diagram; sung vowel [i] at G4; focus point at soft palate

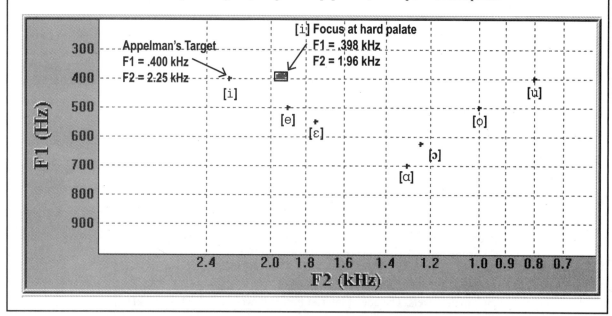

Graph 48A and B shows the [i] being sung with a focus point at the soft palate. Graph 49A and B shows the [i] being sung with a focus point in the middle of the hard palate. Graph 50A and B show the [i] being sung with a focus point at the front of the hard palate, and Graph 51A and B shows a focus point at the teeth. All four are as sung and defined by the singer. The ear perceives these sounds as going from "dark" (Graph 48) to "very bright" (Graph 51) with Graphs 49 and 50 being gradients in between.

As you compare the four graphs, notice that the first two formants in all four graphs remain in an acceptable range for vowel [i], with acceptable being defined as within 50 Hz for F1 and 100 Hz for F2 (Appelman 224), although the F2 in the extreme examples are borderline. However, all four examples are perceived by the ear as [i], maybe not a very good [i], but clearly an [i].

Figure 48 - 51 continued

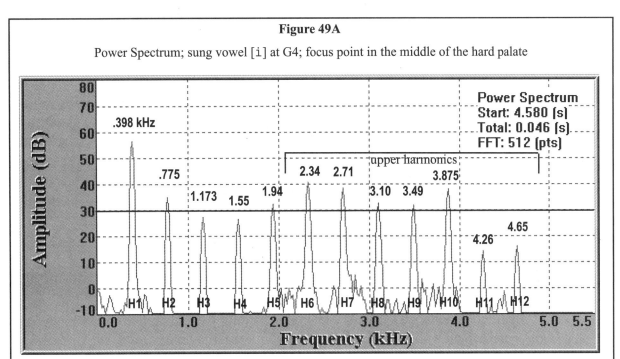

Figure 49A

Power Spectrum; sung vowel [i] at G4; focus point in the middle of the hard palate

Figure 49B

Vowel space diagram; sung vowel [i] at G4; focus point in the middle of the hard palate

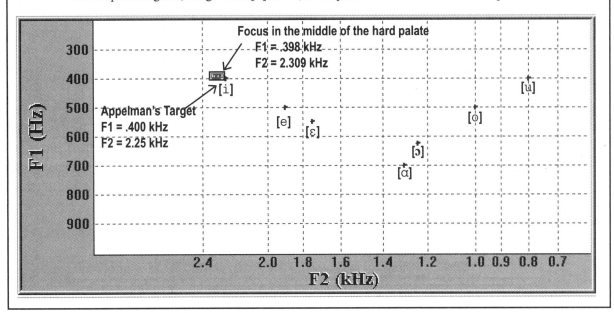

The main difference in the four graphs is apparent in the upper harmonics (harmonics labeled from left to right H1, H2, H3, etc.) From about H6 on, the upper harmonics get gradually louder from 48A to 51A. A line has been added at 30dB for the purpose of comparison. Notice how the frequencies between the brackets in each graph are different, indicating a change in color or focus. As the upper harmonics gain in dB, the sound is perceived as becoming "brighter," overbalanced with the *chiaro* color of the *chiaroscuro*.

     The singer has demonstrated four different focus points for the same vowel on the same pitch. The ear and sensation of the singer, and the ear of the singer's teacher will determine which one is "correct." Some teachers or singers prefer a warmer quality in all vowels. Some prefer more brightness. The exercises later in the chapter are designed to help individual singers identify these various focus points and to be able to choose when each is appropriate. As mentioned earlier, the standard in art song singing is described as *chiaroscuro*, a balance between front and back focus points or a balance between "dark" and "bright."

Figure 48 - 51 continued

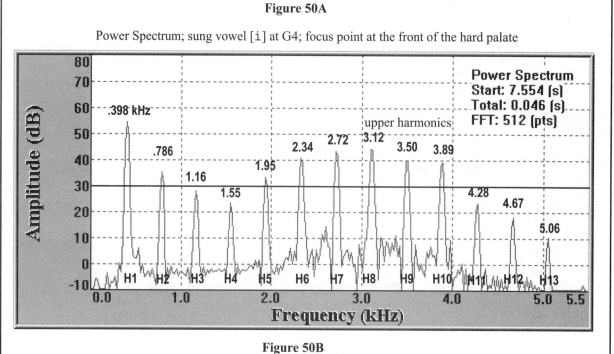

Figure 50A

Power Spectrum; sung vowel [i] at G4; focus point at the front of the hard palate

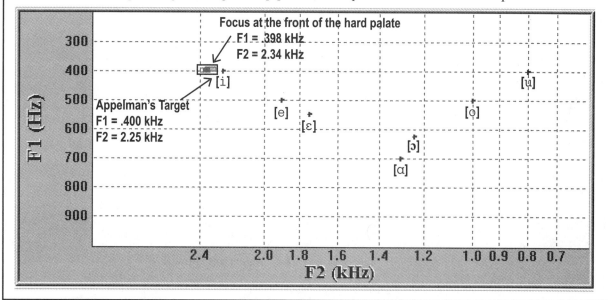

Figure 50B

Vowel space diagram; sung vowel [i] at G4; focus point at the front of the hard palate

Figure 48 - 51 continued

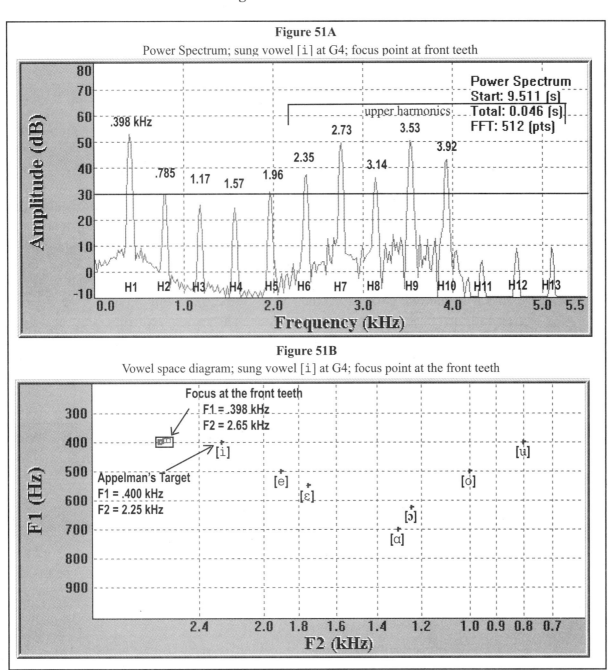

Figure 51A
Power Spectrum; sung vowel [i] at G4; focus point at front teeth

Figure 51B
Vowel space diagram; sung vowel [i] at G4; focus point at the front teeth

Voice scientists have also identified a "super" formant that is present in trained voices which is a clustering of F3, F4, and F5. This is called the "singer's formant." When it is present in a voice, we hear a ringing, bright quality, sometimes called "ping" or "ring."[25] All of these acoustic phenomena contribute to this sensation of "focus of the tone." Vennard says that " 'focus' or 'ping' is the *sine qua non* of good singing" (Vennard 156). It is indispensable.

Ingo Titze tells us that there are maximum points of pressure in the vocal tract as singers produce various vowel sounds ("Is There a Scientific" 167) as outlined above. For example, air pressure is high in the hard palate for vowel [i], high in the soft palate for [u], and high in the pharynx for [ɑ]. He points out that singers may rely on those

---

25   A comprehensive discussion of the various formants in singing and the singer's formant can be found in Sundberg, 93-133.

high-pressure feelings to shape and modify vowels. Scientifically, these are probably the sensations that singers and teachers are describing when they feel the "focus of the tone" or the "placement of the tone." We also know that these points of focus seem to vary with pitch. This variance of focus with pitch presents us with the counter-intuitive concept of vocal line and vowel modification. In order for singers to have consistency of tone throughout their range, they must make focus adjustments as they sing: more open for higher notes, more closed or gathered for lower notes.

Having defined "focus," we now need to come back to our dynamic equilibrium. When we hear good singing, we value tone that seems to be focused, or that comes to a point, giving it a ringing quality. But we also value warmth and depth of tone. Beautiful singing is a balance between these values, not too dark, not too light, but with elements of both, the *chiaroscuro* tone.[26] This quality gives dimensionality to a singer's performance and when cultivated well, it gives a singer many different options of color and emotion as the balance shifts from darker to lighter, (or vice versa) always keeping both values, but in appropriate balance for the mood and text of a song. This is a complex skill, requiring all of the various elements of beautiful singing to be in harmony or in balance with each other. The Spiral of Singing graphic (see *Figure 1*, page viii) although perhaps simplistic, attempts to represent this complexity of skill and thought. Serious students of singing, including singers AND teachers AND conductors, are continually on this journey of harmony and balance to create beautiful and expressive singing.

Exercises to Encourage
the Focus of Tone

The following vocalises are some suggestions for a practical means to experience and maintain a focus of the tone. As always, the assumption is that you have released tension, aligned your instrument, and are cultivating the concepts of *appoggio* breath management and well-coordinated onsets and releases. In addition, you are working with the concept of an open vocal tract, which includes a comfortably low larynx, an open pharynx, a flexible tongue and jaw, and a lifted soft palate, which all contribute to a freely produced tone.

Begin Exercise 120 using an [m] hum, with your lips together and your teeth apart. The sound should feel buzzy on your lips, but easy at your larynx. You should not have any tension in your lips, but as you are singing you should be aware of the forward buzz quality on your lips.

Exercise 120

---

26 *Chiaroscuro* is a term borrowed from visual art that describes a painting that has both qualities of "light" and "dark." In Italian, *chiara* means "light" and "*oscuro*" means "dark."

Now repeat Exercise 120 using an [n] hum, with the tip of your tongue behind your top front teeth and your lips separated. Can you feel how the focus point has shifted from your lips to your hard palate? Now do the exercise with [ŋ]. Can you feel the focus point shift back a little toward your soft palate?

Think about the little pocket that is right behind the place where your upper teeth and hard palate touch (see *Figure 52*). It is just about the right size for a little "red hot" candy to fit, like you find around Valentine's Day. Now repeat Exercise 120 using [ni]. Can you direct the sound into that little pocket? The point of these three exercises is to help you feel and understand that you can shift this forward focus point around.

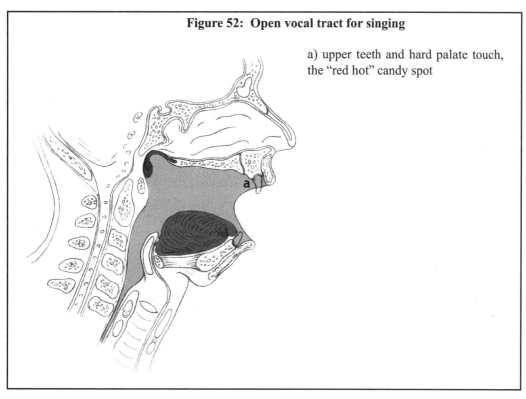

Figure 52: Open vocal tract for singing

a) upper teeth and hard palate touch, the "red hot" candy spot

Exercise 121 uses the French "u" or the German "ü," written in IPA as [y]. This vowel is shaped with your lips in the [u] position and your tongue in the [i] position and is defined when both your tongue and lips are in their most forward position. (Some choral conductors say, "Put your lips in the [u] position and say [i].") Sing the exercise and ascend by half steps with each repetition. Can you feel the focus point move slightly backward as you modify or open the vowel? Remember that the focus point is different on every vowel and every pitch. Think of the thousands of combinations!

Exercise 121

[n— ny————————]

Exercise 122 uses the syllables [mi ni] "meanie", [mɪ ni] "Minnie", and [mɛ ni] "many." Feel how the focus shifts from your teeth and hard palate toward your soft palate as you switch vowels and ascend.

Exercise 122

[mi ni mi ni mɪ ni mɪ ni mɛ ni mɛ ni mɛn]
meanie   *Minnie*   *many*

Now use a straw with exercise Exercise 123 to feel the focus point in front of your face at the end of the straw. On subsequent repetitions, use [u], [o], and [ɑ], which in some singers can be sung too far back. Especially feel the forward focus point for these "back" vowels as you descend; this will contribute to an evenness of line through your range and keep the bottom of your voice from getting muddy.

Exercise 124 uses the French word *bon,* which contains the nasal [õ]. Keep the sound

Exercise 123

1. With straw
2. vowel [u]
3. straw
4. vowel [o]
5. straw
6. vowel [ɑ]

bouncy and bright.

Exercise 124

[bõ bõ bõ   bõ bõ bõ   bõ bõ bõ]

Exercise 125 should be sung cheerfully and brightly. The [z] sound keeps the focus point forward and that is carried into the final syllables, zee, zah, and zoh.

Exercise 125

zing - a   zing - a   zee   zing - a   zing - a   zee
zing - a   zing - a   zah   zing - a   zing - a   zah
zing - a   zing - a   zoh   zing - a   zing - a   zoh

zing - a   zing - a   zing - a   zing - a   zee __
zing - a   zing - a   zing - a   zing - a   zah __
zing - a   zing - a   zing - a   zing - a   zoh __

Exercise 126 trains the concept of singing "open" with increasing space as you ascend and gathering the tone (i.e focus) as you descend. Sing the vowels suggested to train the jaw and other articulators to open gradually as you ascend. Then sing with only one vowel, but modify that vowel toward its more open counterpart as you ascend, and modify back to the original vowel as you descend.[27]

Exercise 126

[ni___   a___   e_____]
[ne_____   o___   u_____]
[ne_____]
[no_____]
[na_____]

Some Common Images
Used to Encourage the Focus of Tone

♫ Put your index finger about two inches in front of your nose. Sing directly to your finger.

♫ Choose a spot on the far wall of the room you are singing in. Imagine that your voice is a laser beam directed precisely at that spot.

♫ Experiment singing through a kazoo. Can you feel the focus in front of your face? Keep that image when you sing without the kazoo.

27   For a comprehensive discussion of vowel modification, see Appelman, 216-247.

VII

Focus of the Tone

♫ Use a hair comb and a piece of wax paper. Place the wax paper on top of the hair comb (teeth facing you). Put the paper and comb up to your mouth and gently croon "oo," like "who." Can you make the paper rattle? Remember that feeling when you sing.

♫ Feel as if you are sifting the tone from under your eyes.

♫ As you approach the high note in a phrase, point with your finger, "up and over."

♫ The focus of the tone in your voice can be compared to the various focal points available in the vewfinder of a digital camera. You can focus the picture to emphasize the background or focus more on the foreground. It is the same picture with a different focus. Likewise your voice can sing the same vowel with a different focus of the tone.

♫ Look at a common kitchen funnel, ideally about three or four inches at the wide end. Imagine that this wide end is your pharynx (open throat). The narrow end is a perfect image for how the tone comes to a focal point in front of your face. (See *Figure 53*)

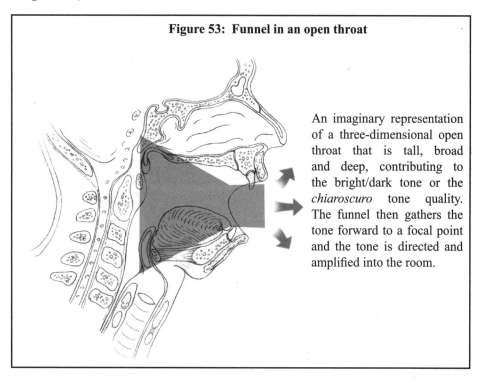

Figure 53: Funnel in an open throat

An imaginary representation of a three-dimensional open throat that is tall, broad and deep, contributing to the bright/dark tone or the *chiaroscuro* tone quality. The funnel then gathers the tone forward to a focal point and the tone is directed and amplified into the room.

Especially for the Choral Conductor

Different sections in your choir may have different focus issues. For example, young sopranos and tenors may lack focus in the lower range of their voices and then become too bright on the top, producing a shrill or overly loud tone. Altos, in general, become foggy and indistinct as they descend, and basses are notoriously heavy and muddy in their lower range. How you correct these problems and train your choir will depend on the choral tonal ideal you have developed in your mind's ear. Some choral conductors build their sound from the bottom up, ideally with a rich bass section, a fairly brilliant tenor section, a light but warm alto section and a light flute-like soprano section. This tonal value enables spectacular tuning and a flawless blend, but at its extremes can be monochromatic in color. Another tonal example is the model that values disparate voices in each section and through careful seating and blending of voices, the choir is able to express many different colors and emotions, bringing more meaning to the texts. Your singers need to understand and share your tonal ideal, and one of your many tasks is to give them guidance and training in how to attain that sound.

The following is a suggested sequence of exercises to use with your choir to help them feel and produce a forward focused tone quality.

♫ Use Exercise 120, page 120, to help them feel different focal points. [m] emphasizes lips, [n] emphasizes hard palate, and [ŋ] emphasizes a little further back toward the soft palate.

♫ Now invite them to sing Exercise 122 on page 122. The [m] and [n] consonants coupled with vowels [i], [ɪ], and [ɛ] will help all sections to get a forward, brilliant sound. This is especially helpful if you are training to sing Baroque music that requires a bright, bouncy texture.

♫ Exercise 125, page 123, now introduces vowel [ɑ] and [o]. Listen carefully and make sure that these more "back" vowels stay forward and focused.

♫ Exercise 126 practices the concept of opening space as you ascend and gathering the sound as you descend. Do the exercise with the suggested vowel changes, and then practice on one vowel, but be sure your singers allow the vowel to modify to more space as they ascend, and allow the vowel to gather a bit as they descend. This is the principle of vowel modification (in Italian: *aggiustamento*). Altos and basses generally need to be reminded to close or gather the tone as they descend. Sopranos and tenors generally need to be reminded to release as they ascend, especially through the *passaggio* areas.

♫ Exercise 127 trains flexibility for your choir as they practice both forward focus and vowel modification. Do it first with the built-in open vowels suggested, and then on a single vowel, modifying appropriately on the high notes.

VII

Focus of the Tone

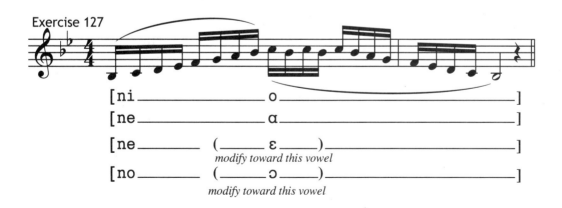

VII

Focus of the Tone

Summary

♫ The concept of the focus of the tone in singing is dependent on sensation or feeling in the singer.

♫ Singers develop this skill by "remembering how it feels" and reproducing that feeling consistently.

♫ Focus of the tone is another example in singing of a balance of two disparate feelings or actions. Focus is a balance between the sensations of space and point.

♫ Scientifically, there are two explanations for the sensations of focus.

> 1. Lack of breath energy creates breathy singing. If breath management is improved, the singing focus will improve.
>
> 2. Different vowels and consonants have different points of maximum air pressure in the vocal tract. The scientific explanation is a function of formants three, four, and five in the vocal harmonic spectrum. These formants (like all formants) are primarily determined and defined by the relationship between the shapes of the pharynx and the mouth. Singers can learn to control and manipulate these relational shapes to produce an optimal balance between space and point, warmth and brilliance.

♫ The balance between space and point will vary with vowel and pitch. Although it seems counter-intuitive, these pitch-related changes help to create a consistent vocal line. This technique of opening vowels as you ascend and gathering them as you descend is commonly called vowel modification or vowel migration. The Italian term is *agguistamento*.

♫ When tone contains both elements of "light" and "dark," it is called the "*chiaroscuro*" tone. Highly prized in singing, this tone gives dimensionality to a singer's performance and allows a broad range of color, emotionality, and expressiveness in performance.

Chapter VIII

ARTICULATION

Independence of the jaw, lips, tongue, and soft palate is cultivated to form consonants and vowels. Articulator movements are coordinated with the diaphragm to energize consonants. Vowel/consonant and consonant/vowel joins are swift with no anticipated or shadowing. Diphthongs are precise and appropriate.

Articulation

Chapter VIII

Articulation

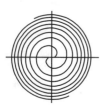

Background and Scientific Approach

We are making good progress in building our singing voice "castle in the air," as quoted from Mr. Lamperti in the Introduction. Our examination of this marvelous, magical "castle" has necessarily been linear, but remember that the principles of the Spiral of Singing are a gestalt construct: the individual parts are so integrated that they become a functional unity that is greater than the sum of the parts. As we continue on this journey of singing, each time we revisit an element we are able to go deeper in our understanding of it and how the various parts interrelate with each other. In the previous chapters we have examined several steps that now lead to the point of forming and singing words. As we add words and consonant articulation to our study, the interdependence of all these concepts becomes even more apparent.

Voice scientists use the term articulation to mean any action in the vocal tract during phonation. By this definition, articulation means the movements required to shape vowels as well as consonants. But for our purposes here, when we speak of articulation, we are talking about the actions required for consonants: the articulating movements that interrupt the stream of vowel sounds that emanates from the vocal tract. All the principles we have examined so far are a delivery system designed to produce a tension-free stream of tone that begins with the singer's thought and ends with delivery to the listener's ear. But, of course, singing is much more than beautiful tone; this is the great advantage we have over instrumental music. We have articulation, the accompanying enunciation, and pronunciation, which are the primary components of diction. We get to use language and words to express thoughts and feelings and to tell stories! This is that "castle in the air."

Zemlin (304) states that consonants by definition are characterized physiologically by an obstruction of the vocal tract. In singing, these obstructions create sounds that irregularly (and ideally briefly) interrupt that vowel flow that we have worked so hard to create. Consonants are actions made audible, and they bring language to our singing. Our singing articulators, usually defined as the jaw, lips, teeth, tongue, and the hard and soft palate, produce these actions. The cheeks and the glottis should also be added to that list, as they both assist in certain sounds. These articulators were described in Chapter 2 "Opening the Vocal Tract" (page 14). One of the goals in that chapter was to make you aware of these articulators and remind you that you have some control over them, as long as they remain tension-free. In this chapter we are concerned with maintaining freedom and developing independence of these articulators in order to facilitate clear and precise diction.

Phoneticians classify consonants in three categories: 1) voiced or unvoiced, 2) the place in the vocal tract where they are articulated, 3) and the manner in which they are articulated. *Figure 54* on page 130 contains this information in chart form.

1. Voiced or Unvoiced
(Included within each articulation category on the chart)
Your vocal folds are either vibrating (voiced) or not (unvoiced).

2. Place of Articulation
Labial or bilabial: at the lips
Labial dental: lips and teeth
Dental: teeth
Alveolar: at the gum line behind the teeth
Palatal-aveolar: at the hard palate
Velar: at the soft palate
Glottal: at the vocal folds

3. Manner of Articulation
Stop: complete stoppage of airflow
Fricative: incomplete closure of the vocal tract creating a noise excitation in the vocal tract
Affricative: the sound begins as a stop and is released as a fricative
Glides and liquids (sometimes called semi-vowels): voiced, and the tone emanates from the mouth with no nasal coupling
Nasals: voiced, and tone emanates from the nose. There is a constriction at the lips, or at the tongue as it contacts the alveolar ridge, or at the tongue as it contacts the hard or soft palate.
Glottal: made by narrowing or completely adducting the vocal folds

Consonant Chart

Figure 54

Manner of Articulation ↓ / Place of Articulation →	Labial or bilabial (lip or lips vibrating) Voiced	Unvoiced	Labial dental (upper teeth and lower lip) Voiced	Unvoiced	Dental (tongue at the teeth) Voiced	Unvoiced	Alveolar (tongue at the gum line behind the teeth) Voiced	Unvoiced	Palatal alveolar (Tongue tip at the hard palate) Voiced	Palatal alveolar (tongue blade at the hard palate) Voiced	Unvoiced	Velar (back of tongue at the soft palate) Voiced	Unvoiced	Glottal (at the glottis) Voiced	Unvoiced
Stop/Plosive: (complete stoppage of the airflow)	[b]	[p]					[d]	[t]				[g]	[k]	[?]	
Fricative: (incomplete closure of the vocal tract)		[hw]	[v]	[f]	[ð]	[θ]	[z]	[s]		[ʒ]	[ʃ]				[h]
Affricative: (begins as a stop and is released as a fricative)										[dʒ]	[tʃ]				
Glides and liquids: (voiced with no nasal coupling)	[w]				[ɫ]		[l]		[r]	[j]					
Nasals: (voiced with tone emanating from the nose)	[m]						[n]					[ŋ]			

130

In summary, consonants (defined as an obstruction of the vocal tract) are a product of four different things: 1) a movement of the articulators, 2) no vibrations or vibration of the vocal folds, 3) the place where the articulation occurs, and 4) the manner in which the obstruction occurs.

Now, again, you might be thinking, "Too much information!" But as singers, we do need to be concerned with how all these things work together. The ability to tell our stories and to express our thoughts and feelings depends on our ability to coordinate and execute those four things, those "actions made audible."

The enemy of these actions is tension. In order for us to keep a beautiful vocal line as we sing with clear diction, the consonants, which are interruptions, must be very quick and agile. If an articulator is holding tension, it will be impossible for that action to be swift, and the vocal line will be disjointed and the diction will be compromised. Think of consonants like the blinking of your eyes. You probably blink thousands of times a day. Is your vision impaired? No, because your eyelids move without tension and very quickly. This is why we must cultivate a tension-free jaw, lips, tongue, and soft palate. The rule to follow is to use only the minimum but necessary amount of muscular involvement to form consonants. This is especially true of consonants like the American "l, r, d, n, and t." For these consonants, use only the tip of your tongue (minimum but necessary) to form them, not the entire tongue.

Another facet of clear diction is the independence of each articulator. Sometimes particular articulators develop an affinity with another. An example of one affinity would be if every time you released your jaw back and down, your tongue retracts also. Or some singers raise their tongue in the back every time they raise their soft palate. Or perhaps every time the tongue "fronts" for a forward vowel, the soft palate lowers. These are all issues of articulator **non**-independence, and singers must cultivate the ability to consciously separate the action of one articulator from another, so each articulator may become increasingly independent.

Consonants require much more breath energy in singing than they do in everyday speech. Additionally, in singing, voiceless consonants require more muscular effort and more airflow than voiced consonants (Edwards, 23). Singers must learn to energize all consonants by actively coordinating with the breath flow. Without an extra boost of energy, consonant sounds will not project into the room and will not be heard. This is certainly true for solo singers, but it is imperative for choirs to exercise this discipline of connecting diction to breath management.

In the context of singing an uninterrupted vocal line in English, most syllables must begin with a consonant and end with a vowel, similar to the way French is spoken.[28] This facilitates the "blink of an eye" articulation. While singers are sustaining a vowel, they must take care to not anticipate the coming consonant, as this practice "colors" or taints the vowel being sung. This can be problematic with all consonants, but it is especially troublesome in English with the American "r" and "l." In the case of the [l], the sound should be quickly formed with the tip of the tongue, with minimal

28 This method of diction, in which each syllable appears to end with a vowel, historically was advocated by Niccolo Vaccai, the nineteenth-century Italian pedagogue. The purpose was to allow the singer to dwell on the vowel to facilitate *canto legato*, and to facilitate swift and immediate articulation of the consonants (Vaccai, 3).

involvement of the middle and the back of the tongue, similar to the way most Americans say the sound in "leaf." In addition, the American "r" in singing, should be minimized, especially at the ends of words. Most of the time it is enough to think the [r] but not sing it, and your audience will still understand it.

Another issue concerns vowel/consonant and consonant/vowel joins, either in the middle of a word or between words. Some singers develop the undesirable practice of singing a shadow vowel [ə] after a consonant, as in come-uh-with-uh-me, or in International Phonetic Alphabet (IPA) [kɔ mə wi θə mi]. Sometimes this shadowing occurs when a singer is trying to be emphatic, but to the listener it almost always sounds affected except in rare cases of emotional emphasis. Vowel/consonant and consonant/vowel joins should always be swift and supple. Diphthongs in English (two vowel sounds in the same syllable) follow a similar rule: elongate the first vowel as long as possible and then deftly and precisely add the second vowel just before the next syllable. An example would be "But who may abide the day of His coming?" from Handel's *Messiah*. For a beautiful vocal line the phrase must be sung as follows, diphthongs in bold and underlined:

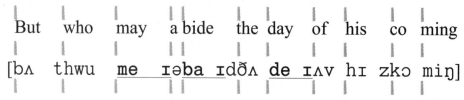

To sum up, clear diction in English requires swift movement of the articulators with a minimal but necessary amount of muscular involvement, freedom and independence of each articulator with no affinity of movement between any of them, and all sounds and movements coordinated with breath energy for clarity and optimal projection.

Finally, a word needs to be said about the age-old discussion regarding what is more important: the words or the music (tone). Of course, both are important. In popular singing and in musical theater, the words will always take precedent over a vocal line (as defined by high culture art song singing). This is as it should be and becomes painfully obvious when classically trained singers ignore this guideline and sing popular songs on national TV. However in *bel canto* or "classical" singing there are certain acoustical and physical properties dealing with pitch and resonance that just can't be ignored. Although it is incumbent on every singer to cultivate and practice the rules of clear diction as stated above, there are times when the vocal line and beauty of the voice must take precedent. This should be celebrated and enjoyed. It is an example of the sum of the whole being greater than the sum of the parts. Certainly, the texts are what primarily convey our thoughts and feelings, but beautiful, consistent tone quality has its own value that contributes greatly to the combined aesthetic and meaning of words and musical sounds. Although very important, word clarity should not be at the expense of vocal quality. This means that sometimes the quality of the vowels, the uninterrupted vocal line, will take precedence over the consonants that constantly interrupt that line, and sometimes words may be hard to understand. But after all, that is why we call it *bel canto*, beautiful singing.

Exercises to Encourage Clear and Precise Articulation in Singing

To differentiate and clarify the three nasal sounds, sing Exercise 128 and 129. Can you feel the movement of your tongue as you progress from [m] to [n] to [ŋ]? Does it feel effortless? Can you keep the space open behind your soft palate as you articulate these three nasals? In other words, can you keep your funnel from collapsing? (See *Figure 53* on page 124.)

Exercise 128

Exercise 129

Exercise 130 requires that you use both voiced and unvoiced fricatives and toggle back and forth. Remember that the unvoiced of the pair always need more airflow and muscular effort (but not tension), so be sure to exert yourself. Can you feel the connection to your abdominal muscles, your breath management?

Exercise 130

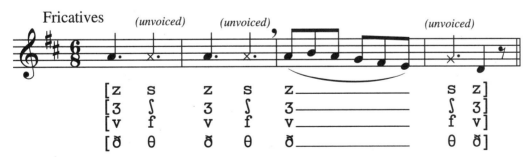

Exercise 131 now adds stops and affricatives. Keep all the sounds unvoiced and feel the connection with your abdominal muscles. Exert yourself! Exercise 132 is a combination of the three sets in Exercise 131. Experiment with dynamics and see if you can hear the "train leave the station."

VIII

Articulation

Exercise 131

All unvoiced!

a)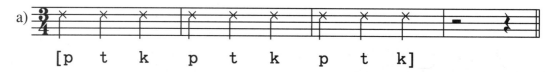

[p   t   k   p   t   k   p   t   k]

b)

[f   s   ʃ   f   s   ʃ   f   s   ʃ]

c)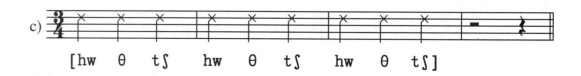

[hw   θ   tʃ   hw   θ   tʃ   hw   θ   tʃ]

Exercise 132

All unvoiced!

[p   t   k   f   s   ʃ   hw   θ   tʃ]

Exercise 133 trains the tricky American "r." In this example an [r] is at the beginning of most words. Sing them quickly, almost like a vowel sound and try to minimize the hard rrrrr sound.

Exercise 133

Round the rough and rug-ged rock the rag-ged ras-cal ran.

Adapted from Kenneth Crannel Voice and Articulation

Exercise 134 will encourage you to sing the American [l] with the tip of your tongue. Sing this exercise as fast as you can, but only use the tip of your tongue to form the [l].

Exercise 134

Lie low li - on,   lie low li - on,   lie low li - on, lie   low.

Exercise 135 trains the glide, the [w] sound, with some [l] and [r] thrown in. Be sure all the consonants are quick, like the blink of an eye.

Exercise 135

Wan - da weighed   wal - nuts   wea - ri - ly.

Exercise 136 trains another glide, the [j], here spelled with a "y" as you would encounter it. See if you can accent all the "y" spellings without slowing down. The accents activate your abdominal muscles; the [j] requires you to move the middle of your tongue quickly.

Exercise 136

Yes,   yel - low   yeo - men   Yell   and   Yap

Exercise 137 exercises the tip of the tongue consonants [l][d][n][t][r]. (Kathleen Darragh tells her students to imagine that the front third of their tongue is on a little hinge, and that is all of the tongue you should use on this exercise!)

Exercise 137

La   Da - ra   na - da   Ta - Da!

Exercise 138 uses Sieber's famous syllables again. Now we use them as a diction exercise, practicing each of the initial consonants as the blink of an eye.

Exercise 138

me ni po tu   la be da me   ni po lu la

be da me ni   po tu la be   da me ni po tu.

Exercise 139 gives an opportunity to practice the glottal sound [?] (see Consonant Chart, page 130) that we use often in English and German. See how softly you can make the sound and have it still be clear. It should <u>not</u> sound like "i yate teggs zat teight." Use the "silent h" concept to get a good separation between the words that will still be musical, but clear.

Exercise 139

I ate eggs at eight and on-ly at eight.

Exercise 140 practices the diphthong [aɪ]. Make sure that the vowel you elongate for as long as possible is [a] and not [ɪ]. An added bonus is that you get to practice the difference between [w] and [ʍ] in "wide" and "white." Now do the same exercise with "how now brown cow," practicing the [au] combination. Another option is "shout foul mouth crowd," which is very challenging. But either way, be sure to elongate [a] as long as possible before adding the [u].

Exercise 140

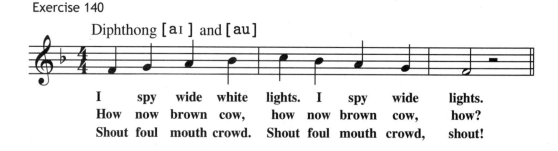

I   spy   wide   white   lights.   I   spy   wide   lights.
How   now   brown   cow,   how   now   brown   cow,   how?
Shout foul   mouth crowd.   Shout foul   mouth crowd,   shout!

Some Common Images Used to Assist in Clear Consonant Articulation

Your eyes blink thousands of times a day, but your vision is not impaired. Think of your vision as the vowels and the consonants like the blinks. The vowel stream is not disturbed if the consonants are swift.

Think of your tongue like an anteater's tongue — so fast you can hardly see it.

Mentally divide your tongue into thirds from front to back. Now imagine that the front third of your tongue is attached to the other two-thirds by a hinge that allows it to flick up toward your upper front teeth. Do not use the back two-thirds of your tongue to form those tip-of-the-tongue consonants.

Especially for the Choral Conductor

Training a choir to execute clear and effective diction is a double duty for the choral conductor. All of the skills mentioned in the above section must be trained individually. The independence of the articulators and the coordination with the abdominal muscles are of particular importance. The added dimension is that the choir members must do all that and do it precisely <u>together</u>. It is kind of like the old Ginger Rogers' story — she had to have the same technical skill that her partners did (individual dance training), and she needed the further skill of coordination with her partner (doing it backward and in high heels). In addition, in choral singing, all diction must be exaggerated; this adds another layer of complexity to the skill of clear diction or articulation.

All of the articulation exercises suggested previously in this chapter are appropriate technical training for choral use. Be sure you are watching and listening for swift articular movements and abdominal muscle involvement. Remember, consonants are <u>actions</u> made audible. If you note problems with a particular sound not being clear, isolate it and train. Lack of clarity is probably because of an absence of articular independence in some of your singers; give them the opportunity to develop this skill by offering them stand-alone exercises that require them to do only one thing at a time.

At the same time, you should be encouraging and training your singers to articulate precisely together. This is an issue of rhythm and duration; sometimes it is enough to draw their attention to it. Other times, they need to develop the technical skill and the listening and ensemble skill to do it together. Exercise 131 and 132, page 134, are especially good for training an ensemble feeling, both for duration and dynamics, as you experiment with tempo and intensity.

Many times diction problems are breath management problems. If the consonant actions are not coordinated with air pressure activity, they will not be heard in the room. Review with your choir the breath management principles in Chapter 3 and be sure they are engaged and exerting themselves as they sing (and articulate). Exercise 130, page 133, is especially good for connecting breath to diction.

For example: you are working on Thomas Morley's madrigal, *"Fire, Fire."* (See Exercise 141, page 139.) The text is "Fire, fire, my heart, Fa la la la la la. . . O help, alas! Ah me! I sit and cry me, and call for help, alas, but none comes nigh me. Fa la la la la la la."

You have noticed that:

1)   the singers lose tempo on the opening "fire, fire"
2)   the "t" of "heart" seems to be silent
3)   the "Fa la la's" bog down and are not together

Possible remedies:

1)   Using Exercise 130, train them to coordinate their breath by articulating fricatives, especially [v] and [f] . Start at a slow tempo and gradually go faster. Another

time, use Exercise 131, but perhaps only the fricative example (b). Again start slow and add tempo as they are ready to do it precisely in time. Now speak the opening in rhythm using ONLY the fricative [f] sound instead of the word "fire." Now add back the words, and remind them to minimize the final "r" in the word "fire" or to leave it off all together, first speaking and then singing

2)   Have each section speak its part in rhythm and have the singers place the final "t" on the appropriate beat **together.** Remind them that they need extra breath pressure and exertion for this unvoiced plosive sound to carry into the room. Have them now sing the opening phrase, "Fire, fire, my heart," overemphasizing the "t" but making it rhythmically precise. If it is too much, ask them to back off maybe 10%.

3)   The problem is most likely that they are not using the tip of their tongues for the "la la la la's" and that is what is slowing them (or some of them) down. Practice exercise 137 "la da ra na da ta da" using **only** the tips of their tongues, and then apply it to the "fa la la's."

Here are some other possible pitfalls with this text:

Problem	**Remedy**
"h" not audible in "help"	Activate diaphragm
"sit and" run together sounding "sitand"	Add gentle glottal before "and"
"d" of "and cry" and "b" of "but none" are inaudible	Activate diaphragm and consider adding slight [ə] between words. [æ ndə kraɪ mi], (and cry me) [bʌ tə nʌ nə] (but none.)
"and call" sounds like "an call"	[æ ndə kɔ̣l] , (and call)

Exercise 141

Fire, Fire!

(SSATB, Unaccompanied)

Thomas Morley (1557-1603)

Forcefully

VIII

Articulation

Cantabile

VIII

Articulation

O help! O help! A-las! O help! Ah_____ me! Ah_____

help! O help! A-las! O_____ help! Ah me! Ah

O help! O help! A-las! O help! Ah me! Ah

O help! O help! A-las! O help! Ah me! Ah

Ah me! Ah

____ me!_____ I sit_____ and cry me, And call for

me! I sit and cry me,

me! I sit and cry me, And call for help, a-las, but

me! I sit and cry me, And call for help, a-las, but

me! I sit and cry me,

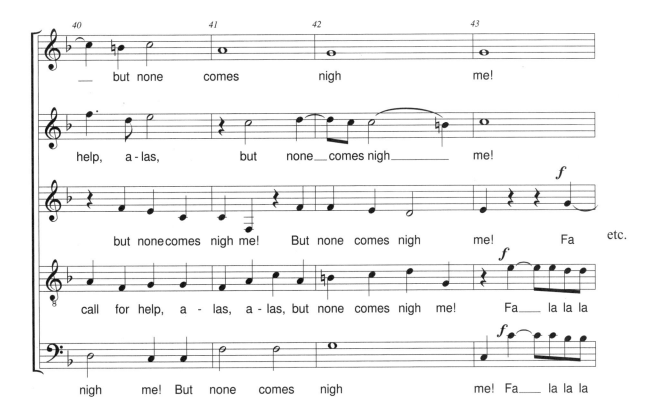

Articulation or diction is one area where the general rules between individual *bel canto* singing and choral singing may differ. As noted earlier, in *bel canto* solo singing, there are instances when beautiful tone must take precedence over clear diction, because of physiological and acoustical considerations. In choral singing, because of the different voice parts usually singing in different ranges, clear and precise diction should always be the goal, and is nearly always possible. It does require, in some cases, a different level of energy, using an enunciation style that would seem affected in solo singing. But the nature of choral singing requires constant diction vigilance on the part of the director in order to avoid the "mashed potato mouth" syndrome that occurs when careful attention is not given over to articulation.

Summary

- ♫ Articulation in singing means any action in the vocal tract, but for our purposes here, articulation means the addition of consonants to the vocal line created by vowels.
- ♫ One definition of consonants is "actions made audible."
- ♫ The components of articulation, enunciation, and pronunciation, enable us to sing our stories and express thoughts and feelings.
- ♫ Phoneticians classify consonants in three categories:
     1. Voiced or unvoiced
     2. Manner of articulation
     3. Place of articulation
- ♫ Clear diction is a result of swift, tension-free movement of the articulators.
- ♫ Singers must have complete independent control over each articulator. An articulating action must be independent of any other articulating action.
- ♫ In singing, consonants require more breath energy than consonants we use in speech. Also, unvoiced consonants require more airflow and muscular effort than voiced consonants.
- ♫ Consonants must be energized and coordinated with the diaphragm and abdominal muscles.
- ♫ Choral singing has an added dimension for clear diction: each singer must have the technical skill to perform clear and precise consonants, and the consonants or articulations must be executed in strict rhythm, <u>at the same time</u> in unison with the other singers.
- ♫ In choral singing, all articulations must be exaggerated.
- ♫ Choirs must especially train abdominal muscle involvement for clear diction.

Chapter IX

Musical Expression

MUSICAL EXPRESSION

Vocal technique supports performance storytelling and emotional content. The goal is to sing emotions, thoughts and ideas, not technique. To that end, vowels and pitched consonants have precise intonation. Sostenuto and legato are maintained at all times. Voice has flexibility and agility. Dynamics are appropriate for intended emotional effect. Vibrato is appropriate and controlled.

Chapter IX
Musical Expression

Background and Approach

Every word written, every idea expressed so far in this book has been leading up to this chapter. Our goal is artistic, beautiful, expressive singing. Perfect technique by itself is not enough; beautiful diction is not enough; even the most perfectly produced, resonated tone is not enough. Neither is perfect intonation and rhythm. All of these things are a means to an end, and that end is our singular human ability to communicate and share our thoughts, feelings and stories with other humans through singing. This ability begins in our souls. We sing because we have to; our spirits demand it. We cultivate excellent technique, diction, resonance, intonation, and all the other aspects of beautiful singing because they enhance this metaphysical experience that we humans crave.[29]

The Greek philosophers commented on this unique aspect of our human experience. Plato's *Phaedo* is an account of the last hours of Socrates, before he commits suicide by drinking the hemlock. In his usual manner, Socrates is debating with his followers the existence of the soul and whether it is immortal. He puts forth the argument that one of the ways that we can "know" our souls is through various musical metaphors. In particular, he reminds his followers, by the example of his own life, that one of their tasks in their search for knowledge (knowledge defined here as ideas of the "soul" as opposed to the "body") is to "cultivate the arts," which is sometimes also translated as "cultivate music" (*Phaedo* 60E). Other metaphors that he uses to help his disciples understand metaphysical ideas include allusions to musical instruments, the mechanics of tuning an instrument, and references to harmony in general as personified in music. He also reminds them that swans (when forewarned about their death by Apollo, the god of music) **sing** their "swan song" to express their soul's joy of what is to come (*Phaedo* 84E-85B). Clearly, Socrates believed that singing was a direct access to the aspect of "soulness" in humans.

But we don't need Socrates or Plato to tell us that music touches us in an "unearthly" manner. Music (singing) enriches our lives; we need it to make our lives more than just a physical existence of eating, sleeping, and reproducing. Those of us who have been gifted in creating music (singers, instrumentalists, conductors) have a special role: not only do we access our own souls when we sing, we enable our audience to be in touch with their spirits also. This is the meaning of the last line of Lamperti's metaphor about singing being a castle in the air (printed in the Introduction). When we build our castle in the air, the soul inhabits it.

---

29 These concepts are not exclusive to singing and music. All of the fine arts share this ability to access the human soul, and other disciplines like dance, drama, and visual art all share the ability to access the metaphysical.

So when we perform, it is not enough to have perfect singing technique, diction, and intonation. Your audience wants a "soul" experience, an emotional experience. They want you to create a whole world for them. You become the character in your song and you take your audience there with you. We call this "being in character"; Aristotle called it "imitation" (*Poetics* 1448a20). Singers create this world out of their imaginations with the help of the text, the music, and the accompanist. Conductors create this world out of their imaginations with the help of their singers, the music, the text, and the accompanist, if one is required.

To state the obvious, this is why you must **know** the text and the music; your brain needs time to cultivate all the different aspects of your performance and make it into artistry. This requires cultivation of both the text and the music, similar to how gardeners grow flowers or vegetables. They work with the soil, adding what is not present. They plant seeds and make sure that there is sunlight and water. They pull weeds. Sometimes they bring in experts to help them with particular aspects. Are you getting the similarities to singing? Only after this kind of cultivation (like pursuing the principles of the Spiral of Singing) can you expect to create an emotional world for your audience.

This is the artistry or creativity of singing, and this is the best part of being a singer. It's not the hours in practice and lessons, nor learning languages, nor figuring out what to do with your tongue (or throat or lips or whatever). The artistry of singing is about sharing the unique world that you have imagined in your head with an audience and getting the feedback of, "Oh yes, that is exactly the way I have felt too" or "I never thought of it that way before, but now I get what you mean."

Of course, you must have something in your head in order to create this world. You spend a lot of time in lessons and rehearsals working on technique, just so you don't have to worry about your voice not responding the way you want it to when you perform. When you are overly concerned with technique in your performance, your audience is aware of it. They view it as a break in character. ("There he goes, reaching for the high note" or "Whoops, the choir didn't quite make that phrase altogether, huh?") Even the most supportive audiences cannot help but be distracted by these kinds of lapses, which is why you work so hard to have seamless and flawless technique. But there must come a point when you put technical concerns aside (momentarily) and deal with the thoughts, feelings, and attitudes you use to create an emotional world for your audience. You must identify the emotions that the music rouses in you, and then portray and "imitate" those emotions so that your audience, vicariously, can experience them through you. "Emotion" comes from the Middle French, meaning "to move." Your goal is to "move" your audience.

Can this be done spontaneously? Absolutely. Some of the best performances happen when a performer seems to be discovering something new in the music as the audience is watching and listening. Usually, though, this skill comes from a lot of thought and practice in advance, so that the performer has a large palette of emotions and expressions to draw from during a performance. The more colors a performer uses, the more the listener's experience is enriched. As performers we must cultivate many emotions beyond happy and sad.

Exercises to Encourage
Musical Expression in Singing

An experienced performer trains the emotional and expressive elements of performing as systematically and conscientiously as the technical aspects. It is not one or the other; you must embody both technique and expressiveness when you endeavor to "move" your audience and enable them to have an emotional journey with you as you perform.

Below are two sets of strategies to help a singer develop a large reservoir of emotions, feelings, and attitudes to draw on during performance. The first strategy outlines a relatively quick process that can be done in a lesson, rehearsal, or class. The second is a more comprehensive method that will assist you in finding deeper and more complex emotional content for your performances. All of these suggestions assume that you have 1) studied the music, 2) read through the text several times, 3) if the text is in a foreign language, you have examined at least one poetic translation and perhaps compared it to others and have written out a word-by-word translation, 4) glanced through Appendix Two, page 170, *List of Feelings or Emotions,* to start your brain thinking about the myriad of emotions you can portray. Although your teacher or choral conductor may assist you with this basic work, ultimately, the responsibility is yours as the artist who will be interpreting this story for your audience.

Strategy #1 — A preliminary text study

After you have read through your text several times, begin this strategy by ending the following sentence: "This is a story about. . . ." You should be able to do it in one or two succinct sentences. For simplicity, let's work with the English folk song *Early One Morning.*

Exercise 142

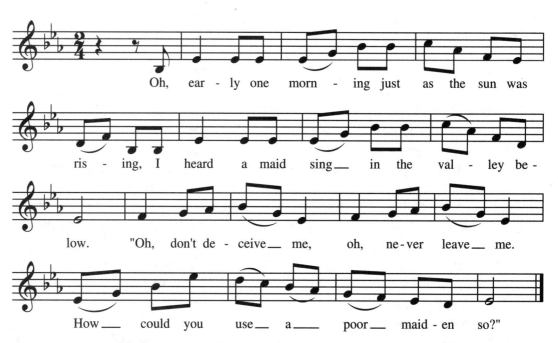

For example: "**This is a story about** a young woman who fell in love with the wrong kind of man. She has spent a sleepless night and she is singing to herself, knowing that sooner or later her lover is going to hurt her." This initial summation can be as simple or complex as you like. The goal is to get you thinking about as many aspects of the song as you can.

Now start to flesh out your interpretation. Put yourself in the text. Answer the following questions about the singer, no matter how obvious they seem. 1) Who am I? 2) What do I want? 3) What am I feeling? 4) What words define or accomplish this?

In *Early One Morning* you have to decide whether you want to interpret from the narrator's point of view or the young woman's point of view. 1) Is the narrator the young woman's lover? 2) Does he intend to hurt her? 3) Is he just an innocent bystander? 4) What is he feeling? 5) What does he think she is feeling? You can see that even a simple text can bring up a lot of different feelings and interpretations.

Now spend some time with the musical aspects of the piece. 1) How do the various elements of the melody either support or refute your initial summation? 2) Although not included in Exercise 142, how might an accompaniment support or refute this initial summation? Does the accompaniment function as a subtext?

Strategy #2 — A more comprehensive text study

First complete the sentence "This is a story about. . ." in your head as outlined above. Then copy the text on a sheet of paper. If it is not in English, then also copy the word-by-word translation underneath it and perhaps a poetic translation under that.

With the text printed in front of you, complete the following ten steps to comprehensively flesh out your unique creation, enabling this particular musical piece to come alive to you and your audience.

1. Is it a poem? Does it have a rhyme scheme? Did the composer follow the poetic form with his or her music?

2. How many characters are there, including the narrator? Remember that sometimes an inanimate object or an abstract idea can be a "character."

3. Give each character a name. (Remember that it is up to you to create this world — if it isn't in your head, it cannot be communicated to your audience.) Create the following details for each named character.
    a. Age, height, and weight
    b. Eye and hair color
    c. Skin color and texture (dark? bronzed? delicate? acne?)
    d. Fragrance (perfume? cologne? body odor? outdoorsy?)
    e. Hair (long? short? curly? silky? wiry? bald? facial hair?)
    f. Clothing in detail, including socks and shoes if any (is it stylish? new? old? worn? ragged?)

4. What is the setting of your creation? What can your characters see around them? What could the audience see if the scene were real? Create all of that in your mind.
    a. Are you indoors? In a house, a palace, an office? What are the furnishings? Include the flooring, the wallpaper, the view from the windows. What kind of furniture is there?
    b. Are you outdoors? In the city, country, suburbs? In what country? Is there vegetation, water, a river or a lake? Are there mountains, fields, a beach, trees, flowers? What are all the colors you envision?
    c. What is the temperature? What are the weather conditions? What season is it? What does it smell like? What is the humidity? Is it moist, dry? Is your character physically comfortable, shivering, sweating?

5. What is the main message of each character in one or two sentences?

6. What is the poetic idea of the whole song in one or two sentences?

7. What is the one thing you want the audience to take away from your artistic creation?

8. Create a backstory: What happened two weeks ago that set off this course of events or this story line? Two days ago? Yesterday? Two hours ago? What happened just before your character started to sing? Emotionally, why are you singing *this* song and text instead of something else? Be specific!

9. Now get very specific with feelings and attitudes. Look over the feelings list in Appendix Two, page 170. Identify several of the feelings (at least 15) that your character(s) might have at particular times during your song. As you sing through the piece, do **not** sing just syllables, notes, and rhythm; do **not** sing just vocal technique. **Do** sing emotions, thoughts, and ideas. Write your preliminary emotional ideas down on your text page near the words you will be singing when you express that emotion.

10. Where in the music can you use dynamics, tempo, or diction to convey the feelings you have listed? These elements should come directly from the emotions you have identified. Does your interpretation match the composer's? If you do not agree with the composer's interpretation, be sure you are making informed decisions. Usually, it is wise to honor what the composer has written down, especially in music written after the 19th century. But if you have a compelling reason or feeling for changing tempos or dynamics, you should go with what your heart and head are telling you.

11. What gestures and facial expressions will support the emotional content of your performance? Make note of these actions near the emotinal words. Are your gestures and expressions organic and authentic to the text and music? Be sure to develop *many* options and interpretations, and practice them in front of a mirror.

12. How does the accompaniment contribute to your creation? What other clues has the composer given you that you must observe?

This is a lot to think about, even for a relatively simple song like *Early One Morning*, never mind a masterwork like Schumann's *Dichterliebe*. But the more you access your own imagination, the more you will be able to share that with your audience. If you have nothing going on emotionally with a song, your audience is not going to have a very emotionally rich experience.

Seasoned performers may not have to go through this kind of precise analysis because they have a full "reservoir" of expressive ideas from many years of experience. But even the most experienced singer will continue to cultivate this kind of rich, emotional imagination in order to keep performances interesting and sounding fresh. On the Spiral of Singing (*Figure 1*, page viii) technical aspects of "Musical Expression" are identified, including intonation, *sostenuto*, *legato*, flexibility, agility, dynamics, and vibrato. These techniques (and many others) are employed by singers spontaneously, as the emotion of the piece demands. An authentic singing performer is not interested in a technical display just to show that they can do it. Technique is only a means to the end of an expressive performance. I have listened to hundreds (maybe thousands) of performances over the years, some very skilled and some not so skilled. The most memorable, the ones that have moved me, were the ones when the performer was completely in the moment, experiencing the emotions of the music, and able to unselfconsciously share those feelings with the audience.

Especially for the Choral Conductor

There is magic that occurs between choral conductors and their singers as they work to interpret music together. This magic is truly another example of the whole being greater than the sum of the parts. The process works something like this:

1) Conductors choose a piece of music, usually because it has some emotional value or connection for them.

2) They do the kind of preliminary work that was outlined previously in this chapter, to create a potential emotional world for the piece in performance. Only after this study can they be prepared to share their emotional vision with the singers.

3) In the course of teaching and rehearsing the piece with their group(s), they communicate to their singers the emotional context of the text and music through verbal instruction and, intuitively, through their conducting gestures. This means that every singer must be emotionally tuned (in harmony!) with the emotional vision of the conductor. This is hard work and it requires strong leadership. The magic is that every rehearsal or performance of a piece can turn into a different expressive journey, and this is usually communicated non-verbally from conductor to singers by the conductor's "hand" or gesture. The conductor may not even be fully aware of the interaction going on. It can be a thoroughly intuitive process, from the conductor's brain to the gesture perceived by the individual singer who is intuitively in harmony with the other singers. That combination creates an emotional experience, not only for the audience but for the singers and the conductor as well. This outcome is not unlike the experience of an individual singer, but it does have the added benefit of other humans sharing the same performing experience. These are the kind of performances that no one forgets; neither the audience, singers, or conductors. It is a magical experience that touches our souls and makes us feel fully human and alive. This is the "soul" experience that we humans crave.

Now look at the technical skill that choral conductors bring to this scenario. First of all, they must be strong musicians, sometimes with years of voice study and/or training with some other instrument. They have studied conducting technique so they are able to use their gestures effectively to communicate not only emotion, but also proper singing technique to their singers. They choose music that they are interested in and that will also appeal to their singers, and is within the ability level of their groups. They study the music for the expressive elements that will make it come alive for their singers, and they are engaging teachers, able to plan rehearsals that are interesting for the singers as they learn the music. They are inspiring leaders so that the singers will listen and integrate the conductor's expressive ideas into their singing. And the conductors create a trusting environment, so that the singers are willing to risk their emotional ideas with each other, the conductor, and the audience. Not only is it magic when all of this comes together, but from this description, it sounds miraculous, a true example of the sum being greater that the individual parts.

The earlier chapters have included many vocalises that are meant to be used with choirs (as well as individual singers) to teach particular vocal techniques. But the reader has been constantly reminded that the goal of the exercises is to enable the expression of thoughts, feelings, and story telling. Unfortunately, any book on singing is going to be a linear account of a very non-linear or intuitive process. So the next layer of complexity for you to consider is how you can make your rehearsals an expressive experience for your singers, as well as how you can encourage their technical skills. The following are some suggestions to encourage emotional content in your rehearsals.

♫ Encourage your singers to have their own individual story lines running in the music you are preparing. Be sure that they have enough information to do this, including translations and background information on the composers and the historical times in which they were writing. Ask them to individually finish the sentence, "This is a story about. . ."

♫ Expand the vocabulary of emotions for your singers to consider. Provide them with a list like that found in Appendix Two, page 170, so that they can get past the usual ones of "happy" or "sad."

♫ Be sure you verbalize your own emotional journey as it pertains to the piece(s) you are rehearsing. Share personal stories that are appropriate to the repertoire. It makes you more human and encourages a sense of trust in the group. It will also trigger similar experiences in their own lives that they will individually apply as they sing.

♫ Every vocalise should be organically musical and expressive. Teach from a sense of the art, not from a sense of the technique. The goal is beauty, not perfection. As you are practicing a vocalise, suggest a particular emotion or scenario that your group could be imagining as they sing it. Your conducting gesture should reflect the particular emotion that you have suggested.

♫ Use the proper expressive terms (like *legato*, *messa di voce*, *piano*, etc.) and make sure your singers know what they mean. Integrate those terms into your vocalises and repertoire. Again, be sure your conducting gesture is encouraging the particular concept that you have verbally suggested. Then reverse the process, and with only your gesture, non-verbally define the emotion you are communicating. Does your choir reflect your emotional idea?

♫ Remind your groups to sing thoughts, ideas, and emotions, not notes, rhythms, and technique. Recently, I heard a choral conductor exhort his professional choir to "please stop 'singing' and let the music happen." That is an interesting anecdote to include in a book that is all about "singing," but it is a quick way to remind your singers that we sing **music** and not **technique**.

Musical Expression   IX

♫ Here are five steps to create an emotional and animated performance:

1. Finish this sentence about your song: "This is the story about..."

2. Create a back-story with a timeline that brings you directly to the moment your character starts to sing.

3. Identify at least 15 emotions that you think your character might feel.

4. Attach these emotions to particular words or phrases in your text and music. Write them down!

5. Explore several ideas about facial expressions and gestures that enhance your emotions. Practice them in front of a mirror in anticipation of your performances.

Musical Expression IX

Summary

♫ One of the main goals in singing is sharing and expressing human emotion, not just displaying perfect technique.

♫ Singing is one way we have to access and experience insights into the human spirit or soul.

♫ Greek philosophers identified this ability of music and other arts to help humans understand and share knowledge about metaphysical "soul" subjects.

♫ Singers create an emotional world in their minds and then share that world with their audience, creating a mutual emotional experience. Conductors create a similar scenario, directing a group of singers to create a mutual experience for the conductor, the singers, and the audience.

♫ Performers that are preoccupied with technique are likely to be perceived by the audience as "out of character." Successful performers use technique as a means to portray an emotional moment that does not draw attention to themselves or the technique.

♫ The most successful singers and conductors use a rich variety of emotions and images to create and communicate their thoughts, feelings, and stories. These emotions and images, cultivated in rehearsal, will lead to spontaneous emotional connections during performance between the audience and the performer, an example of the whole being greater than the sum of the parts.

Chapter X

Vocal Health

Chapter X

Vocal Health

Background and Scientific Approach

In the introduction, it was mentioned that the goals of artistic singing are beauty, freedom, strength, and health. All of the ideas and principles of this book spring directly from the premise that singing artistry encompasses beauty (sometimes hard to describe, but apparent when we hear it), freedom (not only technical freedom, but emotional freedom), and vocal health. For our purposes here, vocal health is not only the absence of pathology or sickness, but is a proactive attitude about the well-being and care of a precious, irreplaceable gift that singers have been given, and that they must learn to manage and cultivate.

Singers' voices are not only used for art, but for everyday living and communication. These same singing and speech organs are also integral to eating and everyday breathing. Singers have been gifted with their instruments; how they individually care for and manage these personal tools is an important and sometimes overlooked part of their training.

Once again let's look to instrumentalists for a parallel. Think about a violinist who possesses a valuable violin. When she is not using her instrument, she stores it in a case that is especially designed to protect it. She knows where that case is every minute of the day. The case probably has a humidifier in it that maintains or at least indicates moisture levels so the violin can be protected from dryness or humidity. The violinist protects the case (and the violin) from rough handling; it would be unthinkable to expose it to bad weather or to play it improperly or in a way that might damage it. She is alert to any minor daily wear and tear or maintenance problems and deals with them before they become big problems. When she travels, her first consideration is how her instrument will be transported. She expects to make her living as a violinist and teacher, and she plans to keep the current violin until she can afford a better one. All of this concern is for an instrument that may be irreplaceable in its individuality, but certainly, this particular violinist can find another instrument to perform on and continue to practice her art.

Now let's look at an aspiring singer. To pay for his voice lessons, he works as a server in a popular restaurant, but it is very noisy. He is an extrovert and really likes people, and he finds himself talking a lot, and in a loud, high-pitched voice so he can be heard. Because of his heavy work (or school) and singing schedule he drinks a lot of coffee in the morning and caffeinated beverages the rest of the day to keep him going. He rarely gets enough sleep and his hours are not regular. Eating is a low priority and food choices are based on convenience. He usually eats a really late dinner. It is not unusual for him to wake up in the morning with a dry throat and congested nasal passages and aching sinuses. He takes some cold medicine with antihistamines and hopes the pills will clear it all up and that he is not getting sick. He socializes with friends that are smokers, and finds that an occasional cigarette helps him to relax. He also is a social drinker and is sometimes careless and has a few too many the night before a performance. He usually has those drinks in a noisy bar, where again he has to speak loudly and in a higher pitch to be heard. He is constantly clearing his throat and complaining of phlegm and dryness. He is very serious about pursuing singing as a career.

The contrasts in this fiction are clear. The violinist has been instructed about the value of her instrument and understands how to care for it even though she intends to replace it. The singer has not made the connection that his body **is** his instrument. He is doing just about everything wrong, showing little or no care for his voice, an instrument that he can never replace. So let's examine some vocal health concepts that might help our fictional singer maintain his instrument in tip-top condition so he is able to sing consistently with beauty, freedom, and creative expression.

HYDRATION

Start with a good defense

As discussed in earlier chapters, consistent singing is dependent on consistent vibrations being emitted from the vocal folds and then acted upon in the resonance cavities. This desired consistency is one of the reasons we are so concerned with dynamic equilibrium in breath management and in how resonance is shaped. But neither breath nor resonance can make up for a dry mucus membrane (the covering of the vocal folds, see *Figure 35*, page 59) that is unable to vibrate consistently because of abuse or pathology. Moist, non-edematous (not swollen) vocal fold tissue vibrates with less lung pressure and produces less trauma to that tissue. And as in football, the best offense is a good defense. So our fictional singer would be well advised to defend his vocal folds from any circumstances or environment that might contribute to drying.

Systemic Hydration

Initially, the best plan is to keep the entire body systemically hydrated, the common wisdom being to drink at least eight glasses of water a day. There is some controversy about the actual optimal amount, but if you pay attention to your body, you will know when you need hydration. Although it seems simplistic, don't ignore the signs of thirst. When you have a dry mouth or feel light-headed and are craving water, drink! Another sure sign of dehydration is dark urine; the axiom is: sing wet, pee pale. These two indicators, thirst and dark urine, are your best signs that you need more water intake, not necessarily an arbitrary number of glasses of water per day.

Surface Hydration

If you are dehydrated, you can also hydrate your mucosa superficially or directly; the most-efficient method is by inhaling steam. It is <u>not</u> recommended that you stand over a pot of boiling water with a towel over your head and inhale. But you can run hot water in a sink and inhale the rising steam safely. Or you can take a hot shower and inhale through both your mouth and your nose to deliver steam directly to your vocal folds. Probably the best method is to purchase a "steamer," sometimes labeled as a "steam facial" and inhale the controlled steam that it produces. For most people, inhaling steam for five to seven minutes twice a day is enough time to hydrate their vocal folds.

X Vocal Health

Humidify

Singers can also defend against dryness by sleeping in a moist environment. Check the humidity level in your bedroom. Optimal humidity for your voice is about 50 to 60 percent; if the humidity is much lower in your sleeping room, you are habitually drying out your vocal folds for five to eight hours each night. This can be avoided by running a humidifier or vaporizer in your bedroom while you sleep. The caveat here is that they must be kept clean to avoid bacteria and mold growth. If you can't be fastidious about cleaning, it might be counterproductive to introduce a further irritation into your sleeping quarters.

Medications

Many singers use an over-the-counter mucolytic drug generically called guaifenisin. This drug helps to liquefy phlegm and can help keep a hydration balance in the mucosa of the vocal folds. It is best activated when you take it with a large glass of water. This is the same drug that is found in over-the-counter cough medicine. But be careful that you are not taking dextromethorphan in combination with the guaifenisin; dextromethorphan is a cough suppressant and a drying agent. Some other medications are drying agents as well; singers should tell their prescribers or pharmacists that they are concerned about drying and ask if their regular medications can contribute to dehydration. Certain cold, allergy, and anti-depressant medications can contribute to dryness and should be avoided if at all possible. A medical doctor (ideally a laryngologist who is familiar with singers' issues) is the best arbiter in these potential conflicts.

Life choices

As stated earlier, the best offense is a good defense. Caffeine and alcohol are drying agents. Singers should limit their intake of these drugs, especially prior to singing. And aside from the legal ramifications, singers would do well to avoid most recreational drugs, such as marijuana and cocaine. They are also highly drying of mucosal tissue and can lead to behaviors that are detrimental to vocal health. These are all personal lifestyle choice issues, and they should be weighed against future goals and career choices.

LARYNGEAL INFLAMMATION AND ILLNESS

Illness

Singers live intimately with their instruments. When they are sick, their instruments are sick. The ability to manage common illnesses or avoid them altogether is a key factor in a singer's ability to progress technically and have a reliable instrument for a career in performing or teaching. Here are some defensive strategies to avoid getting a viral cold in the first place.

Cold viruses are primarily transmitted from your hands to your nose, where they invade the mucus membrane that lines your nasal passages. "Colds" are really **viral rhinitis,** characterized by a runny nose, postnasal drip, and nasal congestion. Unfortunately for singers, your nose drains down to your throat and vocal folds, irritating and inflaming your vocal tract. Again, the best defense is to avoid the virus initially. As a rule, try to keep your hands away from your face and nose. Wash your hands many times a day, at every opportunity you get. Clean and sanitize all your mobile devices, phones, tablets, and computer keyboards. Sanitize or wash your hands after using communal keyboards and phones. Make a determined effort to keep the inside of your nose moist. If your nasal mucus membrane is not dried out, then you have a fighting chance of keeping viruses out with the natural barrier that a moist mucosa provides.

If you do succumb to a cold, you can make yourself a little more comfortable. But the truth is that viruses run their course in seven to ten days, and there is no real clinical evidence that you can affect that time frame very much. Treatment includes increasing your fluid intake to maintain hydration, using steam to directly increase moisture on your vocal folds and throat, taking a decongestant to help you breathe through the night, and resting as much as possible. Be very careful with decongestants; they can be ultimately drying, and the nasal sprays can have a re-bound effect that makes you more congested than when you started. Also avoid antihistamines; "drying you up" is the whole purpose of these drugs. For non-singers, a dried-out mucus membrane may not be a big deal, but for voice users, speaking and singing on a "dried-out" vocal tract can cause worse problems than just dealing with a drippy nose. Of course, it is better to not sing when you don't feel well and when you are physically compromised. But if every singer waited until they were in perfect respiratory health to practice and perform, there would be very little singing in the world. Performances, auditions, evaluations, and juries come along as scheduled, and most singers find that with good hydration (drinking water, steaming, and using an over-the-counter nasal saline spray) and a smart warm-up, they are usually able to perform at 90 percent of normal, and sometimes that is much better than dealing with the consequences of canceling. These are decisions that singers have to weigh with the advice of a trusted teacher and a knowledgeable physician who understand the repercussions of canceling, especially if it happens often.

If a cold does not resolve itself in seven to ten days, and seems to be noticeably worse, then it may have progressed to a secondary bacterial infection. Those symptoms may include congestion and ear pain, a greenish discharge from your nose and throat, white streaking in the back of your throat, aches, fever, and chills. These symptoms must be evaluated by a physician and may require antibiotics.

Reflux

It is not unusual for singers to develop vocal complaints like waking up hoarse, feeling like they have to clear their throat all the time, or having a chronic cough or sore throat. Health professionals have noticed an increase in these sorts of complaints for the past twenty years, caused by the spillover of stomach acids into the airway. When the inflammatory effects are seen in the larynx and pharynx areas, this condition is called larnygopharyngeal reflux or LPR. Inflammation can also occur in the esophagus area, called gastroesophageal reflux disease or GERD. Once diagnosed, these disorders are treated very aggressively, first with changing behaviors and then with medications. These conditions are especially worrisome for singers who by their nature develop a sensitivity to even very small changes in sensations in their vocal tracts, which can be caused by this inflammation. In general, to defend against LPR and GERD, singers should avoid acidic and spicy foods, especially late in the day, and try not to eat at all for several hours before going to sleep. Some people elevate the top of their bed (and their heads) by several inches to discourage reflux from occurring in the first place. These conditions are usually routine for a laryngologist to diagnose with a stroboscopy

X

Vocal Health

examination. If the behavioral measures do not improve the inflammation, a doctor may prescribe over-the-counter remedies (famotidine) and then progress to prescription medications that control acids if the inflammation does not subside.

Smoking and Tobacco Use

Think back to our violinist. You would laugh if I told you that periodically she held her violin over a smoking fire because it helped her to relax and because all of her friends were doing it. It seems self-evident that smoking will only harm your singing instrument, from burning the tissue that you depend on to vibrate consistently to losing the elasticity of your lungs to say nothing of the damage to your heart. The argument that "many great singers smoked" should be followed with the statement "and many great singers who smoked have died of emphysema and lung cancer." Smoking is, of course, a personal lifestyle issue, but serious singers who intend to use their instrument for a lifetime will treasure and protect their most valuable and indispensable asset. For serious singers the mandate is: if you don't smoke, don't start. If you do smoke, stop today and seek cessation counseling that will help with nicotine withdrawal. It is a hard addiction to beat, but your artistry depends on it. A singing career is hard enough; you need every advantage.

Chemicals and Inhalants

Singers need to be alert and constantly aware of the breathing environment around them that might contain toxins that contribute to vocal inflammation. The "sick building syndrome" has received a lot of attention; it is characterized by a new carpet being installed in a large office and followed by all the workers complaining of headaches and coughing. Other irritants include perfumes, detergents, paint, pesticides, cleaning agents, adhesives, fumes from various gasses, carbon dioxide, and smog, among others. Singers must avoid these kinds of toxins and must be proactive in avoiding situations where they might have exposure. Perhaps most insidious is dust and mold exposure in sleeping rooms, where we spend one-third of our time. Removing carpeting, drapes, and other soft materials that can harbor dust and mold, being scrupulous about cleaning and dusting, and using a HEPA filter are all good counter measures for common allergens that can cause vocal irritation and inflammation. Singers will also do well to avoid inhaling extremely cold air, which can seriously irritate vocal tract tissues. Covering your mouth and nose with a scarf when out in cold weather may seem odd, but it may save you some irritation later.

AVOID IMPACT STRESS

Our vocal folds vibrate hundreds of thousands of times a day in normal use. That is a lot of pounding for a tiny stretch of muscle and tissue. Fortunately, our vocal folds are normally pretty resilient, but trauma can produce a variety of pathologies on the vocal folds that will interfere with beautiful, expressive singing. Polyps, nodules, and hemorrhages, among others, are all abnormalities to the epithelial tissue and symmetry that is desired on the edges of the vocal fold, and they should be evaluated by a doctor to determine a course of treatment. Fortunately, singers can minimize the probability of these serious problems by paying attention to behaviors and activities that have the potential of creating damage and then changing them.

As with other issues in vocal health, a singer should be determined to avoid problems, rather that having to deal with them when they occur. Trauma to the vocal folds, or impact stress in singing, can be caused by poor voice training. For example, using lung pressure that is too high, singing with too much tension in the vocal folds when they close (pressed voice), carrying "chest voice" or the heavy mechanism too high in the range, being required to sing too long in a high range of your voice, or singing in a *tessitura* that is not appropriate for your physical mechanism are all factors in phonotrauma (damage to the vocal folds). No ethical voice teacher would ever teach or require any of these dangerous practices of their students and would be constantly vigilant to discourage these techniques if they are observed. Singers who consistently use a poor onset and release technique (*see* Chapter 4 "Onsets and Releases" page 58) can aggravate or cause damage to their vocal folds. Serious singers should never scream, shout, or "holler" and should be mindful in noisy rooms, like bars and restaurants, to not push or strain their voices to be heard. Extroverted personalities need to be mindful that they don't have to speak loudly all the time as they enjoy life. Air travel is especially hard on voices because of the background noise and the inherent dry air; singers are well advised to speak as little as possible when flying. Teachers in general, music teachers in particular, and choral conductors are at risk for voice trauma because of the nature of their work. They should consciously develop strategies to minimize the amount of singing and talking they do throughout the day. These measures are all preventative, and although they may seem overprotective to some, modifying these behaviors are much easier than trying to resolve the physical traumas that can result when precautions are ignored.

Two other negative habits warrant mention here. A persistent, chronic, rough cough should be immediately examined. Is it a nervous habit? Could it be caused by a dry environment or by drying medications? Regardless of the cause, constant coughing can create serious trauma to the vocal mechanism and should be addressed immediately, either medically or by a change of habit. The same caveat applies to nervous throat clearing. Is it really necessary to constantly clear your throat or is it a "security blanket" habit you have maintained as a way of dealing with initial performance anxiety? Either way, develop another way of dealing with this issue because throat clearing violently bangs your vocal folds together, and it is likely to cause problems sooner or later.

PAY ATTENTION TO YOUR NOSE

Your nose is the gateway to your vocal tract and is your natural immune system against viruses and bacteria. Many singers regularly rinse out their nasal passages with a saline solution to clear irritants and dirt, which contributes to a healthy nasal mucus membrane. Many use an aloe vera gel in their nasal passages to encourage hydration. All singers should avoid mouth breathing in general, and when singing, should make an effort to inhale through their nose as often as it is feasible and pragmatic.

LIFESTYLE ISSUES

Nutrition

Unbelievably, some singers do not make the connection between nutrition, their general health, and their vocal health. Like cars that run on gas, humans run on food fuel. And if we feed our bodies improperly, they will not respond optimally when we make heavy demands on them, including the physicality of singing. It is hard physical work to sing correctly; it takes intense mental focus, split-second muscle coordination, and muscle tone, and singing increases respiration effort. Our body temperature rises when we sing, indicating an increase in metabolism. All of this takes fuel, and our bodies require a particular balance of nutrients in order for everything to be nurtured. (Why do you think they call it "nutrition"?) Serious singers will be intentional about eating a variety of healthy foods, well balanced between proteins, carbohydrates, and fats, and they will commit to eating regularly in order to maintain healthy cell replenishment. Voice scientists now strongly believe that a healthy laryngeal mucosa is supported by certain antioxidants like Vitamin C and E and B6 and potassium, folic acid, thiamin, and alpha carotene. Although taking these supplements is a way to insure proper levels in your body, it is always better to obtain these nutrients in natural foods. Singers who expect to have long careers and excellent stamina in performance should be as concerned about their nutrition as they are about their next paycheck.

Stretching Warm-ups

Eager teachers and students who arrived early for good seats at one of Richard Miller's seminars were usually frustrated by being asked to wait outside while the Maestro warmed up prior to speaking and singing all day. As disappointing as it was to not be rewarded for promptness, Mr. Miller was modeling an excellent practice for all teachers and singers. Releasing tension in both large and small muscle groups prior to singing and speaking, at the very least, sets up an even playing field before you start the heavy demand on phonation and breathing muscles that is required for singing. A good warm-up routine for voice professionals will include stretches for the whole body, exercises to establish correct breath management, and exercises to encourage an open vocal tract. (These principles, with suggested exercises, have all been covered in previous chapters.) Singers should start lightly in their middle voice and move into higher and lower ranges, adding more and more demand on the breath. Vocalises that partially occlude the vocal tract like singing through a straw or humming, are especially good for an initial warm-up to begin a day of speaking and singing, and these will be addressed in a later paragraph (*see* page 163). Music teachers, singers, and other voice professionals that establish a regular warm-up routine will find they are less fatigued at the end of the day or practice session and will have better overall stamina in their singing voices.

Address Poor Speech and Singing Habits

How you habitually speak will also affect how you sing. Poor speech habits will make learning to sing resonantly even more difficult. If you listen to the speaking voice of successful singers, like Renee Fleming or Bryn Terfel, you will notice that they speak the way they sing; or perhaps they sing the way they speak! Either way you look at it, they are speaking (and singing) in the resonant part of their voice. Singers should habitually "speak well" and cultivate the "uh-huh" range (the pitch that you use when you are agreeing with someone, "uh-huh") of their speaking voice instead of a range that is too low or too high. In popular culture it has become fashionable to begin and end sentences with a glottal fry – that low, crackly sound. Just like speaking in a high-pitched voice, the glottal fry will tire your instrument and cause tension when you are singing.

If you are trying to correct the placed pitch in your speaking voice, practice speaking and elongating the nasal sounds [m], [n], and [ŋ]. The optimum pitch will usually be where you say "uh-huh" when you agree with someone. These sounds help to find "forward" vibrations and also partially occlude the vocal track, which takes pressure off the vocal folds. Make sure that there is no tension around your larynx;

it should feel "easy," with no undue muscle tension, like you could do it all day. The next step is to carefully add vowel sounds to the nasals, as you speak, without changing pitch, "me, may, ma, mo, moo." Listen carefully as you speak, or listen to a recording. Does your speaking pitch stay in the "uh-huh" range? Does it feel easy, tension-free?

All singers have to cope with times when their voice is not 100 percent. This can be when you are getting over an illness, the result of over-singing, or just general tiredness. In his article, "How to Use the Flow-Resistant Straws," Titze shows that using exercises that partially occlude the vocal tract can reduce impact stress, release tension, and reduce pressure on the vocal folds. One excellent method that he studied uses straws, both stirring and drinking sizes. He advocates singing glides through the range, beginning in the middle range. (When lecturing in his classes, if Dr. Titze felt vocally tired, it was not unusual for him to pass out straws to everyone in the class to sing through. He would make an object lesson out of it while he relieved tension and pressure on his vocal folds.)

Like the nasal sounds and the straw exercises, using your cupped hands is just as effective at relieving the symptoms of a tired, overused voice. You can form an open circle with all your right hand fingers and thumb; place that open circle against the palm of your left hand and with your mouth on the circle formed by your right hand, sing into the circle, feeling the vibration on the palm of your left hand. Like the straw exercise, this has the advantage of quickly soothing (or warming up) your voice and can easily be done back stage or in shared warm-up areas without much volume that disturbs others. With both the straw and the cupped-hands exercise, you should sing fully, using strong air pressure; the double benefit will be to train your breath management muscles also.

Emotional Health

Singing is a very personal activity. Performing is a very public activity. From an emotional standpoint, the two can seem in conflict. Performers need the capacity to be vulnerable in front of strangers, expressing different emotions, which sometimes are very close to the surface. At the same time, they need to pay attention to very personal details about their bodies (their instruments); for example, they must regulate their breath and shape their mouth all the while paying attention to whether their vocal folds are phlegmy. Performing can seem like taking a bath in public. For these reasons, singers need a mental toughness and a strong emotional balance. They need to learn the art of protecting themselves from people and circumstances that they know will be upsetting. Successful singers learn to be proactive about their emotional health, avoiding obvious upsets before major performances and other important opportunities. Singers also have a responsibility to come to their lessons rested and psychologically ready to be able to take full advantage of the time with their teacher. They need to learn to balance emotional highs and lows and to surround themselves with friends, family, and colleagues who can be supportive of the emotional chaos that can accompany singing and performing. Sometimes that support system needs to include a mental health professional that can help sort out conflicting feelings about depression and self-worth that seem to accompany the high-wire act that can be integral to a singer's life. A mature person embraces these difficulties as opportunities for more self-knowledge and applies them to their singing emotional life, making difficulties enriching instead of debilitating. A singer's life is not an easy life, but it is an interesting life, full of beautiful music.

Seek Expert Advice

There are many excellent books that a singer can consult for general information. Dr. Friedrich Brodnitz's book, referenced earlier in the Breathing chapter (page 34) has been used for years by singers. Robert Thayer Sataloff, M.D., D.M.A. continues to publish both books and articles that are excellent sources of current knowledge in voice health and science. His study and research is especially helpful because he is both a medical doctor and a singer.

Books and the Internet are excellent for general information, but every singer needs an ongoing relationship with a laryngologist who is familiar with voice professionals' issues and interests. Word of mouth is the best method to find one; ask all the singers you know!

Especially for the Choral Conductor

Choral conductors are on the front line when it comes to the vocal health of their singers, and they have a responsibility to care for and nurture those instruments both individually and collectively. Choral singing is extremely taxing on the vocal folds, not because of the nature of choral singing, but because of the communal nature of singing that leaves very little control to the individual about how, when, how long, and where they will be singing. Most professional choirs rehearse for three hours, as do most community groups that meet once a week. Church choirs usually have a shorter rehearsal time, as do most university, collegiate, and school choirs. But what all these rehearsals have in common is that the singers are continually singing, with very little rest in the course of a rehearsal. Unlike individual practice and singing, choristers do not have control over when they sing or rest. They are expected to sing on demand when the downbeat occurs. Choral conductors by their nature must be charismatic leaders; their singers want to do well and to please them. In the course of a rehearsal, no one is likely to raise his or her hand and say, "I think we all need a vocal break." This is further complicated by the fact that a lot of the glorious choral literature is very demanding vocally, sometimes written by composers who are more interested in an overall huge sound than in an individual's vocal health. Choral conductors, especially those who are not singers, need to be mindful of all these demands and plan rehearsals so that there is an occasional vocal break in each section. They need to be sure the singers are not constantly singing in only one range, high or low, and only at one volume, soft or loud, for long periods of rehearsal. Although it may seem overwhelming for the choral conductor to have to accommodate the vocal demands of 25 (or 70 or 110) individual singers, it really is in the interest of the conductor to be sensitive to these issues. Choristers who leave rehearsals with tired, "beat-up" voices are bound to be less enthusiastic when it is time to "re-enlist" for another season or year of singing.

The other vocal health issues examined above all apply to choral singers, and it is easy to introduce vocal health information to choral groups in small doses, without having to take 45 minutes of rehearsal time to expound on the nature of laryngeal inflammation. With volunteer groups it would be enough to say, "Singers, be sure you are drinking enough water now that it is cold season" or to use the straw or cupped-hand exercises in the course of the rehearsal to reinforce your concern for their instruments. They will appreciate that you are knowledgeable and interested in their vocal health, and that modeling will go a long way toward your group developing a communal culture that encourages healthy singing.

Vocal Health   X

Summary

♫ Vocal health is not the absence of sickness, but is a proactive attitude about the well-being and care of a singer's instrument.

♫ Regular hydration, administered both systemically and superficially, contributes to moist vocal fold tissues that vibrate with less lung pressure and produce less trauma to the tissue.

♫ Singers should avoid dehydrating agents like caffeine, alcohol, and certain medications, both over-the-counter and prescribed.

♫ There are really no reliable cures for the common cold. Singers should stay hydrated and get as much rest as possible. The best defense is to avoid the causes of a cold. Frequent hand washing along with sanitizing phones and computers will help keep viruses away from the nose, which is the viral point of entry.

♫ Larnygopharyngeal reflux or LPR, which creates inflammation, is becoming a prevalent complaint for singers. Certain behavioral changes can help, and a laryngologist can evaluate and make medication recommendations.

♫ All serious singers will treasure and protect their instruments from irritants like tobacco smoke and other dangerous chemical inhalants.

♫ Heavy impact stress of the vocal folds should be avoided. Causes include poor voice training; heavy voice use, both speaking and singing; talking loudly over background noise; and habitual coughing and throat clearing.

♫ The nose is the gateway to a singer's vocal tract and is a natural immune system. Singers should pay attention to their nasal tissue and keep it hydrated and healthy.

♫ Many lifestyle issues impact a singer's ability to sing expressively and to perform. Mature singers will take responsibility for their nutrition, getting enough rest, warming up the instrument prior to singing, addressing any poor speech and singing habits, and their own mental health.

♫ Singers should be life-long learners about vocal health, and should develop a relationship with a trusted medical doctor to advise them when they are ill.

♫ Choral conductors will find it in their own interest to take care of their singers' voices. Healthy vocal modeling will contribute to a choral culture that values healthy singing and positive vocal health.

Notes

Chapter XI

Vocal Performance

Chapter XI

Vocal Performance

How do I use all this information?
Motor Learning and Deliberate Practice

If you have gotten this far in this book, you have read — and maybe absorbed — a lot of information about what you should know and what you should teach to your students so that you and they can be excellent singers and performers. It seems easy enough, doesn't it? You just have to tell someone what to do, and then they will do it and be beautiful singers. Right? Not only is it that simple, you should even be congratulated for having an interest in voice science and knowledge and for continuing your study so you can use this knowledge to improve your own singing. However, (you knew that was coming, didn't you?) because of new research and scholarship in the branch of cognitive (brain) science called motor skill acquisition, many of our cherished methods of teaching singing have come into question as to their ultimate effectiveness. Knowing "what" to teach your students does not necessarily readily prepare you for "how" to teach your students. It brings up the question of how people learn to improve motor skills. Fundamentally, singing is a motor skill that requires training and coordinating many small and large muscles to work together in a very sensitive and difficult coordination.

This chapter will summarize some of the information that has been studied and reported over the past 20 years about the cognitive science of motor learning and how it pertains to the teaching of singing. Much of this study and scholarship has been spearheaded by Katherine Verdolini Abbot and has been published in her many books and scholarly articles, several of which can be found in the References and Further Reading section in the back of this book. This is an ongoing field of study that is likely to gain more and more attention in the coming years, not only for singing, but for any skill-based activity (sports, dancing, video games) that requires muscle learning and coordination.

HOW ASPECTS OF MOTOR LEARNING
PERTAIN TO THE TEACHING OF SINGING

Learning to sing is dependent on muscle training called motor learning or motor skill acquisition. Verdolini uses the following definition of motor learning:

"Motor learning is a process, which is inferred rather than directly observed, which leads to relatively permanent changes in the potential for motor performance as the result of practice or exposure." (Titze and Verdolini Abbott 219)

This definition is important because it tells us that motor learning is implicit learning (as opposed to explicit learning), it must produce permanent changes in motor performance (not just a one-time anomaly) and that practice is the only pathway to improve that performance. For singing, this means that our traditional way of explicit teaching (*"Please do this, then do this, then do this"*) may actually impede permanent changes or learning for our students. The studies go on to show that there is an optimal method of practice (or repetition), **Deliberate Practice**, that produces the best performance outcomes. (Ericsson, Krampe and Tesch-Romer) This is especially important for singing, because most of the repetition is done by the student, unsupervised by a teacher or mentor. Part of a student's training must be in how to incorporate the aspects of Deliberate Practice into their daily practice. This need for a certain kind of practice has led to behavior studies by Angela Duckworth (2007) and Carol Dwerk (2006), who have provided information about strategies that are the most effective practice and training methods. Their ideas about how to optimize Deliberate Practice will be presented later in the chapter.

So let's examine briefly how motor learning is fundamental to learning to sing and improving your vocal performance skills. Motor learning is dependent on implicit memory (or implicit learning). A simple definition of implicit memory is "learning without awareness." Listed below are some of the important aspects of implicit learning as related to learning to sing. Later in the chapter, particular strategies will be presented.

- ♫ Implicit learning (like motor learning) is governed and enabled by perceptual process, meaning perceived by the senses. In singing, those senses include: sight, sound, and touch (how it feels). Training should be done in the same mode as learning. In the case of singing, training and practice should be related to sight, sound and touch (*"Observe in the mirror how the sound changes when you adjust your jaw"*), not "telling" the student as in *"Open your jaw."*

- ♫ Repetition is required to engender "relatively permanent changes." In singing, this is rehearsal or practice, most of which happens without the supervision of the teacher. This is the most important variable in motor learning and singing, and it is the aspect over which the student has the most control.

- ♫ Practice must be attentional. Learners must be fully engaged and "in the flow." Practice should be perceived as challenging or "hard," requiring the full engagement of the student. Researchers call this kind of practice Deliberate Practice.

- ♫ Practice needs to be "variable" and spaced. For singing, this means that it is better to practice one hour a day for five days than to practice 2 ½ hours two days a week. Practice should be designed to address specific issues, not *"Do this set of exercises exactly like this every day."*

- ♫ Practice should be individually designed and must contain "desirable difficulties," which help the brain neurons and synapses to wire deeper in the brain. "Remembering" (the ability to recall the action for performance) is short-term memory combined with long-term memory. Short-term memory is biochemical. Long-term memory involves anatomic changes; neural pathways are enlarged and deepened. For singing, this means that practice must be effortful and requires much repetition.

♪ Consistency in training is required. Students must practice skills consistently and avoid repeating what they know is incorrect.

♪ Implicit learning, in this case learning to sing, requires feedback from an expert and competent trainer/mentor that provides Knowledge of Results (KOR). For example, *"That was better because it was more forward and sung more freely,"* as opposed to Knowledge of Performance (KOP), *"You did a good job."* The feedback must be specific and individualized. For singing, this means one-on-one training and/or small class sizes to engender skill acquisition and performance improvement.

♪ External locus of attention is better for training than an internal locus. An external locus of attention focuses on the result of the motor skill, whereas an internal locus of attention focuses on mechanical aspects of the motor task. External locus of attention for singing includes watching oneself practice in a mirror, spectral analysis feedback, teacher manipulation and manipulatives like a balloon, exercise ball, belt, students' manipulations of their body, a funnel, and Hoberman's sphere. Less effective internal locus of attention methods would include explicit instructions: *"Lift your soft palate, lower your larynx and release your jaw."*

HOW ASPECTS OF BEHAVIORAL SCIENCE PERTAIN TO THE TEACHING OF SINGING

Integrating knowledge about motor learning into our singing and teaching leads to a lot of questions: If you are more talented, can you practice less? Can you make up for less talent by practicing more? How much repetition (practice) do I have to do? Can I practice in my car? Are grades the best motivators for practicing? What exactly do I have to do to be a successful performer or successful teacher? Let's look at how behavioral science studies answer some of these questions.

Behavioral and cognitive scientists have examined the nature vs. nurture (talent vs. learning) argument as it pertains to motor learning and skill acquisition. In every study, across many different disciplines, it has been shown that "talent" (some kind of innate ability) is not part of the success equation (except in basketball, when height was shown to be a genetic advantage). Moreover, in a field such as music, the presence of "talent" is unknown and unknowable. In study after study, the most important indicator of success, and the one that was under the control of the subject was the amount of time spent in "Deliberate Practice." The presence of "talent," or lack of it, was shown to be irrelevant because without effort and training there is no evidence of it; talent evidently vanishes without cultivation.

So what does lead to success? Those same studies showed that people who had reached mastery in any given discipline had spent about 10,000 hours (about ten years) in Deliberate Practice, defined as an effortful activity that is designed to optimize improvement in performance. Elements of Deliberate Practice include the following: the subject is completely engaged (in the "flow") and the work is effortful. Many repetitions are needed. Practice sessions are spaced and practice is varied. Practice is consistent and individually designed to improve performance. Perhaps most important to student learners is that practice is not supposed to be fun, it is supposed to be challenging to garner results. In short, but effortful practice is the **ONLY** path to improved performance. (Ericsson, Krampe and Tesch-Romer)

One of the most difficult aspects of learning to sing is the ability to engage in Deliberate Practice and maintain the motivation to do it **a lot** — up to six hours a day for professionals, around two hours or more a day for advanced singing students. Angela Duckworth (Duckworth 2007) has extensively studied the characteristic of "grit" across many disciplines. She defines grit as maintaining perseverance and passion while pursuing long-term goals. People who exhibit grit are able to sustain focused effort over time in spite of failure, adversity and plateaus in performance. They are able to overcome disappointment and boredom. The application to the studying of singing is apparent. Students must engage in hours of study, not only technical motor learning, but languages, musical theory, performance practices, etc., and sustain that interest for many years in their journey toward a career in music. Duckworth has shown in her research that "talent" is not a determining factor in achieving long-term goals, but that grit is the characteristic that appears to be the common denominator in people who achieve performance goals.

Can singing students develop and improve their "grit factor"? Clearly the first step is to develop motivation. What motivates young singers to carry through with Deliberate Practice, especially since it has been identified as essential to their growth? Daniel Pink (Pink 2009), drawing heavily on the work of Edward Deci, Richard Ryan and Richard Koestner, among others, postulates that the old theory of "carrot and the stick" is no longer as effective in a 21st century world that requires creative, critical, independent thinking and action. He pointed out in his book *Drive* (Pink 2009) that external rewards and punishments, although effective for algorithmic and repetitive tasks, soon become less and less effective. He advocates an approach that encourages autonomy, mastery and purpose as motivators for creative undertakings. He defines autonomy as being self-directed, especially in the areas of time, task, team and technique. Mastery is defined as becoming ever better at something you care about. Purpose is a yearning to do what we do in service of something larger than ourselves. Providing and enabling singing students with these three behavior incentives is challenging, but it appears to be one path to encouraging and developing more consistent Deliberate Practice.

Carol Dwerk (Dwerck 2006) at Stanford University has further studied the personality traits of people who can work hard at something over a long time period. In her research, she has identified a particular mindset with a number of attributes that contributes to the quality of "grit." She calls this a Growth Mindset. People with a Growth Mindset hold certain beliefs about themselves as follows:

1.   Intelligence or skill can be developed like a muscle.
2.   Challenges are welcomed because they offer opportunity for growth. Learning is better than "looking smart."
3.   Practice is expected to require hard effort.
4.   Criticism is viewed as information from which to learn.
5.   Other people's success is seen as inspirational, because everyone can learn and grow.
6.   "Talent" is not a goal.

She contrasts this Growth Mindset with a Fixed Mindset. People with a Fixed Mindset believe that:

1. Intelligence and skill is static, an entity. (*"I am the way I am."*)
2. Challenges are hard and I might fail, so I will stick with what I know I can do well.
3. Practice is hard work and doesn't pay off (*"I am the way I am"*), so I avoid it.
4. Criticism is personal. I don't like it, so I'll ignore it.
5. Others' success reflects badly on me and makes me feel judged.
6. "Talent" needs to be protected from judgment.

Dweck's continuing research is around developing methods to cultivate and encourage a Growth Mindset for use in all disciplines. Developing this Growth Mindset belief is essential for singers in order to be able to sustain Deliberate Practice and reach long-term goals.

So here is the path or thread that leads to mastery or success in singing:

1. Singing is a motor skill that is acquired through effort and repetition.
2. Although there are many different skill sets that a singer must study, the most important to mastery of singing skills is Deliberate Practice.
3. Deliberate Practice, in itself not "fun" and requires what Angela Duckworth (Duckworth 2007) has identified as "grit." She defines this as being passionate about, and able to persevere in, a long-term goal.
4. Persons who demonstrate grit are highly motivated, operating autonomously, seeking mastery and purpose. (Pink 2009)
5. Contributing to this ability to remain motivated and passionate while persevering is what Carol Dwerk (Dwerck 2006) has identified as a Growth Mindset, as opposed to a Fixed Mindset.

Along every step of the way, students training in singing need high standards, nurturing, an individual course of study provided by a teacher or a mentor, and honest and regular Knowledge of Results feedback that is specific and individualized.

GUIDELINES FOR DELIBERATE PRACTICE

Although there are many aspects to your learning process, establishing attentive and Deliberate Practice habits are the main method for you to improve your performance in singing. This is the aspect in your study over which you have complete control. Here are the steps to follow to cultivate strong habits:

♫ Determine exactly <u>where</u> you will practice each day during the week. At a minimum, there should be a mirror and a keyboard present, but it should be a place where you feel comfortable experimenting. This may seem like a small and unimportant detail. But your goal is to remove all obstacles to your practice regime, so be sure you know that on Tuesday it will be Practice Room B and on Wednesday at my home, etc. This removes temptations to do something else while you figure out where to practice. (*"Wanna go to a movie? Yes! That will help me figure out where to practice!"*)

♫ Determine exactly <u>when</u> you will practice every day and put it on your calendar. Your practice should not be when you don't have anything else to do, or when you feel like it. If you can't make your practice a priority, you will not make progress in your performance. It is better to space out the time than to do blocked practice. For example 40 minutes, five times a week is better than 2 ½ hours, twice a week.

♫ Your goal when you practice is to get into a sense of "flow"; some athletes call this "being in the zone." This is the state of mind when you are doing your most effective learning and you usually lose track of time. Every time you are interrupted, you lose that state of mind and the learning/memory that goes with it. Of course, it is impossible to ignore the demands of your phone and mobile devices. If you want to improve your learning, and your performance, turn off (really OFF) your phone and minimize any other interruptions. If you are a "clock watcher," set an alarm and put your watch (or phone) out of sight.

♫ Decide on one or two small, achievable goals that you can accomplish during your practice time. Ideally, you determined these goals at the end of your last practice session. Here is an example: "*1) Work on the two exercises my teacher gave me, targeting my ideal sound and working to maintain a stable rib cage. 2) Sing through my Italian song and practice adding new emotional content. If time, learn the melody of the first two pages of my new song.*" Use the Practice Journal template provided in this book to remind yourself how you will use each practice session and to keep track of your goals.

♫ Expect your practice to be "hard" work. If it feels easy and routine (and you feel bored), you need to set harder goals and challenges for yourself. You can only improve your performance by pushing yourself toward more advanced goals. Practice is not supposed to be fun, but it is where you learn and improve for your performances. Think of it as gratifying **work** that pays off.

♫ Keep a positive attitude as you rehearse. Tell yourself, *"I'm pretty good at this, and I'm going to get better."* Quiet your "judging" voice in your head and replace it with *"I am a learning singer. I am improving and growing every time I practice."* Don't practice things over and over that you know are wrong. Practice for results and success, and use any mistakes as opportunities to grow, improve and learn more. If things get really frustrating after many repetitions, write it down in your journal and move on. Take the issue to your teacher at your next lesson.

♫ At the end of your practice time, take two minutes to do three things.

1. Write down one thing you improved, learned, noticed or experienced from this practice.

2. Decide what your goals will be at your next practice and write them in your journal. Example: *"I didn't get to the Italian piece, so I will start with that. I still have some work to do on keeping my ribs out while I sing, so I will continue working on the two exercises from my teacher, and I'll learn page*

XI Vocal Performance

three and four of the new song." (The Practice Journal template provided in this book on page 196 is a handy way to keep track of this.)

3. Congratulate yourself on the progress that you made, and most importantly, that you kept your promise to yourself to do Deliberate Practice. Something like *"Wow, that felt good to continue that work on breathing, and I made some good progress on the* Lieder. *I'm glad that I stuck to my plan to practice on that today!"* Acknowledge your successes!!!! Small as well as large. Remember that practice is your ONLY pathway to improving your singing performance.

GUIDELINES FOR TEACHERS TO ENCOURAGE EFFECTIVE MOTOR LEARNING AND DELIBERATE PRACTICE

Teaching is an art as well as a science. Voice teachers also need the freedom to experiment with teaching styles, keeping the techniques that work and acknowledging when ideas fall flat or become too routine to be effective. Recognizing that learning to sing requires implicit and perceptual learning and memory, experiment with the following guidelines when working with singing students:

♫ In lessons, while the student is practicing new motor skills, stay in perceptual and experiential domain. This means talking (telling) less, but when verbal prompts are needed, using phrases like the following:

> *"What is the difference you notice when. . ."*
>
> *"What is your body telling you about. . ."*
>
> *"Did anything happen inside you when. . ."*
>
> *"Let's explore. . ."*
>
> *"Let's experiment. . ."*
>
> *"Observe how. . ."*
>
> *"Imagine. . ."*
>
> *"I wonder. . ."*
>
> *"Be aware of. . ."*
>
> *"How does it feel when. . ."*
>
> *"Notice that when. . ."*
>
> *"Let's see if. . ."*

Avoid giving a set of explicit instructions such as *"Release your jaw, lift your soft palate and slightly lower your larynx."*

♫ This is especially difficult for new teachers. It is just soooo much easier to tell the student what to do. But remember, your goal is not to impress your students with what you know your goal is to improve the performance (the results) of your singers. "Telling" may get short-term improvement, but allowing them to discover how something feels so they can reproduce it over and over again is a better long-term strategy that will serve them better in performance. Giovanni Lamperti had it right when he said, *"The memory of how it feels is your only method."* Note that this is paraphrased here.

♫ Communicate a "hint" toward a desired destination or an approximation of a desired goal. Let the student struggle, but reward close approximations. Help the student define a goal and then allow them to practice toward that goal. Students retain learning better when they "discover" it on their own. A good metaphor is archery practice. An archer doesn't go out to the field, shoot one arrow and go home. She will shoot until she runs out of either arrows or time. Assure the students that they have plenty of arrows to practice getting closer to the target; it is not a one-shot deal. Use phrases like *"That is getting closer, I wonder what would happen if you felt the tone vibrate more on your hard palate. Try that a couple of times until the tone feels more focused."*

♫ Provide "prior knowledge" outside of practice repetition, perhaps at the very beginning of the lesson before any singing has begun. Give only the information that is needed or that the student asks about. Don't drill or test. If you give a set of instructions (explicit learning), then followup with feeling, hearing or sight cues. Here's an example for cultivating correct stance: *"Your mantra is feet apart; hips, shoulders, ears aligned; your sternum moderately tall."* But then before beginning to sing, *"Do you feel grounded, stable and comfortable in your body? When you look in the mirror, do you look 'important with a noble posture?'"*

♫ Feedback for beginners must be frequent and then decreasing as skill acquisition increases. In more advanced learners, too frequent feedback can inhibit learning. Teachers should self-monitor the given feedback to avoid students "going for the cookie" instead of paying attention to the results of their practice. Feedback should be meaningful and specific. For example, *"Compared to the previous figure, that was more open and forward."* Not, *"Good job, you did very well."* The most effective feedback is Knowledge of Results — KOR — (how close to the target), not Knowledge of Performance — KOP — ("beautiful job"). Don't praise mediocre performance, but be honest and maintain high performance standards.

♫ Assume all students have "talent" and then disregard it in respect to performance. Without effort (practice), talent disappears, so it becomes irrelevant. Make sure to maintain high standards and reward effort, strategies and choices.

♫ Set challenging but attainable goals and be clear about what they are. *"Plan the work, work the plan, you can always change the plan."* At the least, general goals should be set at the beginning of the semester (or agreed on time period) and reviewed at the end for results. Weekly goals should be stated clearly in a provided journal as in, *"For next week, please notice how your middle range feels; is it better focused?"* Then follow up the next week and give KOR, and reward effort as in, *"Your middle voice sounds clearer and more focused. Thank you for your hard work on this."*

♫ Don't allow students to practice mistakes. Help them to self-correct and then move on without comment. If a skill level plateaus after several attempts, acknowledge close approximation, move on to something else and return to it another time with perhaps a different approach. For example, *"The e flat is working well in that register, but the e is not quite there. We will come back to*

XI Vocal Performance

♫ *it next week, but meanwhile, remember to keep that 'easy' feeling in your throat as you are practicing it this week."*

♫ Use of external locus of attention is better than internal locus. A mirror is standard, practical and usually available. Spectral Analysis is strong external feedback, but it can be hard to get past the "gee whiz" factor in private lessons, especially if you are limited to 30- or 40-minute sessions. Other first order external foci (student's action has a direct effect on the body) include: stretchy belt around waist to monitor abdominal muscles; using an exercise ball to monitor breathing movements; finger on chin for jaw release; placing a monitoring finger in the mouth, checking for tension; student monitors rib movements or abdominal engagement with fingers. Second order of external foci (student uses empathy or sees representative external objects) include: focusing on representative pictures or objects of ideal singing (funnel, anatomical drawings); using manipulatives like Hoberman's sphere and flight ring to simulate release of tension; teacher demonstrates and models; teacher manipulates student's body to correct "form."

♫ For varied practice, use a variety of vocalises and mix up the order, not necessarily always going by half-steps. Avoid a set exercise series like, *"Do exercise 1, 2, 3, 4 (every day, every week) and now you are ready to sing."*

Every vocalise should have a clear purpose that the student is aware of and can attain or approximate with some effort. Vocalises should be prescribed by the teacher, practiced during the week and then commented upon at the next lesson. They should not be mindless "warm-ups."

♫ Allow students to experiment and repeat figures and exercises that go well as long as they need to. Allow them to get "in the flow" and don't interrupt them too quickly with comments unless they need feedback to continue.

♫ Cultivate a Growth Mindset and discourage a Fixed Mindset around their singing learning.

♪ Reiterate and reinforce that humans can cultivate improvement in performance through effort. This will probably include the student's definition of "talent." Reinforce that talent without effort does not improve performance. Talent becomes less and less important without Deliberate Practice.

♪ Emphasize that effective learning is better than "looking smart or looking talented." Help them focus on their strategies, choices, process and effort, and praise them for these activities, not for their talent. Example: *"You did a very good job managing your practice time so you could get all four pieces memorized"* not *"You are such a quick memorizer!"*

♪ Treat any mistake or failure as an opportunity to learn. Failures or mistakes should be treated with curiosity and as information for future growth. *"Huh, I wonder how that happened? What did you learn from that particular mishap?"* Don't allow the student's "teller" to outshout the "doer" (Green 16-24). When they say things like, *"I'm not any good at. . ."* counter with *"Yet!!!"*

♫ Allow students as much autonomy as possible. Develop a collaborative learning approach. Avoid if-then rewards because they are ultimately discouraging. Offer information and define standards but don't try to control behavior. Assume that your student wants to improve and then teach "as if."

♫ Encourage mastery — getting better at something that matters to them. Provide meaningful challenges that are not impossible to achieve. As a teacher, don't be afraid to admit that something is too hard for them (repertoire) and move on to something else. Reinforce that mastery is hard and is like the North Star: it can't be reached but it is an important guide to a destination. However, "mastery attracts because mastery eludes." (Pink 125) We want to master something because it is there to master.

♫ Encourage your students to think about their place in the larger picture of music making. They are part of the great line of all musicians like Bach, Mozart, Verdi and Puccini when they join in this human endeavor of creative, high-level singing. Music is important, it makes us more human. We sing because we must share our humanity with each other and because music is one way to access our souls. It is not all about them and how great they are (or not); it is about how we are better people because of our ability to share music. It is about the satisfaction of building Lamperti's "castle in the air," using our muscles, nerves and imagination to create art that our souls can inhabit! (Refer back to page vii for the direct quote.)

CODA

So how is the work going on your personal "castle in the air"? Singing and the teaching of singing are noble and important endeavors. They will change and define your life. Use the space below to write down how singing has made your life more interesting and more satisfying. Share your thoughts on this with your friends and singing colleagues. This endeavor is a lifetime journey of castle building and beautiful singing. Rachmaninov was right! *"Music is enough for a lifetime. A lifetime is not enough for music."*

Now...go practice.

Blank space for written reflections

XI Vocal Performance

APPENDIX ONE
APHORISMS FOR SINGING

An aphorism is a concise statement of principle; a terse formulation of a truth or sentiment, an adage (Merriam Webster's Dictionary). Aphorisms illustrate in either a concrete or metaphorical way the principles being addressed.

Vocal Wisdon, by Giovanni Battista Lamperti is perhaps the best example of this literary construct, and this book has drawn extensively from his wisdom and maxims. Many voice teachers have their own collections of aphorisms, which usually sum up in a sentence or two concepts that may take years to master. The following collection is offered as a stimulus for singers, voice teachers and choral conductors perhaps just beginning their "castle in the air" journey. The intent is to get you started on your own meaningful collection. Authors are noted when known.

We sing emotions, thoughts, and ideas; not notes and rhythms.

Goals of artistic singing: Beauty, Freedom, Health.

Do not listen to yourself sing! Feel yourself sing!
— Lamperti

Difficulties in singing come from three directions:
uneducated hearing,
undisciplined muscles,
untrained breathing.
— Lamperti

Relaxation is acquiring energy and freedom for action.
— Doscher

Tone is soul;
Vowel is the body.
Soul expresses itself through the body
like the tone expresses itself through the vowel.
— K. Darragh

Practice should have a definite aim
— the production of beautiful tone.
— D. A. Clippinger

A lot of tone in the nose; but no nose in the tone.
— Jean de Reszke

Nasality should be thought of as a seasoning, not an ingredient.
A little salt adds flavor to the soup; too much ruins it.
— K. Darragh

Good singers sing on their interest and not on their capital.

To do, first we sometimes over-do.
(And then modify so the action goes from the gross to the fine.)
— K. Darragh

Speech therapy [and singing] begins at the hips
and goes to the lips.
— Zemlin

The singing process is analogous to a snowball on a hill.
If it is begun correctly, (the snowball poised at the top of the hill)
it would be surprising if it didn't continue correctly
(fall on down the hill).
— Adah Mase Curran

Observe how many good singers use the "fiore dalla bocca,"
the flowering of the mouth.

Music is enough for a lifetime. A lifetime is not enough for music.
— Sergei Rachmaninov

"Si canta come si parla." ("One sings the way one speaks.")

Breath is transformed to sound;
Sound is transformed to tone;
Tone is transformed to words;
Words are transformed to meaning;
Meaning is transformed to emotion;
Emotion accesses the spirit or soul.
Spirit and breath mean the same thing.
This is how singing accesses the human soul.
— Adapted from Adah Mase Curran

Tone is disembodied spirit.

There are no great teachers, just good students.
You teach yourself to sing with the aid of a competent teacher.
— Enrico Caruso

When the student is ready, the teacher then appears.
— A Budhist proverb

The secret of training a choir is, of course,
in giving the training dignity and worth.
If choir members are allowed to come irregularly to rehearsals,
and then allowed to slide through slipshod practices,
and to sing publicly when they know that they are only half-trained,
they will never regard the work of the choir with the seriousness it demands.
— John Finley Williamson (Beck 5)

There are eloquences in language simply as sound, as there are in music,
which remain somehow mystical and un-stateable,
but which many of us can sense together - and might even be able to impart
to a few good listeners,
once our purpose is constant and our techniques are secure.
— Robert Shaw (Blocker 118)

As a teacher: present the material and let the student draw the conclusions.
Don't be afraid to give too much information. Just don't drill on it.
Plant the seed and get out of the way of the rain.
Don't dig up the seed each day to see if it is growing.
— K. Darragh

Singing is the highest of all the arts.
One must <u>create</u> an instrument from an abstract thought;
<u>tune</u> it; and <u>play</u> it with proper technique.
— Adah Mase Curran

In fact, all bad habits of the throat are merely
efforts of protection against clumsy management of the breath.
— Lamperti

Maintain the thought; Sustain the breath.
— Adah Mase Curran

To sing wet, pee pale.

The object of art is expression.
The essence of expression is imagination.
The control of imagination is form.
The "medium" for all three is technique.
— Herbert Witherspoon

Imitate your best efforts,
imagining a still better and better quality
based upon what you have already accomplished.
— Herbert Witherspoon

He who does not strive with all diligence
to attain the highest place in his profession
soon begins to descend to the second,
and gradually becomes satisfied with the lowest grade.
— *Pietro Francesco Tosi*

Correct breathing gives the feeling of elation.
Correct singing is always "comfortable."
— *Herbert Witherspoon*

Good technique is like coming home.
It is the way your body always wanted to do it.
— *Steven Dahlke*

The vocal exercise you find to be the most difficult,
or that you dislike the most, is perhaps the one
that has the greatest gift to give you.
— *Nadia Smelser*

First be true to the tone and then true to the vowel.
If one has to be compromised, it will be the vowel.
Vowel modification is not something that you do -
it is something that you allow and encourage but only when necessary.
— *K. Darragh*

"Chi sa ben respirare, et si lavare, sappra ben cantare."
(If you breathe and articulate well, you can sing well.)

When you speak, you undertake to make your audience know.
When you sing, you undertake to make your audience feel.
– *D. A. Clippinger*

Singing is the singer's way of striving to be one with the universe.
– *Adah Mase Curran*

Submit your favorite
vocal aphorism at
www.PavanePublishing.com
[Cantabile tab]

Aphorisms

APPENDIX TWO

List of Feelings or Emotions

A

Abandoned
Abrasive
Absolved
Absurd
Abused
Abusive
Accommodating
Acknowledged
Acquiescent
Acrimonious
Adequate
Adamant
Admonished
Adoring
Adventurous
Affected
Affectionate
Afflicted
Affronted
Afraid
Agitated
Aggravated
Aggressive
Agonized
Agreeable
Almighty
Alarmed
Alienated
Alive
Alluring
Alone
Altruistic
Ambiguous
Ambitious
Ambivalent
Amenable
Amorous
Amused
Angry
Anguished
Animated
Annoyed
Anonymous
Anxious
Apathetic
Appeasing
Appreciative
Apprehensive
Ardent
Argumentative
Aroused
Arrogant
Ashamed

Assured
Astounded
Attentive
Authentic
Awed
Awkward

B

Bad
Bare
Barren
Beaten down
Beautiful
Begrudging
Bemused
Betrayed
Bewildered
Bewitched
Bitter
Blessed
Blissful
Blunt
Bold
Bored
Bothered
Brave
Breathless
Breezy
Bright
Brilliant
Broken
Bruised
Bucolic
Buoyant
Burdened
Burdensome

C

Callous
Calm
Capable
Captivated
Captivating
Careless
Caring
Cathartic
Celebrative
Chagrined
Challenged
Chaotic
Charitable
Charmed
Charming
Chastened

Cheated
Cheerful
Cherished
Childish
Childlike
Clandestine
Clear
Clever
Cold
Collected
Combative
Comfortable
Compassionate
Competitive
Complacent
Completed
Composed
Concerned
Condemned
Confident
Confused
Congenial
Conspicuous
Contented
Contrite
Cool
Cordial
Cornered
Creative
Cruel
Crushed
Culpable
Curious
Cursed

D

Dainty
Deceitful
Defeated
Defensive
Defiant
Dejected
Delectable
Delicate
Delighted
Demure
Depressed
Desirable
Desirous
Desired
Desolate
Despair
Desperate
Despondent

Destructive
Determined
Devoted
Different
Diffident
Diminished
Disappointed
Disbelieving
Discomfort
Discontented
Disgust
Disgusted
Dismal
Dispassionate
Displeased
Disregarded
Disregarding
Distracted
Distressed
Disturbed
Doomed
Dominated
Dubious
Dull

E

Eager
Earthly
Earnest
Easy
Ecstatic
Elated
Electrified
Embracing
Empathetic
Empty
Enchanted
Endearing
Enduring
Energetic
Enervated
Enfolded
Engaging
Enlivened
Enraged
Enraptured
Enthused
Enthusiastic
Enticing
Envious
Eternal
Even tempered
Evil
Exacerbated

Exalted
Exasperated
Excited
Exciting
Excluded
Exhausted

F
Faithful
Fanatical
Fascinated
Fascinating
Fearful
Fervent
Fervor
Fierce
Fiery
Flattering
Flattered
Fluid
Flushed
Flustered
Foolish
Foolhardy
Forbearing
Fortified
Frantic
Fractured
Free
Fretful
Frightened
Frigid
Frisky
Frustrated
Full
Fulfilled
Fuming
Fun
Funny
Furious

G
Galvanized
Genial
Genuine
Giving
Glad
Gleeful
Gloomy
Glorious
Glowing
Good
Grateful
Gratified
Gratitude
Grave
Greedy
Grief
Grieving
Grim

Groovy
Grounded
Guilty
Gullible

H
Haggard
Half-hearted
Happy
Hardened
Harsh
Hateful
Hearty
Heavenly
Heavy
Hectic
Helpful
Helpless
High
Hilarious
Holy
Homesick
Homicidal
Honored
Hopeful
Horrible
Horrid
Horrific
Horrified
Horror-stricken
Hostile
Hovering
Humble
Humorous
Hurt
Hysterical

I
Ignored
Illuminated
Immortal
Imperious
Impetuous
Imposed upon
Imposing
Impervious
Impressed
Impressive
Impressionable
Impulsive
Inattentive
Inclusive
Indulged
Indulgent
Inept
Inexhaustible
Infatuated
Infelicitous
Inflexible
Infuriated

Insane
Insatiable
Insensitive
Insouciant
Inspired
Interested
Intimidated
Intrepid
Intrigued
Intuitive
Inviting
Inward
Irrepressible
Irritable
Irritated
Irritation
Isolated

J
Jaunty
Jealous
Jittery
Jolly
Jovial
Joy
Joyful
Joyous
Jubilation
Judged
Judgmental
Jumpy

K
Keen
Kind

L
Laconic
Languid
Lazy
Lecherous
Left-out
Lethargic
Licentious
Light-hearted
Liquid
Lively
Loathsome
Lonely
Lonesome
Longing
Long-suffering
Lost
Love
Loved
Loving
Lovely
Low
Lukewarm

Lustful
Luxurious

M
Mad
Manic
Martyred
Maudlin
Mean
Melancholy
Merry
Mindful
Mindless
Mirthful
Mischievous
Miserable
Moderate
Mortified
Moved
Murky
Mystical

N
Naughty
Needy
Nervous
Nice
Nonchalant
Nonplussed
Nostalgic
Numb
Nutty

O
Obnoxious
Obsessed
Odd
Opposed
Optimistic
Outraged
Overflowing
Overwhelmed
Over-wrought

P
Pained
Panicked
Paralyzed
Parsimonious
Passionate
Passive
Paternal
Patient
Peaceful
Perky
Perplexed
Persecuted
Perturbed
Petrified

Pitied
Pitiful
Placid
Plagued
Playful
Pleasant
Pleasing
Pleasure
Pleasured
Poignant
Precarious
Pressured
Pride
Prim
Prissy
Protected
Protective
Proud
Provocative
Provoked
Puzzled

Q
Quarrelsome
Quiet
Quivery

R
Radiant
Rage
Rash
Raving
Ravished
Ravishing
Receptive
Reckless
Reconciled
Redeemed
Redemptive
Refreshed
Rejected
Rejection
Relaxed
Relieved
Remorse
Repressed
Repugnant
Rescued
Resentful
Resentment
Resigned
Resistant
Restless
Restrained
Restraint
Reverent
Reviled
Revived
Rewarded
Ridiculous

Righteous
Robbed
Romantic

S
Sad
Safe
Sarcastic
Satiated
Satisfaction
Satisfied
Scared
Secretive
Scattered
Screwed up
Secluded
Secure
Sedate
Seduced
Seductive
Seething
Selfish
Sensational
Sensual
Sentimental
Serene
Serious
Servile
Settled
Sexy
Shaken
Shielded
Shocked
Shrill
Shy
Silly
Simmering
Sincere
Sinking
Skeptical
Smug
Sneaky
Snug
Sober
Soft
Solemn
Somber
Sore
Sorrow
Sorrowful
Sorry
Sour
Sparkling
Spastic
Spirited
Spiteful
Spry
Stark
Startled
Stingy

Stoic
Stranded
Strange
Stressed
Stricken
Static
Stuffed
Stung
Stunned
Stupefied
Stupid
Subdued
Subjugated
Suffering
Sunny
Supportive
Sure
Susceptible
Suspicious
Sweet
Sympathetic
Sympathy

T
Talkative
Tame
Tantalized
Temperate
Tempted
Tenacious
Tender
Tense
Tentative
Tenuous
Terrible
Terrified
Threatened
Thrilled
Thwarted
Tickled
Tight-lipped
Timid
Tingly
Tired
Tolerant
Tormented
Tortured
Touched
Transfixed
Transparent
Tranquil
Transported
Trepidation
Trapped
Troubled
Trusting
Trustworthy
Twitchy

U
Ugly
Unaware
Uncomfortable
Unconcerned
Unconscious
Uncontrollable
Undone
Uneasy
Unfeeling
Unhappy
Unimpressed
Unruffled
Unsettled
Upset

V
Valiant
Vehement
Vexed
Victimized
Violent
Vital
Vivacious
Volcanic
Voluptuous
Vulnerable

W
Warm
Warmhearted
Weary
Weepy
Welcomed
Whining
Wicked
Wishful
Winsome
Wistful
Woeful
Wonderful
Worldly
Worried
Wounded
Wretched
Wronged

Y
Yearning
Yielding

Z
Zany
Zealous

Submit your favorite
emotion or feeling at
www.PavanePublishing.com
[Cantabile tab]

Feelings

A page for you to write your own feelings and emotions

A page for you to write your own feelings and emotions

Feelings

APPENDIX THREE
GLOSSARY OF TERMS

Abduct In anatomy, to move away from a midline, to separate, as when the glottis opens i.e., when the vocal folds move apart.

Adduct In anatomy, to move toward a midline, to approximate, as when the glottis closes i.e., when the vocal folds move together.

Aerodynamic The motions of air and the forces that act on it.

Affinities between muscles Muscle groups that develop a relationship with other muscles groups, causing them to work in sympathy i.e., when the soft palate and tongue **always** move at the same time, which is not necessarily desirable.

Alveolar ridge The gum ridge above and behind the upper teeth.

Aggiustamento From Italian, *aggiustare* to adjust or arrange. In singing, physical adjustments that a singer makes to accommodate register and resonance changes, and facilitate evenness throughout the range.

Amplitude The magnitude of the range of movement in a vibrating object. Humans perceive this aurally as loudness or softness.

Appoggiare la voce Italian: to support the voice.

Appoggio Italian: literally, to lean on. In singing, the establishment of a dynamic equilibrium between the muscles of inhalation and exhalation; also refers to the dynamic equilibrium or balance between breathing, phonation and resonance that results in freely produced beautiful singing. Commonly called "support."

Arpeggio The notes of a chord played individually, one after the other in succession.

Articulation Movement or placement of the articulators.

Articulators The speech organs involved in sound production, including the lips, the teeth, the tongue, the jaw, the soft palate and the hard palate.

Attenuate To make weaker; to decrease the amplitude of a sound wave.

Chiaroscuro Italian: The quality of both brightness and darkness in the same medium. Borrowed from visual art, in singing it refers to a balanced, three-dimensional tone color, which is neither too "bright" nor too "dark."

Clavicular breathing Chest breathing; use of shoulder muscles for inhalation. Provides poor control over exhalation.

Condyle A prominent, rounded process on a bone, in this case on the mandible (lower jawbone.) See *Figure 14* and *15*, page 16.

Constrictors of the pharynx Three pairs of primarily swallowing muscles, that form the back wall of the throat.

Coronoid Process Bony projection on top of the mandible (lower jawbone), in front of the condyle. See *Figure 14* and *15*, page 16.

Cricothyroid muscles Referred to as CT. Intrinsic muscles of the larynx attached at the front of the cricoid cartilages and pulling down on the thyroid cartilages, lengthening the vocal folds.

CT muscles Cricothyroid muscles

Cultivate To improve or develop something through attention and study.

Decibel A unit for expressing the relative sound pressure or intensity of sound waves.

Deliberate Practice A highly structured, repetitive activity undertaken with the specific goal of improving performance.

Diaphragm Large dome-shaped muscle of inhalation that separates the thorax from the abdomen. Literally means a barrier or partition.

Dynamic Equilibrium A balance between what may appear to be opposing or disparate forces. In singing it refers to the balance necessary between the muscles of inhalation and exhalation to produce the *appoggio* breath management technique. It also refers to the balance between the breathing, phonation and resonance functions of the singing voice that produces a healthy, free and beautiful tone.

Edemetous A description of tissue with an excess of accumulated fluid; swollen.

Enunciation To speak clearly and skillfully.

Epigastrium Area between the sternum and the navel, bordered by the edges of the ribs.

Epiglottis The cartilage that covers the entance to the larynx.

Esophagus The tube behind your trachea that connects your mouth to your stomach.

Expiratory muscles Muscles of exhalation including, the external obliques, internal obliques, the transverse abdominis, the quadratus lumborum, and the internal intercostals.

Glossary

Explicit learning   A conscious learning operation to acquire information, dependent on knowing facts. Learning that is "Know-that."

External Locus of Attention   Directing of attention to the results or effect of muscle movement.

Extrinsic muscles of the larynx   Muscles which attach to the larynx, but originate somewhere else.

Fauces   The passage from the mouth to the pharynx.

Faucial pillars   Two folds of tissue on either side of the narrow passage that lead from the mouth to the pharynx. (The tonsils are nestled between the two folds.) The pillars connect the soft palate to the pharyngeal wall, (the palatopharyngeus muscle) and the soft palate to the base of the tongue (the palatoglossus). Also referred to as palatine arches.

Fixed Mindset   A belief held by learners that their talents, intelligence, and abilities are fixed resources, unable to grow or change.

"Floppy" vibration mode of the vocal folds   A multiple undulating mode of vibration in the vocal folds that produces a high number of frequencies in the glottal source.

Flow Phonation   The optimal balance between a breathy phonation (low air pressure and low resistance from the vocal folds) and a pressed phonation (high air pressure and high resistance from the vocal folds) resulting in a coordinated onset of tone.

Formant   A resonance of the vocal tract; an area of strength or reinforcement in the partials or harmonics of a vocal tone.

Frequency   The number of vibrations (or cycles) per second in a tone. A higher number is perceived as a higher pitch.

Garcia position   Named for Manual Garcia, the nineteenth century pedagogue who advocated its use. The singer stands and places hands behind the back with palms facing outward. This position promotes the "noble" posture and allows the singer to manually monitor certain muscles of breathing.

Glosso-palatine pillars   Of the two sets of pillars, the one most forward in the mouth, connecting the soft palate to the base of the tongue. (See faucial pillars)

Glottis   The space between the vocal folds.

Glottal Fry   The phonated sound produced at the lowest possible pitch, characterized by a scratchy quality.

Glotal source   Vibrations produced directly at the glottis of the larynx.

Hard palate   The bony part of the roof of the mouth. It is in front of the soft palate and together they form the complete palate.

Harmonics   Partials of a complex sound whose frequencies are an integral multiple of the fundamental frequency. For example, if the fundamental frequency is 220 Hz, some of the harmonics would be 440, 660, 880, 1100 etc.

Hertz (Hz)   The measurement of cycles per second, named after Heinrich Hertz.

Hyoid bone   U-shaped bone at the base of the tongue. Only bone in the body that is "free floating," not connected to another bone. The larynx is suspended from the hyoid bone.

Implicit learning   Learning without awareness, governed and enabled by the senses. In singing, Implicit learning is achieved by sound, sight and touch (how it feels). Learning that is "Know-how."

Inspiratory muscles   Muscles of inhalation, including the diaphragm, the external intercostals, and also, less desirably, the scalenes and the sternocleidomastoids which in singing are best thought of as assisting in correct initial posture.

Internal Locus of Attention   Directing of attention to a movement itself or the biomechanics of a muscle movement.

Intercostal muscles   The muscles situated between the ribs.

Intrinsic muscles of the larynx   Laryngeal muscles that both originate and insert wholly in the larynx.

Intuitive   The quality of attaining direct knowledge without evident rational thought, inference, or sequential development. The opposite of linear.

Knowledge of Results (KOR)   Feedback that comments on the success of an action in regard to the desired goal. ("Your jaw was much more freely released on that high note.") Contrast with Knowledge of Performance.

Knowledge of Performance (KOP)   Feedback that comments on the quality of success of an action. ("Good job on the high note.") Contrast with Knowledge of Results.

Larynx   An organ of the body, suspended in the neck, that contains the vocal folds, sometimes called the voice box.

Legato   In music, to connect smoothly from one note to the next.

Levator palatine   One of the muscles involved in the positioning of the soft palate. It is a "lifter."

Ligament   Strong, dense connective tissue that attaches two bones or cartilages.

Linear A quality or system that depends, or is based on sequential development or thinking; as opposed to an intuitive or instinctive method.

LPC Spectrum Acronym for linear predictive coding. A method to obtain a spectral graph that is particulatly useful in showing the formants of a particular sound.

Mandible The lower jaw.

Martellato Literally "to hammer." In singing, putting an emphasis on each individual note, using diaphragmatic pulses. Notes are not separated, but still connected. Used extensively in Baroque repertoire.

Masseter muscle A muscle connecting the lower jaw to the skull. Its action raises the lower jaw and assists in chewing.

Messa di voce Italian: placing the voice. A technique used to practice a wide range of dynamics contrasts, and in some ranges of the voice to blend registers. The singer sustains one pitch, beginning softly, *crescendoing* to *fortissimo*, and *decrescendoing* back to *pianissimo*.

Metaphysical Philosophical thoughts and ideas that transcend the physical and scientific world, for example: what does it mean to be human? What is the nature of the human soul? The fine arts and especially music are traditionally thought to be one of the methods that humans have of accessing the metaphysical.

Modification See "vowel modification."

Motor Learning Long term behavioral change in muscle activity, as a result of repetition or practice.

Motor Skill A function which involves the precise movement and coordination of muscles with the intent to perform a specific task or act.

Mucosa The mucous membrane that lines or covers the vocal tract, including the vocal folds.

Muscle antagonism Muscle action where one muscle (or muscles) resists the action of an opposing muscle (or muscles).

Myoelastic-aerodynamic Pertaining to vocal production, muscular action and breath pressure both contribute to vocal fold vibration.

Onset of tone The commencement of vibration at the glottis.

Palatine arches See faucial pillars.

Palatine muscles Muscles of the soft palate: levator palatine, tensor palatine, and uvula.

Palatoglossus muscles Of the two sets of pillars, the one most forward in the mouth, connecting the soft palate to the base of the tongue; part of the faucial pillars; also called glosso-palatine pillars.

Palatopharyngeus muscles The rear faucial pillars connecting the soft palate to the pharynx. Part of the faucial pillars; also called pharyngo-palatine pillars.

Pedagogy The art and science of teaching.

Pelvic girdle The upside-down arch formed by the hip bones and pelvic muscles, that can assist in breath management stability.

Pharyngo-palatine pillars The rear faucial pillars connecting the soft palate to the pharynx. (See faucial pillars.) Also called palatopharyngeus pillars.

Pharynx The throat.

Phonation The vibration of the vocal folds, producing sound.

Phonotrauma Accumulated stress causing injury to the vocal folds from misuse, abuse or over use of the voice.

Pillars See faucial pillars.

Power Spectrum A graphic representation of the many frequencies in a sound. Frequency is shown on the horizontal axis, and amplitude is shown on the vertical axis.

Pronunciation To produce or speak the various sounds in language according to linguistic rules.

Quarter-wave resonator An open-closed tube that predictably responds to certain acoustical conditions relating to resonance. The human vocal tract responds as a quarter-wave resonator in singing.

Raccogliere Italian: To gather, to collect together. In singing, in reference to the focus of the tone.

Raccolta Italian: Derived from *raccogliere*. In singing, refers to a focused or gathered tone.

Release of tone The cessation of vibration at the glottis.

Resonance When vibrations from a sound source are modified (intensified, enriched, enhanced, attenuated etc.) in some other place or way. In singing, vibrations made at the glottis are enhanced, enlarged, reinforced or attenuated in the vocal tract, to produce a beautiful singing tone.

Rotation   Movement or pivot around an axis. In singing, one of the actions of the jaw, when it rotates around a horizontal axis as the jaw releases back and down.

Singer's Formant   A concentration of energy found in the 2800 Hz to 3200 Hz frequency range in a trained singer's voice. This energy peak is the reason why one professional singer can be heard above many accompanying orchestral instruments.

Soft palate   Membrane and muscular tissue that extends back in the mouth from the hard palate. It is also the bottom of the nasal cavity, and separates the mouth from the pharynx. In singing, it can be adjusted to effect the shape of the vocal track and in that manner, effect the singing tone.

Sphenoid sinus Irregular shaped cavities in the body of the sphenoid bone (at the base of the skull) that drain into the nasal cavity.

Staccatto Notes sounded in a short, separated, detached style, indicated by a dot over the notehead.

Sternum The breastbone.

TA muscle   See thyroarytenoid muscle.

Temporalis muscle Large muscle located above the ear and in the temple area that connects the skull to the jaw, and assists in raising the jaw (or closing the mouth). It also assists in chewing.

Temporomandibular joint   Located just in front of the ear, this joint is the place where the jaw connects to the skull.

Tensor palatine   One of the muscles involved in the positioning of the soft palate. It is a "spreader."

Thorax   The chest cavity.

Thyroarytenoid muscle   Also referred to as the TA. The intrinsic laryngeal muscle that is the main component of the vocal folds. It is connected from the thyroid cartilage to the arytenoid cartilages and when it contracts, it shortens and thickens the vocal folds.

"Tone Factory"   A mental image for the pharynx or throat, where tone is "manufactured."

Tonus   The state of a muscle that is ready to act and respond. The optimal state in a continuum between relaxed and tense.

Trachea   The tube that goes from the larynx to the bronchial tubes, sometimes called the windpipe.

Translation   One of the two actions of the temporomandibular joint. When the jaw glides forward, or juts, it has translated, meaning the new horizontal axis is parallel to the old axis. For the other movement see "rotation."

Unvoiced consonants   A speech sound produced by a partial or complete obstruction of the vocal tract by the articulators, and does not include vocal fold vibration.

Uvula   The pendant hanging from the back of the soft palate, that contains the lower end of the *Azygos uvulus* muscle, one of the soft palate muscles.

Velum   The soft palate, as opposed to the hard palate.

Viscera   Collectively speaking, the many organs of the body that are found in the abdominal cavity, including the stomach, the intestines and the kidneys, etc.

Vocal ligament   One of the components of the vocal fold.

Vocal tract   The tube that goes from the larynx to the lips and tip of the nose. Its shape can be manipulated to effect vowels and tone color.

Vocalise   A short vocal exercise, usually without words, that is used for pedagological purposes.

Voiced consonants   A speech sound that includes vocal fold vibration as well as a partial or complete obstruction of the vocal tract by the articulators.

"Vowel Factory"   A mental image for the mouth, where vowels are "manufactured."

Vowel modification   The action that a singer takes, adjusting the shape of vowels, as a method to balance resonance qualities throughout the range. Also called, in Italian, *aggiustamento*.

Zygomatic arch   The cheek bones.

APPENDIX FOUR
GUIDE TO THE INTERNATIONAL PHONETIC ALPHABET
AS USED IN THIS TEXT

International Phonetic Alphabet (IPA) Symbol	English equivalent sound spelling underlined
Vowels	
[i]	s<u>ee</u>
[ɪ]	s<u>i</u>t
[e]	ch<u>a</u>otic
[ɛ]	l<u>e</u>t
[æ]	c<u>a</u>t
[ɑ]	f<u>a</u>ther
[ʌ]	sh<u>u</u>t
[ə]	<u>a</u>bout
[o]	<u>o</u>bey
[õ]	French nasal, no English equivalent; sing a pure [o] with a lowered soft palate
[ɔ]	y<u>aw</u>n
[ʊ]	p<u>u</u>t, b<u>oo</u>k
[u]	n<u>oo</u>n
[y]	No English equivalent; sing [i] with [u] lip shape.
[aɪ]	l<u>igh</u>t
[aʊ]	h<u>ow</u>
[ɛɪ]	sk<u>a</u>te
[ɔɪ]	b<u>oy</u>
[aʊ]	no

Consonants

[b]	<u>b</u>ee
[d]	<u>d</u>og
[f]	<u>f</u>rank
[g]	<u>g</u>ood
[h]	<u>h</u>at
[k]	<u>k</u>ite
[ǀ]	<u>l</u>eaf
[m]	<u>m</u>o<u>m</u>
[n]	<u>n</u>o
[ŋ]	i<u>n</u>k or ra<u>ng</u>
[ⁱŋ] [ᵃŋ] or [°ŋ]	used to denote the subtle tongue changes in the [ŋ] in words like si<u>ng</u>, sa<u>ng</u> and so<u>ng</u>
[p]	<u>p</u>et
[r]	<u>r</u>ed
[s]	<u>s</u>it
[ʃ]	<u>sh</u>ine
[t]	<u>t</u>ip
[θ]	<u>th</u>ing
[ð]	<u>th</u>ese
[v]	<u>v</u>ictory
[w]	<u>w</u>ater
[ʍ]	<u>wh</u>ite
[j]	<u>y</u>es
[z]	<u>z</u>ebra
[ʒ]	vi<u>si</u>on

The IPAlphabet P5024 HL#08301917 by Cristian Grases is the most amazing and comprehensive pronunciation resource of all time. Every letter in 5 different languages: Spanish, Italian, Latin, French and German, in a quick and easy format. A must for every singer and choral director.

Practice Journal

Date: ___/___/___   Time: _____ to: _____

Something I learned, observed, or accomplished:

Goals for next pratice session:

Minutes Practiced:_____

Date: ___/___/___   Time: _____ to: _____

Something I learned, observed, or accomplished:

Goals for next pratice session:

Minutes Practiced:_____

Date: ___/___/___   Time: _____ to: _____

Something I learned, observed, or accomplished:

Goals for next pratice session:

Minutes Practiced:_____

Date: ___/___/___   Time: _____ to: _____

Something I learned, observed, or accomplished:

Goals for next pratice session:

Minutes Practiced:_____

Date: ___/___/___   Time: _____ to: _____

Something I learned, observed, or accomplished:

Goals for next pratice session:

Minutes Practiced:_____

Date: ___/___/___   Time: _____ to: _____

Something I learned, observed, or accomplished:

Goals for next pratice session:

Minutes Practiced:_____

Practice Journal

Date: ___/___/___   Time: _____ to: _____

Something I learned, observed, or accomplished:

Goals for next practice session:

Minutes Practiced:_____

Date: ___/___/___   Time: _____ to: _____

Something I learned, observed, or accomplished:

Goals for next practice session:

Minutes Practiced:_____

Date: ___/___/___   Time: _____ to: _____

Something I learned, observed, or accomplished:

Goals for next practice session:

Minutes Practiced:_____

Date: ___/___/___   Time: _____ to: _____

Something I learned, observed, or accomplished:

Goals for next practice session:

Minutes Practiced:_____

Date: ___/___/___   Time: _____ to: _____

Something I learned, observed, or accomplished:

Goals for next pratice session:

Minutes Practiced:_____

Date: ___/___/___   Time: _____ to: _____

Something I learned, observed, or accomplished:

Goals for next pratice session:

Minutes Practiced:_____

REFERENCES AND FURTHER READING

Adler, Kurt. *Phonetics and Diction in Singing.* Minneapolis, MN: University of Minnesota Press. 1974.

Appelman, D. Ralph. *The Science of Vocal Pedagogy.* Bloomington, IN: Indiana University Press. 1986.

Beck, Joseph G., ed. *Selected Writings of John Finley Williamson.* Bloomington, IN: AuthorHouse. 2004.

Blocker, Robert. *The Robert Shaw Reader.* New Haven, CT: Yale University Press. 2004.

Brodnitz, Friedrich S. M.D. *Keep Your Voice Healthy.* PRO-ED, Inc. 1988.

Bunch, Meribeth. *Dynamics of the Singing Voice.* 3rd ed. New York, NY: Springer-Verlag. 1995.

Conable, Barbara. *The Structures and Movement of Breathing.* Chicago: GIA Publications, Inc. 2000.

Conable, Barbara. *What Every Musician Needs to Know about the Body,* (Revised Edition). Portland, Oregon: Andover Press. 2000.

Crannell, Kenneth C. *Voice and Articulation,* (Third Edition). Belmont, CA: Wadsworth Publishing Company. 1997.

Dickson, David Ross, and Wilma M. Maue. *Human Vocal Anatomy.* Springfield, IL: Charles C. Thomas Publisher. 1970.

Doscher, Barbara. *The Functional Unity of the Singing Voice,* (Second Edition). Lanhan, Md., & London: The Scarecrow Press, Inc., 1994.

Duckworth, Angela. "Grit: Perserverance and Passion for Long Term Goals." *Journal of Personality and Social Psychology,* 92 (6): 1087-1101. 2007.

Dwerk, Carol S. *Mindset: The New Psychology of Success.* New York: Random House. 2006.

Edwards, Harold T. *Applied Phonetics* (,2nd Edition). San Diego, CA: Singular Publishing Group, Inc. 1997.

Ehmann, Wilhelm and Frauke Haasemann. *Voice Building for Choirs.* Chapel Hill, NC: Hinshaw Music. 1982.

Ericsson, K. Anders, Ralf Th. Krampe, and Clemens Tesch-Romer. "The Role of Deliberate Practice in Acquisition of Expert Perfroamnce." *Psychological Review,* 100 (3): 363-406. 1993.

Feldenkrais, Moshe. *Body and Mature Behavior.* London: Routledge & Kegan Paul Limited. 1949.

Green, Barry and W. Timothy Gallwey. *The Inner Game of Music.* New York: Doubleday. 1986.

Kent, Raymond D. *The Speech Sciences.* San Diego, CA; Singular Publishing Group, Inc.

Lamperti, Giovanni Battista. *Vocal Wisdom,* (Enlarged Edition). New York: Taplinger Publishing Company. 1957.

Marafioti, P. Mario. *Caruso's Method of Voice Production.* New York, NY. Dover Publication, Inc. 1981.

McNevin, Nancy H, Charles H Shea, and Gabriele Wulf. "Increasing the distance of an external focus of attention enhances learning." *Psychological Research,* 67: 22-29. doi:10.1007. 2003.

Miller, Richard. *The Structure of Singing.* New York: Schirmer Books. 1986.

Netter, Frank H. M.D. *Atlas of Human Anatomy.* Summit, NJ: Ciba-Geigy Corporation. 1989.

Ohrenstein, Dora. "Insights Into Training Aural and Kinesthetic Awareness." *Journal of Singing,* 60 (1): 29-35. 2003.

Palmer, John M. *Anatomy for Speech and Hearing,* 4th ed. Baltimore, MD: Williams & Wilkins. 1993.

Pink, Daniel H. *Drive.* New York: Riverhead Books. 2009.

Reid, Cornelius L. *Bel Canto.* New York: The Joseph Patelson Music House. 1972.

Robison, Clayne W. *Beautiful Singing.* Provo, Utah: Clayne W. Robison. 2001.

Sataloff, Robert, T. "The Human Voice." *Scientific American* 267.6 (1992): 108-115.

Sieber, Ferdinand. *Thirty-Six Eight-Measure Vocalises.* New York: G. Schirmer.

Sundberg, Johan. *The Science of the Singing Voice.* Dekalb, IL: Northern Illinois University Press. 1987.

Titze, Ingo. "How to Use the Flow-Resistant Straws." *Journal of Singing* 58.5, May/June 2002: 429-430.

Titze, Ingo R, and Katherine Verdolini Abbott. *Vocology: The Science and Practice of Voice Habilitation.* Salt Lake City, UT: National Center for Voice and Speech. 2012.

---. "Is there a Scientific Explanation for Tone Focus and Voice Placement?" *Journal of Singing* 37.5, May 1981: 26-28.

---. *Principles of Voice Production.* Englewood Cliffs, NJ: Prentice Hall. 1994.

Vaccai, Niccolo. *Practical Italian Vocal Method.* New York: G. Schirmer. 1894.

Vennard, William. *Singing: The Mechanism and the Technic,* (Revised Edition). New York: Carl Fischer. 1967.

Verdolini, Katherine. "Principles of Skill Acquisition Applied to Voice Training." Chap. 8 in *The Vocal Vision: Views on Voice by 24 Leading Teachers, Coaches and Directors.* Milwaukee, WS: Applause Books. Accessed October 2, 2014. 2000.

Verdolini-Marsten, Katherine, and David A. Balota. "Role of Elaborative and Perceptual Integrative Processes in Perceptual-Motor Performance." *Journal of Experimental Psychology: Learning, Memory, and Cognition,* 20 (3): 730-749. 1994

Witherspoon, Herbert. *Singing.* New York: G. Schirmer, 1925.

Wulf, Gabriele. Prinz, Wolfgang, and Markus Hob. "Instructions for Motor Learning: Differential Effects of Internal Versus External Focus of Attention." *Jounral of Motor Behavior,* 30 (2): 169. Accessed September 23, 2014. 1998.

Zemlin, Willard R. *Speech and Hearing Science: Anatomy and Physiology,* (4th ed. Boston, MA: Allyn and Bacon, 1998.

Index

A

Abdominal muscles   2, 5, 38, 41, 42, 43, 45, 47, 51, 52, 53, 55, 133, 135, 137, 144
Abduction   67
Adduction   67
Affricative consonant   129, 133
Alveolar consonant   129, 174
Appoggio   34, 35, 37, 41, 45, 46, 47, 49, 55, 56, 81, 84, 90, 99, 105, 107, 110, 120, 187
Articulation   2, 12, 15, 48, 64, 65, 79, 85, 127, 128, 129, 131, 133, 136, 137, 144, 186
Articulator   64, 123, 128, 131, 132, 137, 144, 186, 192
Arytenoid   v, 58, 59, 67, 96, 97, 98, 192
Azygos uvulos   17

B

Back Wall of Throat   18
Belt, cloth   42, 47
Bilabial   129
Breathing for Singing   iii, 2, 34, 186
Breathy onset   60, 61, 114
Buccinator   15

C

Cartilages of the larynx   59
Castle in the air   vii, 128, 146, 178
Chest register   94
Chiaroscuro   28, 78, 80, 91, 117, 120, 124, 126
Choral Conductor   vii, 11, 30, 54, 66, 89, 108, 124, 137, 151, 164
Clavicle   38
Closed/open tube   73, 80
Closed glottis   97, 98
Condyle   7, 8, 16, 187
Consonant chart   130
Consonants   16, 17, 31, 65, 125, 126, 128, 129, 131, 132, 135, 136, 137, 144, 192
Constrictor muscles   15, 18, 27
Coordinated onset   60, 61, 62, 67, 68, 69, 80, 114, 188

Corniculates   58, 59
Coronoid process   8, 16, 20
Cricoid   58, 59, 96, 187
Cricoid cartilage   59, 96
Cricothyroid   96, 98, 112
    CT   96, 98, 99, 104, 106, 187, 198
Cross-section of the vocal fold   59
Cuneiforms   58

D

Deep layer of vocal folds   59
Deliberate practice   168 - 172, 174, 176, 187, 198
Dental   129
Diaphragm   2, 5, 19, 35, 36, 37, 39, 40, 41, 42, 43, 52, 56, 138, 144, 189
Diaphragm moves   36
Diphthong   132, 136
Dynamic equilibrium   3, 12, 34, 37, 38, 41, 45, 56, 60, 61, 62, 78, 80, 89, 99, 114, 120, 157, 174

E

Emotion   61, 120, 147, 150, 151, 152, 154, 179
Epigastrium   iv, v, 5, 42, 187
Epiglottis   14, 58, 59
Epithelium   59
Exhalation   iv, 19, 20, 31, 34, 35, 37, 38, 40, 41, 42, 43, 44, 46, 58, 67, 81, 186, 187
Expiratory muscles   34
Explicit learning   169
Exterior intercostal muscles   37
External locus of attention   170, 176
External oblique muscle   39
External obliques   39, 187

F

False vocal folds   97, 98
Fauces   18, 24
Fixed mindset   172, 176
"Floppy" vibration   60, 61, 67, 69, 114
Flow phonation   60
Focus   iii, vi, 80, 88, 110, 113, 114, 115, 116, 117, 118, 119, 120, 121, 122, 123,

124, 125, 126, 161, 191, 199
Formant   v, 74, 75, 76, 77, 109, 115, 116, 119, 126, 188, 189, 191
Fricative consonant   129, 133, 137, 138

G

Garcia, Manuel   40, 47, 94, 188
Glides and liquids   129
Glottal   47, 48, 60, 61, 65, 66, 68, 69, 72, 73, 74, 81, 91, 104, 114, 129, 136, 138, 162, 188
Glottal attack   60, 61, 66
Glottal source   v, 61, 72, 73, 74, 91, 188
Glottal stroke   61
Glottis   38, 58, 61, 72, 73, 77, 79, 88, 91, 94, 97, 98, 99, 128, 188, 190, 191
Growth mindset   171, 172, 176

H

Hard palate   14, 18, 19, 88, 116, 117, 118, 119, 121, 122, 125, 129, 186, 191, 192
Head register   94
Heavy mechanism   94, 95, 96, 97, 101, 106, 107, 108, 109, 112, 161
Hyoglossus   15
Hyoid bone   17, 18, 19, 58, 177

I

Icons   ii, vii
Implicit learning   169, 170
Inhalation   2, 15, 17, 18, 19, 20, 24, 31, 34, 35, 36, 37, 38, 41, 43, 44, 46, 47, 49, 50, 52, 53, 55, 56, 58, 60, 61, 66, 67, 81, 83, 186, 187, 189
Inspiratory muscles   34
Instrument   vi, 2, 3, 9, 11, 12, 14, 15, 19, 30, 35, 38, 41, 42, 45, 54, 58, 60, 61, 62, 67, 69, 81, 89, 94, 99, 100, 109, 110, 120, 146, 151, 156, 157, 158, 160, 162, 165, 180

203

ABOUT THE AUTHOR

Katharin Rundus, DMA, is a singer, a voice teacher and a choral conductor. She is the Director of Vocal Studies at Fullerton College where she teaches voice and oversees the more than one hundred and fifty students studying voice either privately or in classes. During her tenure there, she has conducted the Fullerton College Chamber Singers and the Women's Chorale. She also maintains a voice studio at California State University, Long Beach.

Katharin performs frequently as a recitalist as well as a concert and chamber soloist in Southern California. She continues to cultivate her love of choral music singing as a professional chorister with the John Alexander Singers in Orange County, California.

Adept at explaining complex scientific vocal concepts in an engaging and practical manner, Dr. Rundus is regularly invited as a guest lecturer in vocal pedagogy at many universities, colleges, high schools and churches. She has also been an invited clinician at many ADCA conferences, and has lectured about vocal pedagogy and voice science to the NATS-LA chapter.

Dr. Rundus received a Bachelor of Music degree from Coe College, a Master of Music degree from Westminster Choir College and a Doctor of Musical Arts in vocal performance from the Claremont Graduate University. While pursuing the doctorate, she studied and researched the use of spectral analysis in the voice studio. Additionally, she has studied the science of vocal production with Ingo Titze and vocal habilitation with Katherine Verdolini at the National Center for Voice and Speech in Denver, Colorado.

Pavane Publishing

CANTABILE: Voice Class, P5026, HL#145650, $14.99.

- This course text was designed specifically for the undergraduate voice class.

- Retailing at $14.99, it is the most affordable in its genre.

- The content is precise and designed for the classroom, *and* there is no anthology. We provide a free download at the Pavane website that lists anthology content suggestions and how to build your own anthology using free Internet sites and purchasable single copy options.

- Plus, on the Pavane Publishing YouTube Channel we have video lessons by the author providing visual support that match the book.

- Throughout *Cantabile: Voice Class*, you will find itemized references that tie topics together with Cantabile, (P5023), the comprehensive manual.

CANTABILE: Voice Class textbook is clearly and concisely written for 21st century undergraduate voice students. Already tested in lower division voice classes, students' response was overwhelmingly enthusiastic. Twelve foundational "anchors" of voice study are presented with accompanying vocal exercises that build competency and confidence from the first use. In addition to "anchors" on vocal technique, topics such as Deliberate Practice, Musical Expression and Vocal Health are covered. The text is engaging and well-illustrated with photos, drawings and icons.